The Microstructure of Organizations

The Microstructure of Organizations

Phanish Puranam

OXFORD
UNIVERSITY PRESS

OXFORD
UNIVERSITY PRESS

Great Clarendon Street, Oxford, OX2 6DP,
United Kingdom

Oxford University Press is a department of the University of Oxford.
It furthers the University's objective of excellence in research, scholarship,
and education by publishing worldwide. Oxford is a registered trade mark of
Oxford University Press in the UK and in certain other countries

First Edition published in 2018

Impression: 2

Published in the United States of America by Oxford University Press
198 Madison Avenue, New York, NY 10016, United States of America

British Library Cataloguing in Publication Data
Data available

Library of Congress Control Number: 2017962118

ISBN 978-0-19-967236-3 (hbk.)
     978-0-19-967237-0 (pbk.)

Printed and bound by
CPI Group (UK) Ltd, Croydon, CR0 4YY

To my parents
who showed me the joys of a life in research

■ PREFACE

Goal-directed collaboration (which I use synonymously with "organization") is humanity's most important accomplishment. Undoubtedly, organization is present in the animal kingdom too. But impressive as the collaborative efforts of insects and primates are, they pale into insignificance compared to the range, flexibility, and complexity of goals displayed by human collaboration systems, ranging from dyads to corporations. It is our capacity to design organizations that enables us to pursue breathtaking objectives such as building the pyramids, getting to the moon, or curing cancer, that would be unthinkable for individuals with diverse knowledge and interests to achieve by acting on their own. With less arrogance and more accuracy, our species should label itself "the organizer," rather than "the wise" (i.e. *sapiens*).[1]

Research on organizations has grown voluminous over the last century, and arguably contains some of the most exciting developments in social science in the last few decades. Much is known today about the impact of organizations on the welfare of their constituent individuals and indeed on the markets and societies of which they form a part; about the ecological, institutional, and psychological pressures that shape organizations through processes of selection, adaptation, conformance, and categorization; and about organizations as social systems—between and within which power, stratification, connections and culture emerge. The most prestigious peer-reviewed academic journals that publish research on organizations and their management showcase some of the best work on these and related topics.

Yet, our interest in *organizing as a technology*—a technology that allows us to structure collaboration between individuals with diverse knowledge and interests in order to achieve a goal—seems to have flagged. This is arguably still the first order issue for the creators, users, inhabitants and indeed students of organizations. This is also the traditional domain of organization design researchers.

Research on organization design has an illustrious heritage, and the internal structure of organizations has been one of the founding themes in organization studies. In the initial decades that followed the contributions of the Carnegie school pioneers, research on the design attributes of complex organizations that enabled them to adapt to changes in their environment accumulated rapidly. However, it is also true that research on organization design is not very current. It is fairly common to see graduate-level courses in organization

---

[1] Google translate suggests the phrase "*Homo Praeparator.*"

design being taught today from a research base that is decades old, and for scholars to periodically point out the dire need for (and dearth of) new theories.

In this book, I describe a microstructural approach to theorizing about organization design that may help us make rapid progress in both the basic science and the applied technology of organizing. While written primarily for researchers and advanced graduate students in management, it may also prove useful to the thoughtful practitioner. On the "science" end of the spectrum, the microstructural approach claims novelty by placing aggregation issues at the centre stage of the study of organization. On the "technology" side, it is an approach that I believe is strongly complementary to the interests of strategy scholars. Even as research on the structural configurations of organizations waned in the 1980s, research in strategy on inter-organizational and buyer-supplier relationships, on post-merger integration, on subsidiary–headquarter relationships, on corporate forms such as business groups, and on non-contractual organizations based on volunteer contributors (such as Wikipedia and Linux) has flourished. Given the field's central question (i.e. the nature of inter-organizational performance differences), strategy researchers are naturally interested in the antecedents of performance in organizations. Adopting an organization design perspective on the various phenomena noted above, can offer an integrative framework to analyse the common challenge of generating collective goal-directed behaviour that cuts across these contexts.

I do not think this book (at least in this edition) offers a final, polished statement on the microstructural perspective, nor is it meant to be a comprehensive literature review of prior or current work. Instead, it is designed as a brochure, meant to invite others to the exciting journey of developing and sharpening this perspective further.

Phanish Puranam

Singapore
August 2017

◼ ACKNOWLEDGMENTS

Marcel Proust famously wrote that a book is like a cemetery in which the names on tombstones have been effaced. This is a beautiful metaphor for the fact that there are many sources of ideas that make it into a book, but these are seldom adequately acknowledged. But I am not (yet) willing to accept that the ideas in this book are headed for a graveyard. I am therefore happier with the imagery of a book as a vast library, in which the authors' names on the individual book covers are often not as visible as they should be. Let me try, however imperfectly, to rectify that here.

Some of my collaborators stand out in particular for the role they played in helping develop my thinking about the issues at the heart of this book, as well as their feedback on drafts. They include (in alphabetical order): Oliver Alexy, Julien Clement, Ranjay Gulati, Thorbjorn Knudsen, Ozgecan Kocak, Toby Kretschmer, Eucman Lee, Sunkee Lee, Dan Levinthal, Marlo Raveendran, Markus Reitzig, Harbir Singh, Kannan Srikanth, Michael Tushman, Bart Vanneste, and Massimo Warglien. The list is growing with each year, as is the burden of my intellectual debts. I learnt most of what I know about organization design in working with these wonderful scholars, indeed friends.

The European Research Council generously funded my projects through one of their frontiers of science grants ("The Foundations of Organization Design," ERC#241132). Research and Materials Development Grants and a school-endowed chair professorship at London Business School, and the chair professorship endowed through the generosity of Mr. Roland Berger and the consulting company he founded helped support additional expenses.

I was very fortunate to receive feedback on drafts from many leading researchers and practitioners in our field: Phil Anderson, Carliss Baldwin, Oliver Baumann, Markus Becker, Rich Burton, Martin Gargiulo, Giovanni Gavetti, Dorthe Dojbak Hakonnson, Vivianna Fang He, Connie Helfat, Reddi Kotha, Nirmalya Kumar, Siegwart Lindenbergh, Borge Obel, Magda Osman, Madan Pillutla, Hazhir Rahmandad, Shreshtha Yash Raj, Roderick Swaab, Stefan Thau, Bala Vissa, and Nicolay Worren. They were generous with their time, pointing me in various fruitful directions to think and read more about what I was trying to say, and challenging me to say it better.

I tested the patience of PhD students at various schools, but particularly at INSEAD, with early drafts of the chapters; the group comprising Daniel Mack, Sunkee Lee, Maciej Workiewicz, Afonso Almeida Costa, Julien Clement, Arianna Marchetti, Prothit Sen, and Nikhil Madan was the worst hit. They repaid me with excellent comments and suggestions.

Finally, I owe a very special debt of gratitude to Ozgecan Kocak, Marlo Raveendran, and Bart Vanneste for their generous and patient feedback on various versions of these chapters, ranging from the earliest (sometimes oral) versions to the present form.

■ CONTENTS

■ LIST OF FIGURES

■ LIST OF TABLES

1 An introduction to the microstructural approach to organization design

This book presents a theoretical perspective on the design of organizations, which I refer to as the **microstructural approach**. Organization design research is a branch of organization science that is concerned with understanding a) how organizations work in terms of aggregating the actions of their members towards organizational goals, and b) how to make organizations work better.[1] The joint emphasis on aggregation and a normative view on organizations as instruments for attaining goals distinguishes organization design theories from other branches of organization science such as organizational ecology theory, institutional theory, or resource dependence theory.

The microstructural approach to organization design aims to both expand and narrow current thinking. It takes an expansive view on the kinds of phenomena that can be studied in terms of organization design: besides traditional topics like inter-divisional collaboration, subsidiary–headquarter relationships, and re-organizations, this approach has also been used to fruitfully analyze cross-functional teams, strategic partnerships, buyer–supplier relations, alliance networks, mega-projects, post-merger integration, business groups, open source communities, and crowdsourcing.

At the same time, the microstructural approach narrows our focus by abstracting away from the variety and complexity of organizations to a few fundamental and universal problems of organizing (that relate to how they aggregate their members' efforts), as well as a few reusable building blocks, called microstructures (which capture common patterns of interaction between members of an organization). The complexity and variety of organization designs, this approach claims, can be understood in terms of these simpler elements.

The microstructural approach in historical context

If the kind reader is willing to tolerate a little ancestor worship, it will serve the purpose of anchoring the new approach I am writing about within the historical development of the field of organization design.

---

[1] "Organization theory" as a term is ambiguous as to which theory, and ignores the central role of empirical analysis. I prefer the term "organization science."

I believe there have been at least three distinct earlier generations (grouped by similarity of ideas, not necessarily chronologically) of theories about organization designs. The first generation of theorists flourished in the intellectual ecology created by the rise of industrialization. These included Henry Fayol, Luther Gulick, Mary Parker Follett, Frederick Taylor, Lyndall Urwick, and Max Weber. Arguably there were organization design theorists around for millennia before these scholars, including Imhotep (the architect of Egypt's earliest pyramids), Moses of the Old Testament, and more recently Alexander the Great, Chanakya, Caesar Augustus, Tokugawa Ieyasu, and Napoleon. The musings on organization design of these historical characters receive attention primarily because of their great deeds. But the first generation of organizational design theorists I have named were different. They are remembered more for the power and generality of their ideas about organization design, originating from specialized study of the topic, rather than particular applications of organizing.

The second generation, which marks an important intellectual watershed, is that associated with the "Carnegie" school. Richard Cyert, Harold Guetzkow, James March, and Herbert Simon (and indirectly through him, Chester Barnard) were some of the prominent theorists of this generation. Their pioneering attempts to treat organization design as a domain of scientific enquiry (rather than as a set of expedient management principles) made them, quite self-consciously, step away from the strongly normative stance of earlier theorists. The strong foundations of their work in the psychology of decision making enabled the nascent science of organization to take a big leap forward. The Carnegie school's lexicon—bounded rationality, decision-making premises, programs of action, coordination modes, sequential attention to goals, aspiration levels, problemistic search, quasi-resolution of conflict, myopic search, dominant coalitions, decomposability, interdependence, information processing, etc. remains an actively used set of constructs and conjectures that frame organizational phenomena in scientific terms. The mere roll call of these terms generates a sense of awe about the deep impact on the field these pioneers have had. Whatever theories have come since, and may come in the future, will very likely still build on these foundations (as indeed the ideas in this book do as well).

An important and influential third generation of research on organization design took what I will call a "macro-structural" approach. Thomas Burns, Lex Donaldson, Jay Galbraith, Paul Lawrence, Jay Lorsch, Raymond Miles, Henry Mintzberg, Charles Snow, George Stalker, James Thompson, Michael Tushman, Andrew Van de Ven, and Joan Woodward are some of the prominent theorists in this tradition. This approach is characterized by a focus on the organization as a whole; organizations are seen as complicated but ultimately describable as unitary entities. A typical statement of this perspective is that "entire organizations can be portrayed as integrated wholes in dynamic interaction with their environments" (Miles and Snow, 1987: 30). This is very much in the spirit of Cyert and March's analysis of organizational behavior (1963). The key questions have been about how organizations interact with their environment, and the appropriate internal structures needed to confront key environmental contingencies.

The macro-structural approach is concerned with organizational level constructs: size, centralization, formalization, span and depth of hierarchy, the basis for grouping and structural differentiation.[2] There was a corresponding interest in developing dimensions along which to characterize organizational environments, such as dynamism, turbulence and uncertainty, to explain the organizational level constructs through mechanisms of adaptation and selection (also see Levinthal, 1997). The core ideas in this "structural contingency" approach included typologies and configurations, as well as the constructs of internal and external fit (Donaldson, 1995; Miller, 1998; Siggelkow, 2003).

The fourth generation, to which the ideas in this book primarily belong, takes what I call the microstructural approach to organization design. Its two key tenets can be summarized as follows:

- Large, complex organizations can be understood as collections of smaller, simpler, and recurring patterns of "micro"-organizations.
- The fundamental issues in organization design pertain to the universal processes of dis-aggregation and re-aggregation that link the individual to the organizational level in all organizations—namely 1) the division of labor, and 2) the integration of effort.

If the macro-structural approach takes the lead of Cyert and March (1963) in treating the organization as a unitary entity, the microstructural approach may be seen as pushing forward in a complementary manner on the ideas in Simon (1945) and March and Simon (1958) that place aggregation issues center stage. This approach has strong links to the research on Complex Adaptive Systems (e.g. Simon, 1962; Holland, 1998; Miller and Page, 2007). Linda Argote, Richard Burton, Felipe Csaszar, Jerker Denrell, Kathleen Eisenhardt, Sendil Ethiraj, Thorbjorn Knudsen, Daniel Levinthal, Borge Obel, Jan Rivkin, Nicolaj Sigelkow, and Michael Tushman (in particular his later work on structural ambidexterity) are some of the contemporary scholars whose work I see as being very much in the spirit of the microstructural approach.

To elaborate on the two core ideas of the microstructural approach, namely that large complex organizations can be seen as collections of smaller, simpler ones, and that all organizations face the same universal problems pertaining

---

[2] The "macro" in the macro-structural approach signifies the emphasis on organizational level analysis, not necessarily "large n" organizations with a large numbers of individuals. For instance, the study of small, young entrepreneurial ventures can be undertaken from a macro-organizational perspective.

to the aggregation of efforts, some clarity on terminology is essential. I first describe what I mean by an organization, and then discuss the universal problems of organizing.

What defines an organization?

March and Simon wrote that "Organizations are systems of coordinated action among individuals and groups whose preferences, information, interests or knowledge differ. Organization theories describe the delicate conversion of conflict into cooperation, the mobilization of resources and the coordination of effort that facilitate the joint survival of an organization and its members" (March and Simon, 1993: 2). While later scholars have offered their own definitions (e.g., Aldrich, 1979; Burton and Obel, 1984; Etzioni, 1964; Scott, 1998; Stinchcombe, 1965), the various conceptualizations (see Table 1.1) of an organization have always preserved some common features: in essence they portray an organization as a particular kind of system which 1) has multiple agents, within 2) identifiable boundaries and 3) system level goals, towards which 4) the constituent agent's efforts make a contribution (I will use the terms actor, agent, individual, and decision-maker synonymously, for now, to refer to an "entity capable of action").[3]

In a theoretical analysis I conducted with Oliver Alexy and Markus Reitzig (Puranam, Alexy, and Reitzig, 2014), we argued that each of the four elements in this definition is critical and reflects widely accepted conceptions of which kinds of systems can be treated as organizations.

First, the system in question must have more than a single agent. This implies that two agents would suffice for the system to be called an organization, if other criteria were met.

Second, the set of agents under consideration must exist within identifiable boundaries. I do not necessarily mean a legal boundary, as in the case of a business firm, which is a particular kind of organization. Rather, a boundary demarcates the system under consideration from its context; we need it simply to be clear what "it" is we are talking about. The existence of a boundary does not of course imply that organizations are closed systems. They may be quite amenable to the influence of the environment outside their boundaries, and vice versa (Scott, 1998). Further, the boundaries need not be constant over time.

Third, it should be possible to ascribe goals to the system. In essence, we recognize a system as an organization through our understanding of its purpose. In fact, this is implicit in the Greek root of the word "organization",

---

[3] This and the next section draw extensively from Puranam, Alexy, and Reitzig (2014).

Table 1.1 Definitions of "organization"

Authors	Pages	Definition
Barnard, 1938	4	Formal organization is that kind of cooperation among men that is conscious, deliberate, purposeful.
March and Simon, 1958	23	Organizations are assemblages of interacting human beings . . . the largest assemblages have a semblance of a coordinating system . . . high specificity of structure and coordination (vs. diffuse and variable between organizations).
Etzioni, 1964	3	Organizations are social units (or human groupings) deliberately constructed and reconstructed to seek specific goals.
Stinchcombe, 1965	142	By an "organization" I mean a set of stable social relations, deliberately created, with the explicit intention of continuously accomplishing some specific goals or purposes.
Thompson, 1967	10	We will conceive of organizations as open systems, hence indeterminate and faced with uncertainty, but at the same time as subject to criteria of rationality and hence needing determinateness and certainty.
Katz and Kahn, 1978	20	All social systems, including organizations, consist of the patterned activities of a number of individuals. Moreover, these patterned activities are complementary or independent with respect to some common output or outcome: they are repeated, relatively enduring, and bounded in space and time.
Aldrich, 1979	4	Organizations are goal-directed, boundary-maintaining, and socially constructed systems of human activities.
Scott, 1998	10, 23, 25, 24	Organizations are collectivities oriented to the pursuit of relatively specific goals and exhibiting relatively high formalized social structures . . . Most analysts have conceived of organizations as social structures created by individuals to support the collaborative pursuit of specified goals. (A rational systems definition.)
		[Environments] shape, support, and infiltrate organizations. In this view, participants do not necessarily hold common goals or even routinely seek the survival of the organization. Participants in effect have transitory coalitions. [. . . In this view, organizations are] systems of independent activities linking shifting coalitions of participants; the systems are embedded in—dependent on continuing exchanges with and constituted by—the environments in which they operate. (An open systems definition.)
		"collectivities whose participants share a common interest in the survival of the system and who engage in collective activities, informally structured, to secure this end" (p. 24). (A natural systems definition.)
Daft, 2007	11	Organizations are (1) social entities that (2) are goal-directed, (3) are designed as deliberately structured and coordinated activity systems, and (4) are linked to the external environment . . . An organization exists when people interact with one another to perform essential functions that help attain goals
Kates and Galbraith, 2007	1	The organization is not an end in itself, it is simply a vehicle for accomplishing the strategic tasks of the business. It is an invisible construct used to harness and direct the energy of the people who do the work.
Wikipedia, 2012 (as of June, 23)	n.a.	An organization (or organisation—see spelling differences) is a social group which distributes tasks for a collective goal.

organon, that emphasizes the instrumental, tool-like nature of the entity (also see Perrow, 1972). Typically, the goals of an organization—even if defined simply in terms of continued existence—may be understood in terms of exploiting some form of gains from joint action that cannot be achieved by individual members acting in isolation. This approach treats organizations as instruments that help attain such goals, but is agnostic about the specific nature of these goals or the values we attach to the goals.

Organizational goals may well be implicit (i.e. unknown to any member), and even if explicit, need not be identical to the goals of the constituent agents (Scott, 1998). For instance, conventional business firms have explicitly stated goals, which typically include the pursuit of profits. However for most business organizations, the goals of the employees and the organization diverge, because the overall goals of the organization may not directly appeal to its employees, who contribute instead for compensation (Simon, 1951). Finally, it is worth noting that implicit goals for an organization may develop quite independently of its explicit goals, and in a manner that no agent is particularly conscious of (Selznick's description of the institutionalization of the Tennessee Valley Authority offers a striking illustration (1957)).

Fourth, the efforts of the agents in the organization, in aggregate, must contribute towards the organization's goals. This condition is intuitive if organizations are viewed as intentionally designed systems for achieving a goal (e.g., Aldrich, 1979; Stinchcombe, 1965). A gap between this intention and achievement would indicate that the system in question may have been set up with the aspiration of creating an organization, but is not yet one. For instance, if we were to imagine a public sector bureaucracy in which the employees in aggregate contribute nothing towards any discernible goal (bearing in mind that the stated goal is often not the only relevant one), it would not be an organization in the analytical sense defined here. After all, we would not call an object that seems to accomplish no purpose, a tool. Other theories in organization science, which do not share the premise of organizations as instruments, may legitimately reach different conclusions and adopt different naming conventions.

Even in implicit organizations that emerge spontaneously, if we recognize an organization at all, it is because the constituent agents' efforts appear to contribute towards this goal (to us, as analysts, not necessarily to the participants themselves). For instance, the existence of an emergent informal organization such as a community of practice may be recognized by the efforts of the members that seem to further the goals of the community, while possibly furthering their own goals as well.

Thus, if we wish to design a system of agents that accomplishes a goal, we are aspiring to create an organization. Conversely, for any system of agents that we want to study in terms of some goal they seem to be already accomplishing (whether consciously or not), I suggest it is useful to think of it as an organization. In the first sense, an organization is a designed object. In the second, it is a perceived object, that we perceive through a "design stance" (e.g. Dennett, 1995). In both, the concept of a goal-directed system is critical.

This conceptualization of an organization does not preclude short-lived dyads, corporations, or the various departments, units, sub-units and project teams within a corporation. Each of these can be treated as an organization, albeit of widely varying longevity and scale for the purpose of analysis.[4] The customers of the organization may well be included among its participants for some analyses (for instance, consider the user-producers in open source software development communities, or students in an educational organization). Both intentionally designed as well as emergent organizations qualify. For designed organizations, we *expect* that the agent's efforts will contribute towards organizational goals; for emergent organizations, we may infer their existence because the agents' efforts *appear* to contribute to an organizational goal.[5]

So what is *not* an organization? Individuals, goal-less networks and crowds, or in general collectives in which the constituent agents are neither expected to nor seem to make efforts towards achieving organizational goals, are ruled out by our definition. The reader may be curious at this point about the status of phenomena such as crowdsourcing, given this definition (Lakhani, Lifshitz-Assaf, and Tushman, 2012). "Crowdsourcing" is a neologism which gets its appeal from taking the notion of crowds, which are quintessentially goal-less (unlike mobs, which, perhaps terrifyingly, have goals) and showing how these can be organized into a goal-directed activity. I believe it is therefore useful to think of it as a form of organizing (also see Chapter 8 for an analysis of new forms of organizing).

In a microstructural approach to organization design, dyads, teams, groups, communities, committees, departments, divisions, government agencies, corporations, alliances, joint-ventures, and mega-project consortia are all legitimately the focus of analysis as organizations in their own right. To emphasize the point, we may "see" and choose to analyze different co-existing organizations with possibly overlapping memberships for any given set of agents. IBM corporation, and for that matter a much smaller entity like INSEAD, may be analyzed as one or many different smaller organizations, based on what we are trying to understand.

---

[4] Teams are organizations in which the members all interact, are interdependent, share goals, and are embedded within larger organizations (e.g. see Kozlowski and Bell, 2013: definition of teams).

[5] This is the sense in which Milgrom and Roberts (1992) treat a market as a particular kind of organization, whose constituents appear to be working to maximize their utilities through buying and selling.

Why do I insist on such a broad definition of organizations, that imposes no size constraint, neither requires a designer nor awareness of the organization's goals by its members?[6] There are at least two reasons.

First, with an expanded definition, we may learn useful things from our colleagues who have been studying systems of non-human agents. We do not usually think of these as organizations, but in fact they meet the definition discussed above. For instance, a network of computers designed to accomplish a purpose (e.g. support the exchange of cryptocurrencies) meets the conditions for being an organization. Nature has evolved many non-human organizations; a primate or insect colony can be seen as a robust solution to the implicit goals of these organizations (i.e. enhancing the reproductive success of their agents), given their environmental constraints and agent properties. Perhaps we should step back more often to see what we can learn from these, much as engineers can learn something about aircraft design from studying the wings of birds. Under what conditions would these design features make sense for a human organization? Even if the answer is "none," because the environmental constraints and agent properties are quite different, what general principles of organizing can we learn from these examples?

Table 1.2 Terminology used in this book

Organizational structure/organizational architecture: stable pattern of interactions between individuals or groups of individuals, where an *interaction* is interdependence, influence or both.

Formal structure refers to that part of the organizational structure that results from the mandates of *formal authority*—including decisions about grouping and linking roles, reporting relationships, decision systems, incentives, allocation of design and decision rights, and the geographic locus of activities.

Informal structure is that part of the organizational structure that is emergent—only partially and indirectly influenced by the structuring decisions made through formal authority. It includes the emergence of networks of communication, adcise and friendship, informal authority based on expertise and status, as well as values, beliefs and norms.

Organization design (noun): a set of solutions to the universal problems of organizing (i.e. division of labor and integration of effort). Put differently, an answer to the question "how does this organization work."

Organization design (verb): the process of arriving at the choices regarding the solution of the fundamental problems of organizing (i.e. division of labor and integration of effort) that define an organization design (noun). This process may not be carried out with foresight, or indeed by anybody; evolutionary forces of variation, selection and retention may also generate an organization design (noun).

Implicit organization: an organization whose constituent members are unaware of the organization's goals.

The "folk theorem" of organization design: the widely accepted principle that "interdependence between agents must be matched by integrative influence" (see Chapter 4 for a detailed discussion). It is a corollary of the necessity and sufficiency of solutions to the universal problems of organizing for an organization—division of labor must be matched by integration of effort.

---

[6] Groups are often defined as multi-agent goal-oriented systems in which agents are aware of their mutual co-membership in the group (e.g. Hackman, 1990), and teams are sometime stipulated to require at least three members. I do not impose these restrictions on the definition of an organization. This means all groups and teams are organizations, but the converse is not true.

Second, an expanded definition of organization also allows organization design theorists to potentially say something about phenomena that traditionally have not been considered in this way—for instance communities that manage common property, mega-project consortia and social movements. In the not too distant future, we may see teams of robots or mixed teams of humans and robots designed to accomplish particular goals, and we may have something useful to say about the design of such systems since they are, by definition, organizations.

Table 1.2 summarizes the common organization design-related terminology I will use in this book.

Universal problems of organizing

It is well known that any organization must feature the division of labor and the integration of effort (Smith, 1776; Burton and Obel, 1984; Lawrence and Lorsch, 1967; March and Simon, 1958; Mintzberg, 1979). These are, of course, classic dis- and re-aggregation processes.

The division of labor in organizations refers to the breakdown of the organization's goals into contributory sub-goals and eventually tasks, and the allocation of these tasks to individual members within the organization. The integration of effort within an organization requires mechanisms to motivate (cooperative) effort as well as to ensure that the information needed to coordinate efforts is available to the agents (Gulati et al., 2005; Lawrence and Lorsch, 1967). No sequencing is presumed here; solutions to the problem of division of labor may take into account the existence of solutions to the problem of integrating effort. The incentives and task allocations we would design for a group of strangers coming together to accomplish a goal would typically not be the same as what we would use for a pre-existing group faced with the same goal.

The fundamental problems of organizing are universal, not the solutions. There exist many possible ways to divide labor and integrate effort. For instance, contracts, authority and trust represent three qualitatively different solutions to the problem of integration of effort. To take another instance, today integration of certain kinds of knowledge based effort can occur either through face-to-face collaboration or increasingly over the internet (though these are not perfect substitutes). Thus, the possibility of technologies such as internet enabled collaboration must necessarily alter the kinds of division of labor that can emerge for the same goal (Altman, Nagle, and Tushman, 2013).

In our theorizing, Alexy, Reitzig, and I also found it useful to decompose the division of labor and the integration of effort further to yield a set of four problems that are universal to all organizations.

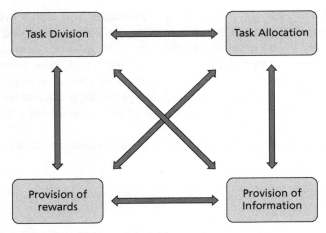

Figure 1.1 The universal problems of organizing

The division of labor can be broken down into the sub-problems of task division and task allocation (Figure 1.1).

Task division refers to the problem of mapping the goals of the organization into tasks and sub-tasks. When this is done consciously by human agents, it typically involves a (non-unique) means-ends decomposition of the goals of the organization. This creates a set of interrelated sub-tasks and information/material transfers that are believed to be necessary for the goals of the organization to be achieved (Newell and Simon, 1972). Workflow diagrams, business process maps and value chains are all ways of representing task division in the typical business firm.

Task allocation refers to the problem of mapping the tasks obtained through task division to individual agents and groups of agents. In the traditional business firm, the designation of formal roles and the recruitment of individuals into them is the usual mechanism to match sub-tasks to the members' skill profiles. This may or may not involve assignation of clusters of similar repeatable tasks to an individual (i.e. specialization), though the benefits of specialization in general are considerable (Smith, 1776). Alternatives include task allocation to minimize interdependence across agents, to increase diversity of tasks, and to assign responsibility for tangible outputs rather than intermediate steps (Hackman and Oldham, 1976). Chapter 3 describes different heuristic criteria for selecting among many possible divisions of labor for a given goal and group.

The integration of effort can in turn be broken down into the sub-problems of the provision of rewards (i.e. ensuring motivation and cooperation) and the provision of information (ensuring competence and coordination).

The *provision of rewards* relates to the idea that any organization must feature mechanisms for providing inducements to its members in order to motivate entry and continuance of membership and contribution (Simon, 1951). For instance, procedures for bestowing monetary compensation as stipulated in the employment contract, and non-monetary compensation in the form of work conditions, the choice of colleagues, and advancement opportunities are the primary reward mechanisms in the traditional business firm (Gibbons, 1998; Prendergast, 1999).

The *provision of information* refers to the problem of ensuring that an organization's agents have the information needed to execute their own actions and coordinate actions with others. Coordinated action requires that enough information exists for interacting individuals to be able to act as if they accurately anticipate each other's actions (Schelling, 1960). Students of organizations know that there are two basic means of solving the information provision problem: either the task division and allocation is such as to reduce the need for such information (e.g. through the use of directives, schedules, plans and standards—as long as each of us obeys them, our actions will in aggregate be coordinated) or the channels needed to generate such information can be enriched (e.g. the opportunity for face-to-face or electronic communication) (Srikanth and Puranam, 2014).

The existence of solutions to the four problems of organizing highlighted here—task division, task allocation, reward provision and information provision—are individually necessary and collectively sufficient for an organization to exist. **These problems are "organizational universals."** Since each of the problems has been defined in terms of choosing a mapping—from goals to tasks (task division), from tasks to agents (task allocation), from value created to agents (reward provision) and from information available to agents (information provision)—that contributes to the goals of the organization, solutions exist if such mappings exist. Solutions must make positive contributions towards organizational goals, but may vary significantly in the extent to which they do so. Higher-valued solutions are the ones that bring the organization closer to achieving its goals, and there may be equifinality in solutions. The contribution of a solution to one of these problems may depend on the solution adopted for another. For instance, the effectiveness of a particular approach to task division may depend on the approach to task allocation. In Chapter 8, I discuss these complementarities between solutions and the implications for the search process through the resulting rugged fitness landscape of organization designs (Levinthal, 1997).

Given the usual behavioral assumptions of bounded rationality and self-interest (Simon, 1947; Williamson, 1975), human organizations must necessarily feature solutions to each of the four basic problems of organizing. Absent arrangements to retain and motivate individuals, and enable them to undertake their assigned tasks (which aggregate towards the organization's goals) in a coordinated manner, one cannot recognize the existence of an organization as defined (i.e. as a multi-agent system with identifiable boundaries and system level goals towards which the constituent agent's efforts make a contribution).

The existence of solutions to the four problems is also sufficient for an organization to exist. If the four problems have solutions, then we have in effect (a) a set of tasks (b) assigned to a set of agents who have been (c) rewarded for and (d) informed about executing those tasks so that their efforts contribute towards the goals of the organization. Thus, for an organization to exist, it is necessary and sufficient that solutions exist to each of the four basic problems of organizing.

The microstructural approach puts these universal and fundamental problems—and the dis- and re-aggregation processes they pertain to—at the center stage of research in organization design. **An organization design is a set of specific solutions to these universal problems of organizing.** If we want to understand the design of a corporation, we must pay attention to how its goals are decomposed into sub-goals and tasks among its constituent divisions, and how their activities are integrated back; to understand the design of the division, the focus must be on its constituent departments, to understand the design of a team, the focus must be on the interactions between its constituent members, and so on.

Authority, which is a particular form of asymmetric influence, is a very important solution to the universal problems of organizing (Chapter 5), but it is not necessarily the only one. For this reason, it neither features as a necessary element in the definition of an organization, nor among the universal problems of organizing I list above.

The solutions an organization embodies to the universal problems of organizing are neither perfect nor permanent. Remedies to these solutions, in the form of arrangements to manage exceptions are often necessary. As I elaborate in Chapters 3 and 4, the organization's environmental attributes, such as dynamism or complexity (Mintzberg, 1979) must also ultimately influence how the fundamental problems of division of labor and the integration of effort are solved. Changes to the organization's environment and its goals therefore necessitate new solutions to the universal problems of organizing or at least improvements on existing ones. This is vital to the process of *organizational adaptation.*

Microstructures as theoretical building blocks

At its core, the microstructural approach exploits the hierarchic nature of interaction patterns in organizations. By this I do not mean anything necessarily pertaining to "fiat" or power (e.g. Williamson, 1975). In its most abstract sense a hierarchy is a pattern of ordered and unordered relationships (I give a more formal treatment in Chapter 6). A particular kind of hierarchy of interactions is known as a *containment hierarchy*. Simon's classic definition illustrates what this means (1962, 1996: 184): "By a hierarchic system or hierarchy, I mean a system that is composed of inter-related sub-systems, each of the latter being in turn hierarchic in structure until we reach some lowest level of elementary sub-system." This is the "boxes within boxes" metaphor: A has two sub-boxes {B, C} each of which has two sub-boxes, {B1, B2} and {C1, C2}, and so on. Simon went on to offer a stunningly simple but powerful explanation for why many complex systems, including organizations, evolve this form of hierarchic structure, which we will return to in Chapter 6.

For now, I want to focus on a particular property of hierarchic structures (including those which are not containment hierarchies): redundancy or repetitiveness. By this I mean the property that in a hierarchic structure, the same pattern may recur multiple times and at various levels of aggregation (Simon, 1962). This implies efficiencies in the description of the structure, as the description will require less information than that represented by the entire structure. If one likes trendy jargon, one may also say (without being dreadfully inaccurate) that organizational hierarchies display fractal patterns, with self-similarity across scales (Mandelbrot, 1983).

To make this concrete, Figure 1.2 shows some basic microstructures that one may recognize as characterizing the relationships between members in a team, departments in a division, divisions in a company, companies within a business group, or firms in an alliance or consortium. The circles are agents—entities capable of action. They could thus be individuals acting in isolation, or representing other organizations, or a decision-making group. The double-headed dashed arrows in each case indicate symmetric interactions, the single-headed bold arrows, asymmetric interactions.[7]

Interactions could take the form of interdependence (a condition in which the consequences to an agent of their actions depend on the actions of others) and/or influence (when one agent can shape the actions of another, possibly independently of the consequences of this influence). As we will see, how the universal problems of organizing are solved affects both interdependence through division of labor (Chapter 3), and influence through integration of effort (Chapter 4).

The " ... " indicates the possibility of scaling the structure by adding more agents. Figures 1.2a and 1.2b represent pure forms, because they portray asymmetric or symmetric relationships only. Figure 1.2c shows mixed structures,

---

[7] I assume in these drawings (to keep them simple) that the interactions are transitive through mediation.

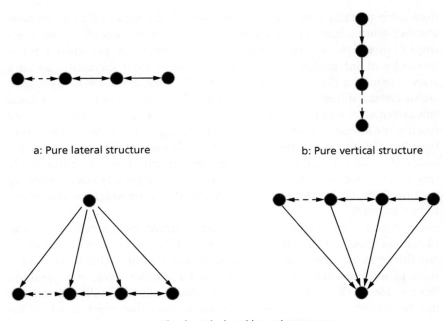

a: Pure lateral structure   b: Pure vertical structure

c: Mixed vertical and lateral structures

Figure 1.2 Instances of micro-structures

in which both types of elements are present. Figure 1.2c can thus be seen as a multiplex network connecting the agents, in which one network represents symmetric interaction (e.g. information flow), and another, asymmetric interaction (e.g. authority).

Figure 1.2a is a "flat hierarchy" with maximum branching = n, the number of agents; Figure 1.2b is a linear hierarchy with maximum branching = 1. Figure 1.2c shows two layered hierarchies with maximum branching = n−1. The structures in Figure 1.2 can also be seen as subgraphs—components from a larger network representing the organization. These are not the only micro-structures we can imagine,[8] but they are among the simplest possible structures with vertical and lateral relationships, and are ubiquitous in organizations (e.g. peer to peer relationships in teams and committees (1.2a), reporting lines (1.2b), one supervisor-many subordinates or matrix reporting (1.2c)). These two dimensions of interaction—vertical (asymmetric) and lateral (symmetric)—are fundamental to understanding structure.

---

[8] There are in fact three possible dyadic subgraphs and sixteen possible triadic subgraphs with directed edges. The number of mutual, asymmetric and null edges in the subgraph (e.g. [1, 2, and 0]) is a useful notation to distinguish them from each other (Holland and Leinhardt, 1976).

More complex structures can be created from these through recursion (each node itself is a microstructure) and scaling (adding nodes where there are dots). Even when dealing with larger and more complex patterns of inter-action than those in Figure 1.2, the basic logic of microstructures as patterns of vertical and lateral interactions will remain invaluable to understand these. The microstructural approach also allows us to draw on a rich body of results from research for each of these dimensions of interaction, and the conse-quences of scaling the organization along these dimensions.

This does not imply that the aggregation is either linear or simple, and we will need more sophisticated machinery from graph theory to represent such structures, and formal models to understand how interactions aggregate in them. The timescales over which these structures operate will be another critical source of variation. In this book, I will keep the technical discussion to the minimum needed for clarity. The details can be found in my original papers referred to in the text.

The microstructural approach thus builds on one fundamental premise about the nature of interaction patterns in organizations; that these patterns look similar *enough*, when seen at any resolution, to make it useful to treat them as identical. I recognize that not all hierarchic systems in nature enjoy the same degree of similarity of operating principles across levels of aggrega-tion. The principles of biochemistry that help explain molecular interactions say little about ecological competition between species (Ahl and Allen, 1996). However, in organizations, interactions at any level of aggregation are often between representative agents—individuals who represent aggregates of other individuals (over whom they may have authority or other asymmetric influ-ence relationships). Consequently, constructs like authority, interdependence, incentives and coordination are useful to understand teams on the shop floor as well as in the board room, as well as strategic alliances and consortia between firms.

I will therefore build on the assumption that regardless of the level of aggregation at which we examine organizations—whether we look at teams, alliances or the M-form corporation—the basic design issues pertaining to solving the universal problems of organizing (i.e. task division, task allocation, information, incentives) are still relevant.[9] The context in which a micro-structure operates is, of course, very important, and we should expect the same microstructure to behave differently in a boardroom and a shop floor.

---

[9] Microstructures are related to the notion of network "motifs"—frequently recurring patterns of interaction that may have functional properties (Milo, Shen-Orr, Itzkovitz, Kashtan, Chklovskii, and Alon, 2002; Onella, 2007). In naturally occurring networks as diverse as phone call networks and gene regulatory networks, the detection of motifs (which requires complex algorithms) has helped to understand the overall functioning of the network. In the hierarchic structure of complex organiza-tions, motif detection may not be as challenging because of the property of repitition, but we may nonetheless be able to gain insights into the aggregate network in an analogous manner.

I assume these differences in context can be considered as differences in parameters that affect the same basic underlying processes, and propose that we see how far we can go with such an approach.

The case for the microstructural approach

There are two basic ideas at the heart of the microstructural approach—first, that large complex organizations can be seen as collections of smaller, simpler ones, and secondly, the key aggregation processes to focus on for organization design pertain to division of labour and integration of effort. What does embracing these ideas do for us? The rest of this book can be seen as a detailed answer to this question. Nonetheless, I sketch out the central arguments here, to return to in more detail later.

IMPLICATIONS FOR THEORY

First, the microstructural approach can give us a better answer to the question of "how organizations work" (which is after all one of the central aims of organization design theorizing) than what can be obtained from either unitary actor or unitary entity models of organization. Models and theories which aim to explain organizational adaptation by treating organizations as unitary actors, largely do so by assumption. Thus organizations, as unitary actors, may be assumed to search locally (Cyert and March, 1963), conform to legitimacy pressures (DiMaggio and Powell, 1983), or exploit brokerage in their network of relations (Burt, 1992). We may also have accounts of varying plausibility for such assumptions: about extreme centralization of power and knowledge that effectively turn an organization into a unitary actor, or about committees, politics and coalitions that produce problemistic and local search (e.g. Cyert and March, 1963); and we may even observe organizational behavior that is consistent with these assumptions. But our ability to rule out alternative explanations and in particular to make normative interventions will remain limited, as long as these assumptions remain assumptions (also see Coleman, 1990).

The problem is not with the unitary actor assumption per se, but rather in it's application to the same level of aggregation as what is being explained. When one is interested in understanding an ecology of organizations or the structure of an industry, assuming that the constituent organizations are unitary actors can be a good analytic strategy. However, even if one can build a perfectly serviceable wall with a "black box" theory of a brick, one cannot hope to truly understand and improve the strength and flexibility of the brick in this way. This can be expressed in more general terms with reference to the specific layer of the hierarchy of phenomena that a theorist is interested in: "assume a simple structure for entities at layer k if the interest is in explaining phenomena at layer k + 1" (counting from bottom up). Thus if one wants to explain market structure, for instance, treating the firm as a unitary entity may be sensible. It is less sensible when the goal is to understand how firms work, and possibly improving how they work.

Within the field of organization design, the "macro-structural" theories of Burns, Stalker, Mintzberg, Miles, and Snow answer the question of how organizations work by assuming the organization to be an internally complex but ultimately, unitary entity. In the work of these authors, an organization is characterized by properties such as its degree of centralization, formalization, differentiation, etc. which are implicitly assumed to apply to the entire organization. These properties can then be explained on the basis of the adaptive advantages they confer to the organization given the particular set of environmental attributes it faces. We should see this approach as being a very important move in the right direction towards unpacking the black box of how organizations work, but not as the final step. The microstructural approach I believe helps us to take another step, because it allows for a recognition of the internal diversity and complexity of organizations by focusing on units at lower levels of aggregation (modeled via representative agents) as well as on the relationships between them. Understanding the micro is necessary, if not sufficient in order to truly understand and re-design the macro.

Second, the microstructural approach embraces the spirit of consilience. The term was popularized by E. O. Wilson, who described it as being the normal approach to the natural sciences, but which he chastised the social sciences for lacking (Wilson, 1998). Consilience encourages explanation at one level of aggregation, on the basis of knowledge of lower order phenomena: organizations or markets as aggregation of individuals; individual actions as a result of cognitive modules, etc. Consilience in the context of the science of organization design requires a) scientifically derived knowledge of lower level phenomena, and b) a theory of aggregation. Wilson articulated and popularized what is widely held to be true across many fields of science: that consilience, through pressure towards local consistency of explanation, can improve global understanding.

By making explicit the links from individual behavior to increasingly complex organizational aggregations, the microstructural approach encourages, perhaps even forces, consilience. At the same time, it does not force an infinite regress. To study organization designs, we need a sound understanding of human behavior, but not necessarily the cognitive mechanisms underlying that behavior, or the neurobiology, chemistry or physics underneath these mechanisms. This is because our interest is in the aggregation from individual behavior to organizational outcomes. Like Popperian falsification, consilience is a powerful heuristic rather than a strict necessity; it is sometimes possible to construct theories of higher-level aggregates with scant knowledge of lower-level elements, as Simon acknowledged (1996: 19). Such a blackboxing approach, as I have noted, comes with the two critical drawbacks of being unable to develop explanations that satisfyingly rule out alternatives, and being unable to intervene effectively to improve the system as needed.

In this book I will build very explicitly on a clearly articulated set of behavioral assumptions, for which we have significant evidence (Chapter 2), and try to stay close to these assumptions at all times. This also implies that I will have to strike a balance between coordination and motivation based approaches to the analysis of organization designs. Traditionally, organizational scholars have focused (though not exclusively) on the problems of coordination between individuals with limited rationality. This perspective sees communication, authority and procedures as central to the design of organizations. Organizational economists have focused (again, not exclusively) on the problem of motivating self-interested individuals to act in accordance with the best interests of the organization; the spotlight is on incentives, shirking and relational contracts. An approach to theorizing about organization design that intends to stay true to behavioral foundations must necessarily aim at both these issues, however challenging that is.

IMPLICATIONS FOR METHODOLOGY

The microstructural approach emphasizes studying organizations in terms of the interactions between lower level entities, and how these aggregate (for instance strategic alliances may be seen as organizations in which the participating firms interact via representative agents). This opens up a range of powerful research methodologies for the organization design researcher. We may underestimate the value of methodology, perhaps seeing it at best as the handmaiden of theory; yet careful analysis of major theoretical breakthroughs reveals that they are often triggered by innovation in methodology (Greenwald, 2012). Methodologies for studying aggregation, in particular agent based models and lab experiments are obviously complementary to the microstructural approach (Puranam, 2012). Detailed ethnographic observation of aggregation processes will very likely play an equally important role, to guide the formulation of models and experiments.

IMPLICATIONS FOR PRACTICE

The microstructure approach also holds forth the promise of being able to explore normative questions with greater confidence than before. As accessing and analyzing large volumes of "big data" on internal organizational processes becomes feasible, the need for simple and robust theoretical principles that help make sense of this data deluge will grow stronger. Data on how individuals act within organizations can only be meaningfully analyzed to improve organization designs **if we have theoretical frameworks to think about how structures influence individual behavior, and individual behaviors aggregate up to organizational goals.** The microstructural approach is unique in aspiring to provide both; unitary actor and unitary entity theories of organizations by definition do not compete in this space.

The increased importance of teams and work groups as primary organizational units (e.g. Kozlowski and Bell, 2013) also implies a direct applicability of microstructural thinking to their analysis. These micro-organizations form and disband, drawing upon the resources of the macro-organization they are part of, and are embedded within the context of the latter. A theory of organization design must be able to confront such nested systems and offer insights on how to improve them.

Beyond studying existing structures, I also believe that by developing a set of well understood general principles of disaggregation and aggregation processes in organizations, and using the tools to simulate and test how these may interact and unfold, we may be able to push forward on the agenda to prototype organization designs *in silico* as well as in the behavioral lab and through field experiments (Zelditch, 1969; Burton and Obel, 1980).

RELATED APPROACHES

This bundle of ideas—aggregation, compatibility with evidence on human behavior, and abstract reusable building blocks—is uniquely brought together in the domain of organization design through the microstructural approach. But it has close relatives in other domains, as I discovered during the course of writing this book.

In the field of strategy, the concept of organizational routines (Cyert and March, 1963; Nelson and Winter, 1982) is an intellectual progenitor, with its careful attention to aggregation and behavioral plausibility. The microstructural approach emphasizes the design and topology of interaction patterns more explicitly. Recent interest in behavioral strategy, micro-foundations and strategic human capital all have at least some elements in common with the organizational microstructure agenda (Levinthal, 2011; Barney and Felin, 2013; Helfat and Peteraf, 2015).[10] In sociology, Levi Martin's work on social structures also has several features in common. As he notes: "We have somehow managed to almost entirely avoid the fact that large structures, including

---

[10] See also the Behavioral Strategy Wiki maintained by INSEAD PhD students: https://www. behavioralstrategywiki.org/.

institutional structures such as organizations, are generally concretes of smaller structures, and even more important, the larger structures tend to be the result of historical processes in which small structures were progressively aggregated" (2009: 30). Organizational economics (e.g. Gibbons, 2018) shares broadly the same approach to thinking about aggregation and building blocks. The push towards thinking of teams as dynamic open systems (Arrow, McGrath, and Berdahl, 2000) shares a similar theoretical sensibility to the microstructural approach, as well as an appreciation for similar methodology.

Coleman's emphasis on understanding the micro-to-macro linkage is foundational for all of these approaches (1990). I think it best to let readers make up their own minds as to what is unique and useful about the microstructural approach I describe here vis-à-vis these intellectual fellow travelers. Organizations are sufficiently complex phenomena that a diversity of perspectives on them is probably desirable, at least at the current state of our understanding.

Conclusion

The microstructural approach tackles the problem of organization design by "thinking small." Large organizations can be analyzed as aggregations of smaller organizations. These smaller organizations form recurring patterns that we call microstructures. Understanding the microstructure allows us to then model the macro-structure, through principles of scaling and recursion.

Is the microstructural approach "reductionist"? It depends on what one means by the term. If by reductionist we mean "reducing to mechanisms of cause and effect," then of course the answer is Yes. The alternative, as Daniel Dennett points out, too often is a wishful reliance on skyhooks (Dennett, 1995; also see Hedstrom and Swedburg, 1998). If we cannot explain a phenomenon in terms of underlying cause and effect, then we have not really explained anything. On the other hand, if by reductionist we mean "reducing to individual level properties alone," then the answer is No. Microstructures are building blocks of (possibly non-linear) interaction patterns between individuals, which are necessary to understand aggregation processes.

This approach leans heavily on the idea that regardless of scale, organizations face the same universal problems in order to exist—division of labor and integration of effort. This is the key principle that connects the micro to the macro. An organization design can be seen as a set of specific solutions to these universal problems of organizing; it is an answer to the question "how does this organization work?" In the microstructural perspective, every organization (to qualify as one) must have a design. But not every design comes from the imperative of a designer (i.e. the case of emergent and implicit organizations).

Organization design*ing* as a process is the search for solutions to the universal problems of organizing that are relevant and feasible for the organization in question. The search does not presume "one best way" that applies to all organizations. Even for an organization, if the "one best way" exists, it is very likely impossible to find it (or even know when we have found it). This follows from the interaction between the nature of human cognition and the search environments typical of design problems (Levinthal, 1997).

However, none of this precludes a) efforts to find improvements for organizations—which is what the practice of organization design is about; b) the scientific study of the organization design process as a phenomenon; or c) the application of the scientific method (i.e. the quest for causal mechanisms underlying observed phenomena) to understand the nature of organization designs (Simon, 1962). The microstructural approach aspires to be a useful meta-representation that is relevant for all these objectives.

There is so much that we still do not understand about how organizations work that it would be foolhardy to claim that the microstructural approach, with its strong functionalist stance, will alone suffice to understand it all.[11] Rather, I see it as a part of a theoretical toolkit, complementary to the macro-structural approach and others.

THE REST OF THIS BOOK IS ORGANIZED AS FOLLOWS

In Chapter 2 ("Behavioral Foundations"), I explicitly introduce the conceptualization of individual behavior in organizations that I use for the rest of the book, and describe its key elements: goals, representations and choice process. I show how this tri-partite classification can flexibly be used to describe many kinds of rationalities that may co-exist within organizations. Organization design is argued to influence individual goals, representations and choices through three basic mechanisms: sorting, framing and structuring.

Chapters 3 and 4 deepen the analysis of the universal problems of organizing I introduced in this chapter, illustrating the arguments with simple dyadic microstructures, as well as matrix notation to scale to arbitrarily large structures.

Chapter 3 focuses on the division of labor. After considering various criteria by which tasks may be clustered and assigned across individuals, I analyze two important heuristic bases for clustering tasks—by object and by activity. I also give the conditions under which a choice between these forms of division of labor arises—the conjunction of a non-decomposable task structure and a decomposable product structure.

---

[11] It is worth pointing out that a functionalist stance requires neither equilibrium nor global optimality assumptions. I do not make either.

Chapter 4 turns to the integration of effort. I discuss the necessary conditions for the integration of effort, and describe how knowledge and motivation related problems may independently and jointly impede it (and when the consequences of these problems can be localized). I also discuss integration of effort as a search (dynamic) vs. execution (static) problem, and what the difference implies for design.

In Chapter 5 ("The Exercise of Authority") I discuss the role of authority in generating, enforcing and correcting solutions to the universal problems of organizing. I use a triadic microstructure, featuring two peers and an authoritative superior, to illustrate concepts such as delegation, decentralization, centralization, and conditional decentralization, as well as why authority may be useful as an organizing principle even when it is not necessarily wielded by the wise.

In Chapter 6 ("Hierarchies of Authority") I define a hierarchy of authority and distinguish it from other hierarchies that may be present in organizations, particularly task hierarchies. A simple process model of hierarchic growth is outlined, and a key distinction is made between integrated hierarchies (where the authority and task hierarchies are aligned) and separated hierarchies (where they are not). I then discusses two aggregate features of hierarchies—control and information loss—and point to their possible adaptive benefits. The chapter concludes with some thoughts on why hierarchies are often disliked, despite their ability to organize large numbers of individuals effectively.

In Chapter 7 ("Formal and Informal Structure of Organization"), I focus on the interactions between formal and informal aspects of organizational structure. I will argue that the emergence of the informal organization can be shaped by choices about the formal organization. In turn, choices about the formal organization are partly constrained and shaped by the informal organization. After illustrating the basic logic in the context of microstructures, I describe a multiplex network approach that enables analysis of this complex phenomenon at the macro-structural level.

Chapter 8 ("New Forms of Organizing") focuses on what exactly is a new form of organizing—and what makes it new. Drawing on the universal problems of organizing introduced in Chapter 1, I will argue that a new form of organizing solves the problems of division of labor and/or integration of effort in a novel manner relative to organizations with comparable goals. Novelty in organizing therefore need not imply theoretical novelty of underlying solution, but may suggest opportunities for theorizing about novel combinations of older solutions.

Chapter 9 ("Methodology for Microstructures") is a reflection on the variety of methods one may use to study organization design in general, and microstructures in particular. There are distinctive strengths (and limitations) to each method when used in isolation or conjunction with others, and I offer some thoughts on these as well as speculations on further developments.

2 Behavioral foundations

It seems only natural to want people, not paragons (or parodies), at the heart of our theories of organization design. But if we aim to build theories on the foundations of evidence about human behavior (as opposed to assumptions), we immediately confront enormous complexity. This arises from the subject matter itself, as well as from terminological and methodological incompatibility across the various fields that concern themselves with the topic. We cannot avoid confronting this complexity as organization designers, as ultimately "The behavior of individuals is the tool with which the organization achieves its targets." (Simon, 1947: 108).

In articulating the behavioral foundations to develop the concepts in this book, I will therefore be unabashedly pragmatic. My aim is to paint a crude, but hopefully useful picture of behavior based on current thinking in the relevant social sciences that is useful for constructing arguments about how organization designs influence and aggregate individual behavior. The picture will look quite coarse to those who are interested in understanding human behavior for its own sake. It will also be coarse in an idiosyncratic way: I readily concede that stylized pictures about human behavior constructed for other purposes (such as theorizing about the effects of public policy on individual choice, of marketing campaigns on consumer behavior, or of parenting styles on child development, for instance) may look different from the one provided here.

The picture I present builds on three hierarchically linked components that have traditionally been used to characterize behavior in the organizational sciences (e.g. Simon, 1946; Cyert and March, 1963): Goals, Representations and Choice process (see Figure 2.1). The particular way in which these elements are linked can be roughly summarized in the statement that **individuals tend to make choices that, in their representations, increase the possibility of attaining goals that are currently important to them**. It is worth highlighting what is not in this proposition: it does not assume constancy of goals, accuracy of representation, or choice as maximization.

The objectives for this chapter are as follows: First, I elaborate on these three elements (Goals, Representations, Choice process), providing an overview of the diversity that is typical in these across individuals, and across situations even within the same individual. Second, I show how the goals/representations/choices framework can be used to understand different conceptions of rationality—global, bounded, adaptive, or concerned with appropriateness— that are useful in studying the design of organizations. Third, I argue that

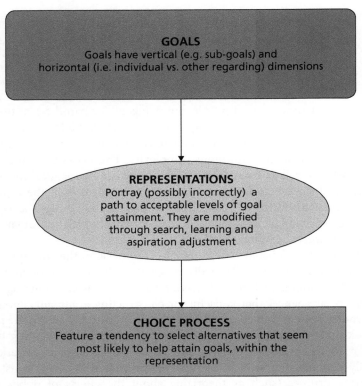

Figure 2.1 Elements of behaviour—goals, representations and choice

organization designers have levers at their disposal—sorting, framing and structuring—that can tune the naturally occurring variation in goals, representation and choice processes to desired levels. This aids tractability in the analysis and design of organizations using the microstructural approach.

Elements of behavior

GOALS

Individuals in organizations are purposive, in the sense that they are motivated by a variety of goals. A goal is a mental construct indicating a desirable end-state. It energizes and induces effort towards its achievement. Put simply, goals motivate, and are therefore critical to understanding what people do (and choose not to do).

We can think of goals along both vertical and horizontal dimensions. The vertical dimension refers to the idea that a goal can be factored into a system of sub-goals through means-ends linkages (Simon, 1947; Fishbach and Ferguson, 2007). For an academic researcher, "doing a good job on the research design" can be seen as a sub-goal in a research project, the attainment of which leads him closer to the sub-goal "having the paper published," which in turn makes it more likely that tenure is achieved (merely another sub-goal, despite what some of our colleagues seem to think), which moves him closer to the sub-goal of "having a good professional career" and so on.[1]

Social psychologists have long been interested in developing a parsimonious description of the ultimate goals, or "basic human needs" (e.g. Maslow's hierarchy) that motivate us. Perfect consensus remains elusive, but some of the ultimate goals that make it to most lists today include *self-preservation*, the *maximization of pleasure and minimization of pain*, the *enhancement of self-esteem, autonomy* and *competence* and the *need to achieve a sense of belonging* or *relatedness within a group* (Pittman and Ziegler, 2007: 85; Deci and Ryan, 2000; also see Lindenbergh, 2013).

While the exact content of the lists may vary, three properties of such lists of ultimate goals seem to be common, and are noteworthy. First, the lists tend to be much smaller than the number of sub-goals that we observe people pursuing in everyday life. This implies that there may be many different pathways through sub-goals that link to the same smaller set of ultimate goals. We should therefore expect diversity in the ways that individuals can be motivated.

Second, material rewards do not feature in the list, indicating that most people do not desire cash or its near equivalents as an ultimate goal in itself. This suggests that it may sometimes be possible to avoid material rewards altogether if the attainment of closer to ultimate goals is directly feasible (for instance when the enjoyment of performing a task provides sufficient intrinsic motivation that no extrinsic motivator is necessary).[2]

Third, the list of ultimate goals includes those that are primarily self-oriented as well as those that are primarily other-oriented. A researcher may care not only about the paths to tenure and career stability, but also about her standing in the academic community, how fairly she is being treated vis-à-vis her colleagues and a desire to advance her department in the global research rankings. This introduces the horizontal dimension in the consideration of

---

[1] Some sub-goals may link negatively to ultimate goals (for instance snacking and long term health), but it is the existence of the linkage that I focus on for now.

[2] Misjudging which tasks can provide intrinsic motivation can be a costly design mistake. There is evidence that the temporary provision followed by withdrawal of extrinsic incentives for tasks that provided intrinsic motivation may suppress the level of intrinsic motivation (Deci, Koestler, and Ryan, 1999; Eisenberger and Cameron, 1996). This is most likely when the incentives were behavior-based rather than performance-based.

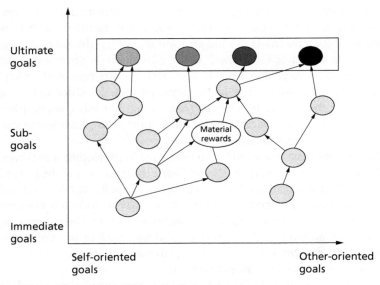

Figure 2.2 Vertical and horizontal structure of goals

goals (see Figure 2.2). This figure helps to place into perspective the role of material rewards in the overall scheme of goals.

The classic dichotomy between individual and collective interests mirrors the distinction between ultimate goals that are individually oriented and those that are socially oriented. The presumption of self-interest is widespread in the social sciences, particularly in neo-classical economics and some streams of rational choice sociology (Ratner and Miller, 2001). The evidence for the existence of other-regarding preferences has however gathered overwhelming weight, and is now simply taken as axiomatic in several fields (such as social psychology, and increasingly in parts of economics—see for instance the review by Cooper and Kagel, 2013). In the Appendix, I reproduce the subset of "human universals" that pertain to goals—these are elements of human behavior or culture that are believed to be present in every single culture or society encountered by ethnographers and anthropologists (Brown, 1991). The large number of other-regarding elements in this list is striking.

Why human beings have these ultimate goals is a question that evolutionary psychologists tend to answer with reference to the reproductive advantages of having them in our ancestral selection environment. In particular, the existence of socially oriented ultimate goals can be understood in terms of the reproductive advantages to the individual of living socially (Caporael, 2007), and are believed to have evolved to sustain human cooperation (Brosnan and De Waal, 2004; Gilbert, Price, and Allan, 1995).

The existence of pro-social motivations varies strongly across individuals. Experimental studies of cooperation in games often report that most individuals are either pro-social (i.e. exhibit a concern for other's outcomes as well as one's own) or pro-self (i.e. purely care about themselves). As we will see, this has implications for designed sorting into organizations.

The pro-sociality may be of a subtle form, as argued in the theory of strong reciprocity (Fehr and Gintis, 2007). Strong reciprocators cooperate if they see others cooperate, and are willing to punish non-cooperators at a cost to themselves. They thus act as if their goal is to uphold the reciprocity norm (a service they perform at a cost to themselves), independent of outcomes received through interaction. Reciprocity (both positive and negative) features in the list of human universals. Experimental evidence from public goods games shows that the majority of participants can be classified as either purely self-regarding or as conditional cooperators (i.e. demonstrating reciprocity) (Fischbacher and Gachter, 2006). Concepts such as reciprocity, particularly when enriched by the possibility of indirect effects (e.g. A's cooperative behavior towards B is observed by C, and C then cooperates with A) can be very powerful in understanding how such interactions in microstructures aggregate up to macro levels (see Vanneste, 2016 for a model of the emergence of inter-organizational trust through indirect reciprocity among individuals).

REPRESENTATIONS

Given their goals, individuals also have *Representations* of how to pursue them. This is their definition of the situation (March and Simon, 1958: 139). Cognitive representations are conceptual structures in individuals' minds that encapsulate a simplified understanding of the reality these individuals face (Newell and Simon, 1972; Rouse and Morris, 1986; Thagard, 2005; Wyer, 2007).[3] I want to focus on two features of representations for goal pursuit that are critical to my purpose. First, representations feature alternative courses of action (i.e. sub-goals) and associated constraints that together shape beliefs about what paths lead to the achievement of relevant goals. Second, they have associated aspiration levels which define the extent to which goal attainment can be considered satisfactory (March and Simon, 1958: 141; Newell and Simon, 1972).

Stated more formally, assume that in the objective task environment, there is a set of possible alternatives A: $\{A_1, A_2 \ldots A_m\}$ which map onto performance outcomes Π: $\{\Pi_1, \Pi_2 \ldots \Pi_m\}$ for the agent in terms of attainment of a relevant goal. The representation for goal attainment held by the agent at time t then

---

[3] I will not distinguish at this point between the possible formats of the representation (e.g. concepts, rules, connections, images or analogies).

consists of a set of alternatives $\{a_{1,t}, a_{2,t} \ldots a_{n,t}\}$ and the associated set of performance outcomes $\{\pi_{1,t}, \pi_{2,t} \; \pi_{n,t}\}$, as well as a performance aspiration level π_t^*. In general, even without knowing the details of the objective task environment ourselves, we can assume that $n<m$ (incompleteness of representation), $\Pi_i \neq \pi_{i,t}$ (inaccuracy of representation) and $\max\{\Pi\}>\pi_t^*$ (aspiration level is below the global maximum).

To illustrate, a fresh PhD taking up a professorial appointment probably has a representation of the path to tenure that includes the possible means to achieve this goal (alternatives), beliefs about their relative effectiveness, what actions are ruled out or are strictly necessary (constraints), and how to judge if progress is satisfactory (aspiration levels). As many young professors go on to discover, representations may be neither complete (i.e. do not cover all possible action alternatives actually available) nor correct (i.e. do not reflect the true possibilities for those actions to help achieve the goal). The correspondence between these mental elements and the states of the world may be a very imperfect one. Representations can thus vary in their veridicality.

Representations can be transformed over time via three key processes: search, aspiration adjustment, and learning.

- Representations are modified through search for better alternatives, if the extent to which desired goals are being achieved falls below aspiration levels. Goals have associated aspiration levels, and if performance in terms of goal attainment is above these levels, then individuals may be satisfied with the current alternatives, rather than continue the quest for the best possible alternative, in order to conserve cognitive processing effort. If our young professor is doing well at teaching and the papers are getting requests for revisions at the best journals, he is unlikely to modify his representations. However when performance falls below aspiration levels, this may trigger a more active search for superior alternatives, modifying the representation of the feasible set of actions (Cyert and March, 1963; also see Greve, 2003, 2008). This is also known as problemistic search.
- Representations also change through aspiration-adjustment processes, based on performance feedback (on own and other's performance) (Cyert and March, 1963; Newell and Simon, 1972). How others in the cohort are doing, and his own performance relative to theirs, may adjust our young professor's aspirations. As aspirations levels adjust upwards or downwards based on past performance, this may trigger or turn off search processes depending on current performance relative to the new aspiration level (Greve, 2003).[4]

---

[4] Instead of aspirations adjusting, the goal itself might also change in response to feedback. An extreme form of this is cognitive dissonance (Festinger, 1957), in which the goal adjusts to accomplishment, rather than the other way round.

- Representations are also modified on the basis of learning about the merits of various alternatives. Learning refers to a change in representation (and consequently behavior), which may arise because of feedback from the task environment on own actions, through sharing representations with other agents, or both. It is convenient to refer to the former as online learning because feedback on actions from the environment is generated and utilized, and the latter as offline learning (Puranam and Maciejovsky, 2017).
- A basic process of online learning that has been of particular interest to organizational scientists is *reinforcement*. This fundamental process and its variants are known under the labels of trial-and-error learning, experiential learning, operant or instrumental conditioning, and "win-stay-lose-shift" rules in the relevant literatures in psychology, computer science, organization theory and evolutionary biology (Thorndike, 1911; March, 1991; Domjan, 2010; Nowak and Sigmund, 1993; Sutton and Barto, 1998).[5] All instantiate Thorndike's Law of Effect: responses that produce a satisfying effect in a particular situation become more likely to occur again in that situation and responses that produce a discomforting effect become less likely to occur again in that situation. This implies that favorable feedback on selecting an alternative tends to positively reinforce the belief about an alternative and thereby make its choice more likely, while unfavorable feedback does the opposite. For our young professor, certain teaching cases and certain journals become favorites while others tend to be avoided.

In sum, problemistic search (typically by expanding the set of alternatives), aspiration adjustment (by triggering problemistic search) and learning processes (by altering beliefs about the viability of alternatives) all modify representations. However, just as representations are imperfect, the processes for updating them are also not infallible. They do not necessarily improve the individual's performance or the veridicality of representations held by the individual. Search is often local. Even when forced to search because performance falls below aspiration levels, search may be restricted to a cognitively local neighborhood. Faced with poor teaching evaluations and rejections from journals, dubious advice from friends in the department (who may not necessarily be expert themselves) may take the place of systematic investment in upgrading teaching or research skills.

Noise and bias in feedback during online learning may lead individuals to learn the wrong lessons from experience and fall victim to superstitious learning (Levinthal and March, 1993). This danger exists in any situation in which establishing a link between individual action and feedback is difficult.

---

[5] It is noteworthy that artificial intelligence researchers began to experience breakthroughs in building adaptive agents after they adopted reinforcement learning and discarded rule-based systems.

Organizations, because they constitute multiple agents whose actions contribute towards an organizational objective, are particularly prone to this challenge because the feedback on an individual's action is very often influenced in unknown ways by the actions of others (Puranam and Swamy, 2016). Offline learning from the experience of others is naturally only as effective as the quality of the representations that others have.

However, representations held by an agent need not be perfect (even if that was ever possible) to be useful. They may be better than, or at least not worse than those of others, and they may serve a coordinative role independent of their veridicality (see the "common prior" effect, in Chapter 4).

A final but important point: representations of social environments are of particular relevance to organization designers. Agents in organizations have representations of whom they are interdependent with, and whether they can trust them (Puranam and Vanneste, 2009). However the basic processes of how these representations change still include search, aspiration adjustment and learning (Vanneste, Puranam, and Kretschmer, 2013; Clement and Puranam, 2017).

CHOICE PROCESS

I assume that agents' choice process is such that they are more likely to choose alternatives that promise the attainment of their currently active goals, than alternatives that do not, within their representation. A representation is a mental model of currently understood to be available alternatives (or paths to those alternatives). Within this available set of alternatives, individuals are more likely to choose the one that appears best, though mistakes or consciously playful or curious attempts to select alternatives other than those that currently appear best, may also occur (also see Luce's choice rule—Luce, 1959). An agent will select with high probability the alternative $a_{i,t}$ that yields the highest expected performance $\pi_{i,t}$, though the probability need not be one. Of course, even if the probability is 1, this does not guarantee global maximization, because of the lack of correspondence between representation and objective task environment.

In other words, individuals tend to exploit what their representations tell them is the best course of action to achieve their desired goals (Camerer and Ho, 1999; Daw, O'Doherty, Dayan, Seymour, and Dolan, 2006; Laureiro-Martinez, Brusoni, Canessa, and Zollo, 2015), but not with perfect reliability. Since representations are not necessarily perfect, escaping the tendency to exploit the current representation in order to explore for better ones by selecting alternatives whose value is unknown in the current representation, or even believed to be inferior, can be useful (March, 1991). But for this exploration to occur, the tendency to exploit must be suppressed (Daw et al., 2006).

A distinction that has become important in contemporary research in psychology is that between automatic vs. deliberative/controlled choice (Stanovich and West, 2000; Evans and Stanovich, 2013). This has been popularized as the distinction between "System I" (automatic) and "System II" (deliberative) thinking (Kahneman, 2011). System I thinking is assumed to not require much working memory. It is described by labels such as "fast, associative, and intuitive." System II thinking requires working memory, and is believed to slower but more accessible to articulation. Its operation is closer (but not identical) to the explicit rule-based approach of a logician.[6] The account of behavior I have given so far—of exploitative choice contingent on the representation of paths to goal pursuit—may suggest a slant towards a System II sensibility. I believe this is a fair characterization, but would add three observations.

First, even when an agent cannot explicitly articulate or be aware of deliberative thinking, his behavior may nonetheless be driven by a non-conscious process involving goals, representations and choices. For instance, there is evidence for reliable patterns of automatic behavior that seem to reflect egocentric biases (Epley and Dunning, 2000). At a minimum, these elements are a modeling convenience, even if individuals do not manifest these in the same way in System I and System II thinking (see Cohen, Levinthal, and Warglien, 2014 for modeling approaches that more directly address habitual behavior).

Second, current thinking suggests that the dichotomy between automatic and controlled processes may be less stark than was previously assumed (Andersen, Moskowitz, Blair, and Nosek, 2007: 142). Controlled processes may become automatic with experience and repetition—so that even routinized behavior, which is arguably a large portion of organizational behavior—may be understood as repeated deliberative choice of preferable alternatives which originated in a representation which may or may not still be appropriate (Dewey, 1930; Nelson and Winter, 1982; Cohen and Bacdayan, 1994). Therefore, to understand existing routinized, automatic thought processes, we may nevertheless benefit from investigating controlled thought processes which might have been precursors (Nelson and Winter, 1982; in particular, see Simon, 1997: 89).

Conversely, controlled thought processes may use chunks that have become automatic through experience. For instance, the research comparing experts and novices in how they solve problems points to the routinization of once explicit problem-solving processes to the point where pattern recognition is sufficient to produce a solution (Ericsson and Charness, 2006).[7] There is thus

---

[6] Stanovich has also argued that System I thinking may be optimized to advance the interests of our genes, whereas System II may be geared towards enhancing our own interests.

[7] In a study comparing experts and novices solving organization design problems, Eucman Lee and I found a pattern of differences very similar to that found in such comparisons in other problem domains: experts relied more on visual representations and analogical reasoning than novices, and made fewer design errors particularly for complex design tasks (Lee and Puranam, 2015).

nothing particularly mystical about "gut-feel" and "intuitive" decision-making, and one should be cautious about succumbing to survivor bias when recommending it as worthy of emulation (or as a student once put it, many people may have the gut, but few have the right feel that comes with experience).

Third, for many problems within organizations, the allocation of attention is a scarce but critical resource (Ocasio, 1997; 2005; Joseph and Ocasio, 2012). Managing attention pertains to deliberately shifting thought processes into the controlled domain (into System II) by altering, bypassing or overriding automatic cognition (Wegner and Bargh, 1998).

Multiple rationalities

This three-part characterization of behavioral elements in terms of Goals, Representations and Choice process is also useful to contrast different forms of rationality that organizational scientists are familiar with. Variations espoused by different theorists can be directly traced to the aspects of variability in goals, representations and choices they suppress or acknowledge.

GLOBAL RATIONALITY

Consider first the classical notion of rationality: As Simon (1977) describes it, "This is what I call full or global rationality: people are making their decisions to maximize utility in a world which they either understand exactly or in terms of a known probability distribution (i.e. they are maximizing subjective expected utility)." In other words, 1) individuals are perfectly aware of the space of their choices, 2) have comprehensive and consistent utility functions, 3) know perfectly the expected utility derived from each choice, and 4) are able and want to make choices that maximize their expected utility.

If the goals pertain to material gain, the choice process is maximization, and representations correspond (at least probabilistically) to reality, we are in the domain of neoclassical economic rationality. If we allow for other kinds of goals (such as self-actualization, or a sense of belongingness) while preserving the other elements, then the resulting model is that of expected utility maximization. This is the form that models of inequity aversion and fairness in economics have taken (e.g. Fehr and Schmidt, 1999). In this expanded view of the utility function, rationality is consistency in optimizing a goal, with a fair amount of leeway in the definition of the goal itself.

Predictions based on this form of rationality depend on both the analyst and the agent knowing the task environment and the application of optimization techniques. Knowing the alternatives $\{A_1, A_2 \ldots A_m\}$ and associated performance outcomes $\{\Pi_1, \Pi_2 \ldots \Pi_m\}$, the analyst can predict that the agent will take the action A that yields the highest Π. In fact if the selection environment is strong enough, even the assumptions about veridical representation and optimization by the agent can be dispensed with, as observed (surviving) behavior is by definition optimizing behavior on the dimension that matters for survival (Alchian, 1965).

ADAPTIVE RATIONALITY

Since bounded rationality is defined by its departure from global rationality, there are many possible ways in which rationality can be bounded. In contrast to global rationality, Simon's notion of bounded rationality "assumes that 1) the decision maker must search for alternatives, 2) has egregiously incomplete and inaccurate knowledge about the consequences of actions, and 3) chooses actions that are expected to be satisfactory (attain targets while satisfying constraints)." Later work by Cyert and March (1963) added problemistic search—which essentially indicates that the search process described above is itself triggered by a failure to meet aspiration levels (also see recent overviews of the tradition of organizations research inspired by Simon, March, and Cyert, by Gavetti et al., 2007, 2012).

This form of bounded rationality, to paraphrase Simon, is really "adaptive rationality" as it emphasizes the process of searching for better alternatives by reacting to feedback (e.g. Simon, 1996). The core notion of "limited rationality is that individuals are intendedly rational" (March, 1994: 9; Simon, 1957: xxiv). In the adaptive rationality approach the analyst needs to understand the agent's representations to make predictions—see through the eyes of the agent, as it were.[8] This requires knowing how the agent represents their task environment at that point of time: alternatives $\{a_{1,t}, a_{2,t} \ldots a_{n,t}\}$, expected performance outcomes $\{\pi_{1,t}, \pi_{2,t}, \ldots \pi_{n,t}\}$, as well as aspiration level π_t^*.

The key differences between adaptive bounded rationality and rationality as expected utility maximization are a) the gap between representation and reality (i.e. ignorance), and b) the lack of search to improve representations as long as performance lies above aspiration levels (i.e. satisficing). In this view, bounded rationality is seen as deviating from full rationality—not in the sense that agents do not desire to pick better over worse options among the alternatives known to them, but rather their inability to do so objectively because of their limited comprehension of the set of alternatives in the task environment (Camerer, 1997; Gavetti and Levinthal, 2000).[9] For Simon, the

---

[8] Implicitly, this approach also assumes that the selection environment is not so strong that we observe nothing but the survivors who happened to display objectively optimizing behavior.

[9] A paraphrase by Richard Nelson captures the spirit of adaptive bounded rationality very well: "I use the term bounded rationality to connote the reasoning and learning abilities of an actor who has

gap between the hypothetical benchmark of global rationality and bounded adaptive rationality does not appear to have been the primary issue of interest; rather, the latter represented a scientific hypothesis about what agents do when it is infeasible to construct accurate and complete representations of the task environment.

An additional possible departure from global rationality is that even within their representations, agents may act inconsistently by not selecting what currently appears the best alternative (i.e. non-exploitative choice). While this aspect was not salient in Simon's original work on adaptive bounded rationality, behavioral economists working within the heuristics and biases research program have documented a number of behaviors that appear to be systematic inconsistencies of this form (Kahneman, Slovic, and Tversky, 1982).

It is not within the scope of this chapter to engage with the so-called Great Rationality Debate (e.g. see Tetlock and Mellers, 2002)—as to whether people are best described as on the whole rational or error prone relative to normative criteria. Rather I want to highlight that even if demonstrated cognitive biases are truly inconsistencies of behavior within the agent's representation (rather than imperfections in representations, or indeed consistent choices within a representation that is not the one the researcher has in mind—see Gigerenzer et al., 1996), these judgment errors can also be a valuable source of exploration (March, 1991). One cannot easily discard an existing representation if acting consistently within it delivers performance above aspiration levels. Inconsistency on the other hand may lead to poor performance, and a reinforcement of the existing representation, but occasionally may also trigger the discovery of a better representation. There is a certain beauty to the fact that one form of bounded rationality (i.e. non-exploitative choice) may compensate for others (i.e. ignorance and satisficing) in an adaptive agent.

THE LOGIC OF APPROPRIATENESS

Distinct from both global and adaptive bounded rationality, the "logic of appropriateness" (March and Olsen, 1989) describes a situation where individuals categorize the situation they are in and choose actions that seem appropriate for such situations. The unique feature is that goals and associated representations are endogenous to the categorization of the situation in the logic of appropriateness. The choice process that then follows may resemble system I thinking more than system II thinking. However, despite these differences, the analytical approach to behavior in terms of goals, representations and choices

a goal to achieve and, on the one hand an at least partially formed theory about how to achieve it (this is the 'rationality' part of the concept), and on the other hand that the theory is likely somewhat crude and perhaps even a bad guide for action, and that success is far from assured (this is the meaning of the 'bounded' qualification to rationality)" (Nelson, 2008).

is useful both for understanding the logics of consequence (to which both neoclassical economic rationality and Simon-style adaptive bounded rationality belong) and appropriateness (also see Goldmann, 2005 and Lindenberg, 2000).

Organization design and its influence on individual behavior

From this account of the vertical and horizontal structure of goals, of the imperfections and mutability of representations, and the fallible nature of choice, it should be clear that for an organization designer, the idea of a constant unitary goal that the individuals in an organization can be counted on to optimize is typically unjustified (whatever its attractions in terms of analytical tractability). But how then should one account for the diversity of goals, representations and choice processes in our theorizing and design? How should conflicts between goals, or even conflicts in representation for the same goal be addressed? Indeed some scholars have grown quite pessimistic about our ability to cope with this diversity as theorists, in particular with the tendency for unverifiable speculations about these internal cognitive processes to become substitutes for rigorous causal inference (e.g. Watts, 2014).

I believe we are actually somewhat fortunate in this regard as students of organization design. The problem of understanding and modeling individuals' behavior in designed organizations is simpler than in society at large (which does not mean it is trivial, of course). There are three mechanisms available to organization designers that make this simplification possible, as summarized in Table 2.1. March and Simon (1958) already made clear that organizations

Table 2.1 Mechanisms for influencing individual behavior within organizations

Mechanism --> Influence on:	Sorting	Framing	Structuring
Goals	Selection into the organization to exploit variation or similarity in goals	Evoking desired goal frames; changing goals to change representations	Manage pro-social and intrinsic motivation through grouping and task design
Representations	Selection into the organization to exploit variation or similarity in representations	Providing common representations	Specify constraints, objectives and decision premises; feedback shapes learning process
Choice process	Selection into the organization to exploit variation or similarity in exploratory tendencies	Changing representations to trigger variation in choices	Incentives and accountability influence exploration in choice

shape what action alternatives, beliefs and values are evoked for individuals within them (e.g. 1958: chapter 3). I focus below on the specific mechanisms through which this evocation process takes place.

SORTING

Sorting exploits *variability between individuals*. If a designer could ensure that individuals are sorted into an organization such that they have the right kind of goals (i.e. display desirable forms of other-regarding preferences, derive intrinsic motivation from the necessary tasks), then this would reduce significantly the challenge of coping with the possible diversity of goals. Even being aware of what goals are important to selected individuals (without being able to choose on this dimension) can still be useful.

While most individuals may display both self-centered and other oriented goals, there may be systematic differences across individuals in the weights placed on them (Griesinger and Livingstone, 1973; de Dreu and Nauta, 2009). Similarly, preferences for tasks are not universal, and people mostly like doing different things (though I suspect there may be some tasks that everybody hates; grading and doing the dishes spring to my mind). As we will see in Chapter 4, certain task allocations are likely to benefit more from evoking pro-social motivations among individuals than others, and in Chapter 8, we will encounter forms of organizing that use self-selection to generate intrinsic motivation by aligning individual and organizational goals, and thus avoid or lower the cost of providing extrinsic motivation.

However, even when individual and organizational goals do not align, knowing this is already useful. In such (perhaps typical) cases, the tasks assigned to individuals in organizations may not generate much intrinsic motivation. When they do not, extrinsic motivators—such as cash, status, power and promotion opportunities—will be particularly important. The greater the mismatch between organizational and individual goals, the greater we should expect the need to rely on extrinsic motivators to be. An important corollary is that autonomy in execution and discretion to choose how to act, within the broad parameters specified by task allocation, can be additional motivators (Hackman and Oldham, 1976; Ryan and Deci, 2000). Managing motivation in organizations is thus a process of managing the delicate balance between the design of rewards (both extrinsic and intrinsic), the allocation of tasks, and the degree of discretion and autonomy on how to execute them. But designed sorting can make this balancing act considerably easier by reducing the space of potential goals to the few that are actually relevant.

As with goals, representations are also to some extent endogenous to organization design—which can shape the set of alternative actions, constraints and associated aspiration levels for individuals (Simon, 1947; March and Simon,

1958; Cyert and March, 1963). In the Carnegie lexicon, representations provide the "decision premises" that guide choice (Simon, 1947). Selection into the organization is an important means of bringing in (or not) diversity of representations (March 1991). Variations in goals contribute to variations in representation—what aspects of the task environment people represent will depend on what goals motivate them. Variations in the familiarity of a situation, as well as variation across individuals in the quality of understanding for a given situation contribute to diversity in representations. Sorting on the basis of variations across individuals in their tendency to explore rather than exploit is another mechanism that organization designers could apply to shape choice processes. Of course, the aim of sorting may not be homogeneity, but in fact diversity.

FRAMING

We know that organizations influence their new members through socialization, and the results contribute to cohesion and coordination (van Maanen, 1978; van Maanen and Schein, 1979). Leadership has broadly similar effects (Waldman, Ramirez, House, and Puranam, 2001). I believe that socialization and leadership can both be usefully understood in terms of the "transmission of framings" of a situation. Accordingly, I explain how framing affects goals, representations, and choices of individuals.

Goals, as cognitive constructs, are selectively activated, with particular ones being triggered by particular framings of a situation (Kruglanski and Kopetz, 2009; Lindenberg and Frey, 1993). Thus faced with the same situation, an individual may behave in a self-interested or collective interest-oriented fashion, depending on how the situation is framed (Pillutla and Chen, 1999). Indeed, behavior in the materially same situation may change, once the situation is framed differently, as was discovered when offers of payment were found to lower voluntary blood donations relative to levels when it was not paid for (Titmus, 1970). This suggests that there may be systematic (and even controllable) *variation within individuals*, based on framing that an organization designer can exploit (e.g. Chester Barnard's "method of persuasion").

To think about framing as a design choice, one needs a parsimonious categorization of possible frames, and how they may trigger particular goals and representations. Lindenberg (2008; also see Lindenbergh and Foss, 2011) proposed a useful theory of three overarching *goal frames*—a set of contextual cues that trigger the activation of particular sets of goals and the means-ends chains linking them to ultimate goals. These frames relate to ultimate goals that may be described as *hedonic* (the desire to improve or preserve how one feels—e.g. self-preservation, pleasure-seeking and pain-avoidance), *gain* (to improve or preserve resources—e.g. material rewards) and *normative* (to act appropriately in the service of a collective entity—related to the need to achieve a sense of belonging). Goal frames govern what stimuli are considered relevant, what alternatives are considered, what knowledge we draw on and what beliefs we hold about the possible behaviors of others (e.g. their trustworthiness). The activation of a particular goal frame has implications for which sub-goals are activated and which ones are suppressed. For instance, both hedonic and gain frames emphasize individual interest, albeit with more (hedonic) or less (gain) immediacy. Thus when they are salient, other-regarding preferences will be subdued, according to this theory.

Goal frames also vary in their baseline strength, with the hedonic frame being the strongest and the normative (social) frame being the weakest (the gain frame is intermediate in strength between the two). Lindenberg justifies this ordering on evolutionary grounds. Individual reproductive success is paramount, with group living merely being a means to this end (Caporael, 2007). This implies that without being reinforced in some way (such as socialization practices or other means of making group identity salient—see for instance Van Maanen, 1978; Van Maanen and Schein, 1979), the normative frame may be pushed into the background by the hedonic and gain frame. But when it is activated, the normative goal frame can unleash a cascade of pro-social behaviors within the group, such as cohesion and collaboration (Tomasello et al., 2005), adherence to and enforcement of group norms (Ostrom, Walker, and Gardner, 1992), and a strong sense of solidarity (Wageman, 1995).

Critically, what goal frame others appear to be operating under can influence one's own goal frames through a contagion process (Aarts et al., 2004). For instance, Lindenberg and Foss (2011) describe how the normative goal frame can be activated (and hedonic and gain goal frames suppressed) to facilitate team production: by making interdependencies and the need for joint contribution clear, through the articulation of a common goal (e.g. through vision or mission statements), and by rewarding actions that support the collective goal (albeit the magnitude of rewards must be modest to prevent the triggering of hedonic or gain frames). Since goal contagion is likely to be stronger from superiors to peers than the other way around (or from peer to peer), what the leaders of the organization do and say therefore becomes critical (Foss and Lindenberg, 2013).

Vision, leadership and planning—primarily framing processes, also shape representations (Gavetti and Levinthal, 2000; Puranam and Swamy, 2016). Indeed, representations may be explicitly provided by an authoritative superior—a point Simon (1981) noted in his observation that the centralization of beliefs may be the distinguishing and useful feature of administrative hierarchies. Authority can also play an important role in generating and maintaining common language representations within the firm—standard terminology being a common instance (e.g. Kogut and Zander, 1996; Srikanth and Puranam, 2013). These framing activities lie at the heart of socialization processes when individuals enter organizations, or organizations merge (van Maanen, 1978).

STRUCTURING

Organizations are multi-agent systems. Therefore, an individual in an organization is surrounded by an easily accessible set of foci for their other-regarding preferences. Some degree of activation of other regarding goals may therefore even be a constant feature of organizational life, as early writers on the process of organizational identification noted (Barnard, 1938; Simon, 1947; also see 1996: chapter 10). However, organizational structure bounds this process further. A particular aspect of formal organizational structure is the decomposition of a complex organization into sub-organizations. This has implications for establishing the salient reference groups that are the focus of other-directed preferences for individuals. In particular, the structuring of sub-groups affects *group-identification* and the operation of *inequity aversion*.

There is a tendency for the goals of one's reference groups to be internalized and preferred when they conflict with those of other groups and the organization at large (see the discussion of sub-goal pursuit in March and Simon, 1958). Upon publicly visible categorization into in-groups and out-groups, people spontaneously experience more positive affect towards the in-group, and favor the in-group in terms of resource allocations and evaluation (Tajfel et al., 1971; Brewer, 2007; also see Yamagishi and Mifune, 2008 for an analysis of the underlying mechanisms based on reciprocity). A sense of group identity can trigger cooperative or altruistic motives in group members, so that they do what is good for the group or each other, rather than behaving according to self-interest (Brewer and Kramer, 1986; Mael and Ashforth, 1992).

The reference group is also the one within which social comparisons processes operate and considerations of equity matter most strongly (Adams, 1965; Fehr and Schmidt, 1999).[10] People care not only about the absolute value of their payoffs, but also about how this compares with what their counterparts and peers receive (Adams, 1965; Ho and Su, 2009). Perceiving inequity, they are motivated to reduce it through actions that are feasible to them (including, in the limit, exiting the organization). A complication is that overconfidence in their own abilities (Moore and Healey, 2008) makes it likely that individuals see receiving less than others as inequity (Martin, 1982; Zenger, 1994), but may not perceive inequity in their receiving more than others (Larkin, Pierce, and Gino, 2012).[11]

---

[10] Equity concerns are believed to have evolved to sustain pro-social behavior (Brosnan and De Waal, 2004; Gilbert, Price and Allan, 1995). Even infants show an aversion to inequity in distributive outcomes (Sloane, Baillargeon, and Premack, 2012) and such behavior is thought to be innate in a number of species (Brosnan and De Waal, 2004; Gilbert, Price, and Allain, 1995).

[11] It is also known that independent of the equity of outcomes ("distributive justice"), individuals value "procedural justice"—which pertains to the perceived fairness of the procedures used to produce the distributive outcome (Folger, 1977; Greenberg, 1987; Lind and Tyler, 1988).

Since formal organizations are often structured as nested (containment) hierarchies of simpler organizations, the strength of other regarding goals for an individual may not extend uniformly from that individual to the outer skin of the formal organization he or she is part of. Instead, the group that is relevant for the activation of such other regarding preferences may be the relevant microstructure an individual belongs to rather than the macro-organization. Thus identification and equity assessment processes may work most strongly within the micro-organizations an individual is part of, losing strength with radial distance moved towards the outer boundary of the macro-organization. Put simply, internal grouping structure of organizations affects goals and motivation, a fact that was deeply appreciated by the pioneers of organization design research (March and Simon, 1958). This also suggests that effective organization design may cluster employees together in order to manipulate reference groups (Gottschalg and Zollo, 2007; Nickerson and Zenger, 2008), to reduce perceptions of inequity and enhance the benefits of identification with the sub-group.

Group identification and inequity aversion are by no means the only relevant processes that shape other-regarding preferences in organizations. However, they are two of the most well studied by researchers interested in understanding pro-social motivation in organizations (Gottschalg and Zollo, 2007; Larkin, Pierce, and Gino, 2012; Lindenberg and Foss, 2011). In fact both can be seen as fairly coarse categories. For our purposes, these are convenient shorthand for a suite of complementary micro-mechanisms whose details psychologists may be better qualified to deal with than organizational scientists. These include social comparison, anchoring, dissonance reduction, reciprocity, justice perceptions and emotional contagion, among others.

At a more granular level, the design of tasks and the allocation of tasks to individuals (i.e. the division of labor) can serve as another channel through which structuring can influence intrinsic motivation (Hackman and Oldham, 1976). Incentive systems may affect the triggering of other regarding preferences through their effects on goal frames (Lee and Puranam, 2017). Pay for performance may encourage a more material/hedonic frame, whereas fixed or group pay may trigger normative frames.

The design of tasks and the allocation of responsibilities are also channels through which structuring may influence representations. Search and learning processes can also be shaped through structuring (e.g. Baumann and Stieglitz, 2014) of constraints and feedback in order to promote exploration—by rewarding it directly, by not penalizing failure, or indeed by penalizing exploitation of current representations (e.g. Lee and Meyer-Doyle, 2017).[12]

---

[12] Some evidence however exists that extrinsic incentives may impede exploratory thinking. McGraw and McCullers (1979) found that the introduction of monetary rewards could narrow attention in unproductive ways for tasks that require creative thinking.

Conclusion

The preceding account sketches a picture of the basic and common elements of human behavior of relevance to organization design—in particular to the centrality of goals, representations and choices. It attempts to outline an updated framework for thinking about organizations as the "psychological environments of choice" (Simon, 1947). There is undoubtedly much diversity in goals, representations and choices across and within individuals. However, the mechanisms of **sorting, framing** and **structuring** can help to reduce this space of possibilities to manageable dimensions. In the resulting account of behavior, alternatives need not be given, their consequences need not be known, and the utilities attached to consequences need not be stable. While far from a fully fleshed out "technology of foolishness" (March, 1963), this chapter offers a simplified framework to understand a variety of forms of rational and non-rational individual behavior as special cases.

Formal agent-based models of the influence of sorting, framing and structuring on shaping the search and learning processes involved in modifying representations have seen remarkable development in the last decade. The analytical structure offered by such models allows a thorough consideration of the dynamics of a system of agents whose representations are co-adapting, and what this implies for aggregate behavior and performance. Much more can be done. For instance, a highly influential definition of "culture" treats it as equivalent to shared representations acquired through learning (Schein, 1993), so that these model platforms may be extremely useful to understand how organizational cultures emerge and evolve. It is fair to say that this is one of the areas where advanced methodology is helping shed light on some of the most fundamental issues in organizations research (see Puranam, Stieglitz, Osman, and Pillutla, 2015 for a review).

How would this picture of behavioral foundations change if we were to describe the behavior of groups rather than individuals? In a microstructural approach, the agents may in fact be organizations in themselves. One approach is to build their behavioral properties bottom-up, starting with individuals, and the ideas about them discussed in this chapter. Another (and these are strongly complementary) is to draw on the empirical research on how group behavior differs from individual behavior. Past research has shown that groups can make more risky choices and have opinions that are more extreme than those of the average individuals in them, and may experience escalation of commitment through dissonance reduction to a similar degree as individuals (e.g. Bazerman, Guiliano, Appelman, 1984). How groups choose differently from individuals is an emerging area of renewed interest in both behavioral economics and social psychology (Kugler et al., 2012; Wildschut et al., 2003). For instance, Wildschut et al. (2003) and others have shown that groups are more competitive than individuals when playing the prisoner's dilemma game.

There is also an enormous body of evidence on the broader question of how teams perform on tasks (see Kozlowski and Bell, 2013 for a recent review). Teams, as I noted in Chapter 1, are organizations in which the agents are all interdependent with each other, share common goals and may be nested within larger organizations. The development of the microstructural approach can thus benefit from what teams researchers have uncovered. One broad result of particular significance is that information aggregation and coordination within teams is a significant challenge even when the interests of the team members are aligned and they interact with each other. Mutual influence processes can enable error correction, but may also prevent surfacing of relevant information, through conformity pressures. How these mechanisms are affected in the presence of conflicting incentives, clustered pockets of interaction and asymmetric influence remains to be explored.

I believe an area of fruitful development that combines microstructural thinking with teams research may be to explore task environments closer to the kind organizational researchers are used to (e.g. team production, project evaluation, resource allocation or candidate selection) along with groups that vary on structural elements (e.g. distribution of decision rights, incentives, flow of information, task division and allocation). A combination of modeling and behavioral lab experiments may help us push the frontiers of our understanding significantly in this area.

■ APPENDIX TO CHAPTER 2: HUMAN UNIVERSALS (BROWN, 1991; PINKER, 2002)

Human Universals relating to Goals	Human Universals relating to Organizing
aesthetics	coalitions
affection expressed and felt	collective identities
attachment	conflict
conflict	conflict, consultation to deal with
empathy	conflict, means of dealing with
envy	conflict, mediation of
envy, symbolic means of coping with	cooperation
ethnocentrism	cooperative labor
fairness (equity), concept of	decision making
generosity admired	decision making, collective
gift-giving	dispersed groups
healing the sick (or attempting to)	division of labor
hospitality	division of labor by age
moral sentiments	division of labor by sex
moral sentiments, limited effective range of	dominance/submission

pride
reciprocity, negative (revenge, retaliation)
reciprocity, positive
redress of wrongs
resistance to abuse of power, to dominance
risk-taking
self-control
self-image, awareness of (concern for what others think)
self-image, wanted to be positive
shame
stinginess, disapproval of
sweets preferred

gossip
government
group living
groups that are not based on family
in-group biases in favor of
in-group distinguished from out-group(s)
institutions (organized co-activities)
kin groups
law (rights and obligations)
law (rules of membership)
leaders
manipulate social relations
oligarchy (de facto)
prestige inequalities
promise
property
reciprocal exchanges (of labor, goods, or services)
sanctions
sanctions for crimes against the collectivity
sanctions include removal from the social unit
social structure
socialization
socialization expected from senior kin
statuses and roles
statuses, ascribed and achieved
trade
succession
triangular awareness (assessing relationships among the self and two other people)
turn-taking

3 Division of labor

If organizations are multi-agent systems with goals (see Chapter 1), there must exist a mapping from organizational level goals to tasks assigned to agents. Such a mapping, at least when explicitly recognized (even if not intentionally crafted) is what we think of as a "division of labor" within an organization. Because the results of the efforts so divided must be integrated back, the division of labor typically results in interdependence between the agents performing the tasks contributing to the overall goal of the organization. This chapter focuses on the process of division of labor and the emergence of interdependence between agents as its consequence.[1] The case of the division of decision rights within an authority hierarchy is considered in Chapters 5 and 6. The consequences of division of labor between actors in an economy are well understood. In a widely quoted paragraph, Adam Smith noted that the division of labor "is not originally the effect of any human wisdom, which foresees and intends that general opulence to which it gives occasion. It is the necessary, though very slow and gradual, consequence of a certain propensity in human nature which has in view no such extensive utility; the propensity to truck, barter, and exchange one thing for another" (1776 [1909]: 19, 20). The most salient consequence is the gain from specialization and trade even if, as Smith assumes in the quotation above, that was not the primary motivation. The origins of this pattern of division of labor that generates gains from trade have provoked some interesting speculation (see for instance the ethnographic studies on trade in pre-industrial societies by Vernon-Smith (1998: 3–6)). The less benign consequences include the suppression of social solidarity and individual motivation (Durkheim, 1893), and the skewed distribution of power between workers vis-à-vis the providers of capital (Marx, 1906; Bendix, 1956).

However, much less attention has been devoted to the process of the designed division of labor within organizations—a process whereby organizational objectives are divided into contributory tasks (task division) which are allocated across individuals (task allocation) (see von Hippel, 1990 for an exception). Incidentally, division of labor also arises in biological systems when they evolve towards differentiated allocation of tasks, but they do so given a task division and an initial undifferentiated task allocation (Rueffler, Hermisson, and Wagner, 2012). The process of explicit task division may thus

---

[1] This and the next section draw extensively from Puranam, Raveendran, and Knudsen (2012), Raveendran, Puranam, and Warglien (2015), and Puranam and Raveendran (2012).

be uniquely important in human organizations, yet remains understudied. Nor do we have a systematic account of the space of possible divisions of labor (and when and why we observe some and not others).

This chapter has three main objectives. The first is to introduce the basic sub-processes of decomposing an organization's goal into clusters of tasks (task division), and assigning these to agents (task allocation). Since these processes must occur whenever an organization is initiated, or when its task environment or its goals change, they are critical to an understanding of effective organizational adaptation. I also introduce a representation of the resulting division of labor that flexibly scales from microstructures with a few agents and tasks to arbitrarily large numbers of both. Second, I provide a detailed analysis of the different options for division of labor, the conditions under which the options become available, and the criteria one may use to choose between them (gains from specialization happens to be just one of these). Third, I point to a fundamental mapping that division of labor accomplishes—it maps interdependence between tasks into interdependence between agents. This sets the stage for the analysis of the mechanisms needed to integrate the efforts of interdependent agents, in Chapter 4.

Division of labor as task division and task allocation

The division of labor in an organization has two logically distinct components: the decomposition of the overall goal into (clusters of) tasks, and the allocation of these task clusters to distinct agents (Smith, 1776). Thus, we may conceptualize the process of dividing labor as involving the search for solutions to two related but distinct sub-problems, namely task division and task allocation.

Task division involves the decomposition of an overall goal into contributory tasks (the completion of which become sub-goals) and the subsequent clustering of tasks (von Hippel, 1990). A task may be thought of as a production technology—it is a transformation of inputs into outputs in finite time. For the purpose of analysis, it can also be thought of as an action or a choice (decision) to be made by an agent, based on inputs, which include knowledge and skills. Whether the task is a design task or a production task will not influence our discussion at this point (see also Ethiraj and Levinthal, 2004a, b), although we should remain mindful that there are qualitative empirical differences between them (Baldwin and Clark, 2000).

Task allocation refers to the assignment of (the clusters of) divided tasks to individuals. It may occur either simultaneously or after task division, or may indeed influence task division, for instance when it occurs on the basis of matching tasks to individual skills.

I will use a notation developed with my colleagues Thorbjørn Knudsen and Marlo Raveendran to describe divisions of labor. Define T^R as the *task structure* of an organization—the most fine-grained means-end decomposition of the organization's goal into its constituent tasks and the dependency relationships between these. Even a group of two individuals, if they meet the definition of an organization, must have a task structure.

Lacking omniscience, boundedly rational agents must invariably work with imperfect representations of the true underlying task structure that leads to the organization's goals (see Chapter 2 for more details on representations). The imperfections of these representations may result in low resolution (i.e. only coarse aggregates of tasks are visible), incompleteness (i.e. critical tasks are missing), incorrectness (i.e. unnecessary tasks are included, or the dependency relationships between tasks are imperfectly portrayed), or some combination of the above.

Representing task structures

There are multiple ways to represent T^R—work flow diagrams, value chains, process maps, responsibility charts, task/design structure matrices, and linear programming models being some of them (Baldwin and Clark, 2000; Burton and Obel, 1984b; Eppinger, 1991; Steward, 1981; Thompson, 1967). For the general case of n tasks, we rely on Task Structure Matrices to represent the pattern of interdependence between tasks in T^R. In this square asymmetric matrix, let a "1" in cell (i,j) denote that there is interdependence between the column-task j and the row task i (as shown on the left in Figure 3.1). This abstracts from variations in the magnitude of interdependence, which can be incorporated if known.

The term *interdependence* in the organization design literature encompasses both asymmetric (one-sided) and symmetric (two-sided) dependence (e.g. "sequential interdependence"). I follow convention and use "interdependence"

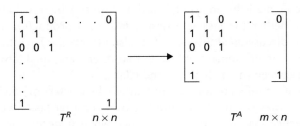

Figure 3.1 Example of T^R and T^A

for both, but specify whether I refer to symmetric or asymmetric inter-dependence when the difference matters.

To define interdependence between tasks, we must rely on the concept of the value of a task. Since tasks have inputs and outputs, they have an associated value (determined by the difference between the benefits of the outputs and the cost of the inputs). This makes explicit that tasks, being production technologies, have outputs and inputs that can be valued. Now, consider a microstructure of two agents, each performing a unique task. We say that two tasks, A and B, are *interdependent* when the value generated from performing each is different when the other task is performed versus when it is not. Conversely, two tasks are *independent* if the value to performing each is the same whether the other task is performed or not. Consequently, the combined value created when independent tasks are performed is the same as the sum of the values created by performing each task alone (e.g., pooled interdependence in Thompson, 1967, where each task makes a discrete contribution to the whole).

This definition of interdependence, that Raveendran, Knudsen, and I developed (2012), encompasses a range of prior conceptualizations of task interdependence. For instance, tasks can be jointly dependent on the same rivalrous and limited inputs (e.g., Burton and Obel, 1984; Malone and Crowston, 1994). In this case of *common input,* performing each task alone will result in different levels of consumption of the input that is in limited supply than will performing both tasks (see Figure 3.2). Therefore, there will also be differences in output and value between the two cases.

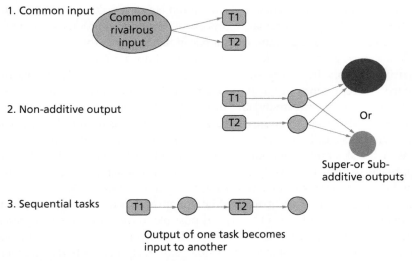

Figure 3.2 Different forms of task interdependence

This form of interdependence is often relevant for tasks that are *similar* in the transformative process they entail (and hence draw on common inputs). Inventory management for multiple production lines, economies of scale and scope (when the fixed cost of inputs is spread over a number of tasks, lowering the average costs of inputs), and economies of experience (when the costs of inputs, typically efforts, decline with cumulated experience of tasks requiring the same kind of effort) are also instances of this form of interdependence. In each case, the amount of input consumed is different under joint vs. individual production.

Tasks can also be interdependent with respect to their outputs, which may be complements or substitutes (Milgrom and Roberts, 1995). In these cases of *super* or *sub-additive output,* performing each task alone will result in different values for each than when performing both tasks. Such complementarity/substitution relationships are explicitly modeled in supermodular (or submodular) production functions (e.g., Milgrom and Roberts, 1990). They are implicit as epistatic interactions in fitness landscapes (e.g., Levinthal, 1997) and dependencies between tasks in Task Structure Matrices (Baldwin and Clark, 2000; Eppinger, 1991; Steward, 1981). This form of interdependence is often present between tasks that are *dissimilar* in the transformative process they entail. The production of hardware and software that is valued as a bundle by customers, or of two competing design choices that interfere with each other are instances of this form of interdependence.

Finally, in *sequential tasks*, the output from the first task (task 1) may form the input to the second task (task 2). In this case task 2 will be (asymmetrically) interdependent with task 1, but the converse need not be true (it will depend on whether the value of task 1 changes with the performance of task 2). This form of interdependence is also common between tasks that are *dissimilar* in their underlying transformative process. A sequence of production stages or screening decisions (e.g. credit card applications) illustrate this.

We can scale the dyadic micro-structure into a m-agent system using matrix notation. In a very simplified manner, a "1" in the Task Structure Matrix T^R represents any of these forms of direct interdependence between tasks (we assume transitivity, and dispense with representing indirect links). There are other ways to do so, of course. Different kinds of interdependencies between tasks can be represented analytically in terms of the different ways that each task's inputs and outputs enter a combined value function. Another approach is to focus directly on the gains from managing interdependence, and how these are distributed (e.g. Kretschmer and Puranam, 2008). However, the advantage of the Task Structure Matrix approach is that it scales very easily to many agents and tasks. Further, it is possible to transform other representations of task interdependence into a Task Structure Matrix, with some loss of information. For instance, sequential and reciprocal interdependencies (Thompson, 1967) can be portrayed by asymmetric and symmetric placement of "1's" about the diagonal, respectively in T^R. Super- or sub-additive outputs and common inputs imply symmetric "1's" above and below the diagonal.

One could also replace the "1" with a real number, capturing weight and sign of the relationship. For instance, there is a deeply significant difference between the cases where two tasks are perfect complements in their joint value function (i.e. the joint value of tasks is zero unless both are performed) as opposed to a case where the marginal rate of technical substitution is less than one (i.e. the value of task 1 performed on its own is positive but less than what it could have been if task 2 were also performed). If initially unknown, it will be easier for agents to detect the existence of the first kind of interdependence than the second (we return to this idea in Chapter 4). For now, all these subtleties are rather brutally ignored (but see Lee, Hoehn-Weiss, and Karim, 2016).

Alternative forms of division of labor

There will typically be many different ways to cluster the tasks in T^R. In addition, these clusters of tasks may be allocated in different ways among the agents in the organization (there are m^n possible ways in which n distinct tasks can be allocated in an unconstrained manner across m individuals). Let the matrix T^A represent the allocation of tasks to agents. Whereas T^R is an n × n matrix where n is the number of tasks, T^A is an m × n matrix, where m is the number of individuals in the organization. Given T^A, we can easily derive T^t the m × m matrix of interdependence between the *clusters* of tasks assigned to each agent, by combining the tasks assigned to each individual.

Since T^A embodies both a decomposition of the overall goal into clusters of tasks as well as an allocation of these task clusters among the agents, it is a concise abstract representation of a division of labor. Consider the original example provided by Adam Smith: pin-making could be divided into "eighteen distinct operations, which, in some manufactories are all performed by distinct hands, though in others, the same man will sometimes perform two or three of them" (1776 [1999]: 5). These would correspond to two different T^A of dimensions n = m = 18 vs. n = 18 and m<18 respectively, for the same underlying T^R, in which the tasks corresponded to the operations known to be involved in pin making.

Why cluster tasks at all? At a very basic level, some division of labor would appear unavoidable to the extent that there are sheer limits on the tasks an individual can carry out, and m<n. However, given bounded rationality and limits on cognitive processing (see Chapter 2), clustering tasks and assigning them to different agents is also a means of rationing attention; an agent assigned a cluster can focus on managing the interdependencies between the

tasks within the cluster, possibly at the expense of interdependencies with tasks in other clusters.[2] This is the idea behind the practice of modularization.

Modularization is a strategy for managing complexity in partially decomposable systems with many interdependencies (Sanchez and Mahoney, 1996; Baldwin and Clark, 2000; Ethiraj and Levinthal, 2004). By clustering elements into discrete clusters that effectively ignore interdependencies with other clusters, local improvements within clusters may be obtained, but possibly at the expense of overall system performance. A good modularization is one that ignores interdependencies across clusters in a manner that least impedes system performance, while grouping elements the joint attention to which yields the highest returns.

Finding a good modularization thus involves detecting clusters of tasks that are strongly interdependent with each other, but independent of tasks in other clusters. It is a computationally challenging task for even relatively simple task structures.

To illustrate this, consider an example: Figure 3.3 shows a popular children's toy sold under the Spin Master trade mark. Since the makers of Spin Master toys want to make assembly easy enough to engage children, they explicitly provide the task structure for assembling this toy in the form of a workflow diagram, with 21 steps (Figure 3.3 shows the last step), and in each step at least four types of task (e.g. reading instructions, picking pieces, fixing, holding) are involved. There are thus $4 \times 21 = 84$ distinct tasks (task i in step j), and potentially m^{84} different ways of allocating these tasks across m individuals jointly engaged in assembly.

Suppose we were to set out to find clusters of interdependent tasks; to do this we would need to know the eighty-four underlying tasks, and construct a task structure matrix of dimension 84×84. Building on the instructions provided by the Spin Master toy designers, we can build a representation of T^R, the task structure matrix, on the reasonable assumptions that a) tasks within an assembly step are symmetrically interdependent (i.e. super-additive outputs), b) all tasks in step j are asymmetrically dependent on all tasks involved in producing the inputs for step j, and c) tasks of the same type (e.g. all picking) across steps are symmetrically interdependent (i.e. generating experience economies, a form of common input-based interdependence).

There exist several algorithms that can help us permute the rows and columns of this resulting matrix to detect clusters (social network theorists refer to these as "community detection algorithms"—see Clauset, Newman, and Moore, 2004; Newman, 2006). I applied one such algorithm that selects

---

[2] Note that in the micro-structural approach developed in this book, the agent in this sentence could be a representative agent, who decided for an aggregation of individual agents—such as a department or a division. An agent is thus a decision-making entity, which may itself represent a collection of agents.

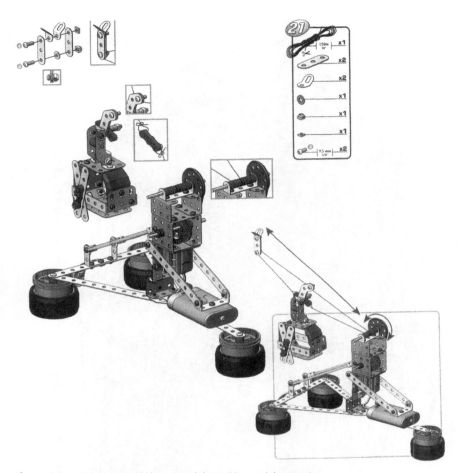

Figure 3.3 A Spin Master (©) toy model used in our lab experiments

clusters to maximize the "modularity" of the network. The modularity for a given clustering is defined as the fraction of edges that fall within clusters minus the expected number of edges within clusters for a random graph with the same node degree distribution as the given network.[3] The results from applying this algorithm to extract a four-cluster solution (i.e. assuming four agents working together to assemble) are shown as a network in Figure 3.4.

---

[3] The modularity score sums over all pairs of nodes v and w given a clustering and is $Q = \frac{1}{2r}\sum_{vw}\left[A_{vw} - \frac{k_v k_w}{2r}\right]\delta(c_v, c_w)$ where the δ function is 1 when v and w are in the same community, zero otherwise. The total number of edges is r, k is the degree of a node, and A is the adjacency matrix entry for the pair v,w. The optimal clustering maximizes Q, and Q = 0 for a random graph.

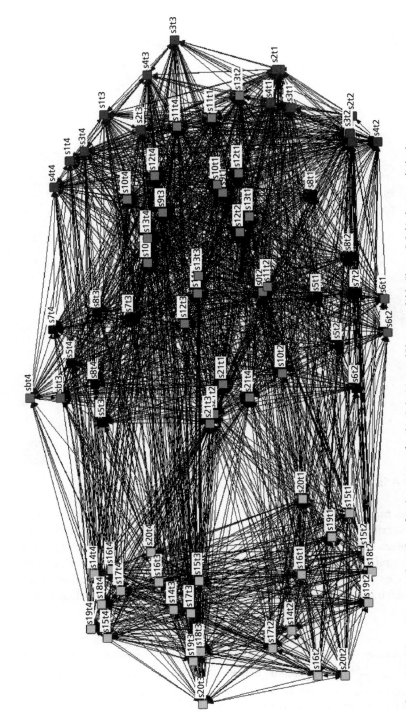

Figure 3.4 Girvan–Newman clustering of task structure for the Spin Master (©) toy model in Figure 3.3 (4 cluster solution)

The nodes that fall into the same cluster have the same color, s1t1 indicates step 1, task 1 etc.

The solution does a good job of identifying sequences of steps that can be worked on in parallel until final assembly (which to be fair, a careful visual inspection of the steps would also have produced—but that was what the Spin Master designers intended). However, note that the clusters vary a lot in the number of tasks, and no cluster is truly independent of the others. Critically, this exercise is premised on an identical weight for all interdependence; this is not a limitation of the algorithm per se, which can be extended to accommodate edge weights, but points to my ignorance about the relative value of interdependencies in this task structure.

The deeper point I want to make here is that it seems extremely unlikely that human beings have the information or the cognitive resources to engage in these kinds of cluster detection exercises purely in their mind, unaided by computers (or even aided by them).[4] In this case, the makers of the toy have been kind enough to enumerate the eighty-four tasks in the task structure and give us strong clues about the shape of the task structure matrix. Nature is not always so generous.

Instead, we must often fall back on heuristics for task division. In my work with Marlo Raveendran and Massimo Warglien (2016), we noted that two archetypes of clusters seem common. First, tasks can be clustered in terms of distinctive intermediate objects they generate, leading to an "*object*"-based division of labor. Intermediate objects exist and have some value independent of each other. The value could reflect a price in a market, but it could also reflect the ease with which a system can be completed, rebuilt or reconfigured given the existence of intermediate objects (Simon, 1962). For instance, in building a table, intermediate objects could be the legs and the table-top. Second, tasks can also be clustered based on how similar they are in how they transform inputs into outputs, leading to an "*activity*"-based division of labor. Thus, the division of labor for constructing a table could also be in terms of activities such as cutting, fixing and varnishing wood which are necessary for each part of the table. A divisional vs. functional structure for a multi-business firm reflects this difference between object and activity-based division of labor.

The distinction between objects and activities mirrors other important psychological distinctions. The ability to decompose one's context into objects (rather than continuous substances), think in categories (rather than relationships) and be fluent with nouns (rather than verbs), all appear to reflect the same or at least very related cognitive processes, which in turn appear to some extent to be culturally influenced (Gentner, 1981, 1982; Gentner and Borodistky, 2001; Nisbett, 2005). Further, the recognition of intermediate objects, as well as of

---

[4] K means clustering is an NP complete problem.

similarity between tasks may be quite subjective. Different individuals may reach very different choices about division of labor for the same task structure.

Two questions naturally arise about object- vs. activity-based division of labor: first, under what conditions does the choice between activity-based and object-based division of labor exist? Second, when the choice exists, which is preferable? These questions are addressed in the next two sections respectively.

DECOMPOSABILITY AND ALTERNATIVES FOR DIVISION OF LABOR

Simon's pioneering work on hierarchical systems (1962 [1996]: 189) introduced the notion of near decomposability—the extent to which a system can be divided into sub-systems that feature strong interactions within them, but weak interactions between them—as a key property of a complex system. Applying Simon's fairly general ideas about decomposability (defined on systems) to the task structure T^R that produces a product, a decomposable task structure matrix is one in which we can permute the rows and columns such that clusters of tasks smaller than T^R can be created with interdependencies within them but not across the clusters (Baldwin and Clark, 2000). If we were to repeat the exercise on each cluster (i.e. recursive decomposition), then a multi-layered hierarchy of tasks will naturally arise (as in Figure 3.5). I argue that this is how a task hierarchy emerges, and we will return to the idea in Chapter 6.

A *strongly* decomposable task structure is one where there are very few interdependencies between the clusters, but many within the clusters (Simon, 1962). Its opposite is a weakly decomposable task structure. For instance, the 84×84 task structure for building the Meccano model in Figure 3.3 is not decomposable—I have verified through Markov clustering that there are no separable components in the network—nor does it look near decomposable even in visual inspection. In the multi-layered task structure in Figure 3.5, the deeper we go (i.e. the more fine-grained the task division), the harder it will be to find clusters with low interdependence between them.

Distinct from the decomposability of the underlying task structure that produces it, we can also discuss the decomposability of a product. A product is highly decomposable when it has components that have relatively few connections with each other, so that parts within a component can be changed without affecting the functioning of other components (Henderson and Clark, 1990; Langlois, 2002; Sanchez and Mahoney, 1996). Thus, a product that is strongly decomposable is one in which the final assembled product can be broken up into two or more freestanding sub-assemblies that have only few connection points to each other (often only at the final stages of assembly). The production of a strongly decomposable product is likely to involve the

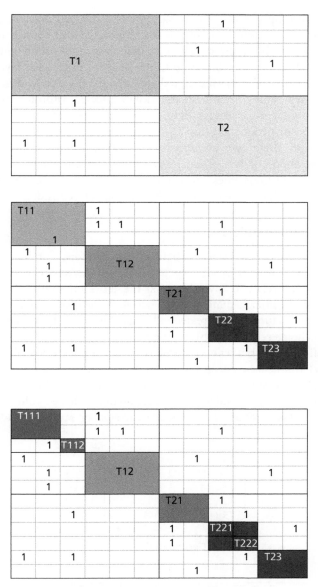

Figure 3.5 A multi-layered task structure produced through recursive decomposition

simultaneous existence of multiple intermediate objects during all but the close-to-final steps. A non-decomposable or weakly decomposable product, on the other hand, may feature just one intermediate product at any point in the production process that develops through stages.

Product decomposability is necessary for object-based division of labor to be an option. For instance, a chair is decomposable, but soup is not. In the production of a chair, there can simultaneously exist many intermediate objects (e.g. legs, armrests, back) up to the point of final assembly. However, from the moment of putting the ingredients into the pot and heating them, the soup has no separable components that can be affected without affecting other components. Object-based task division is therefore viable for producing a chair, but not for producing soup.

Armed with these two constructs, task structure decomposability and product decomposability, we can now outline an answer to the question: under what conditions does the choice between activity-based and object-based division of labor exist? There are three cases to consider.

Case 1: Decomposable Tasks

In this case, there is no distinction between the two forms of division of labor (Figure 3.6). This is because all tasks produce outputs, and a cluster of related tasks that do not relate to any other tasks (i.e. a decomposable task structure) must produce an intermediate object. Therefore, the task clusters in a decomposable task structure can be treated either as object or activity-based clusters; there is no choice required between the two.

An implication is that when the task structure is decomposable, the resulting product will also be decomposable (but the converse is not true: i.e. task decomposability is sufficient for product decomposability, but not necessary). To illustrate this case, consider the production of a collected volume of papers, such that the tasks required to produce each paper are independent of the

	T1	T2	T3	T4
T1	1			
T2	1	1		
T3			1	1
T4			1	1

a. Decomposable

	T1	T2	T3	T4
T1	1	1	1	1
T2	1	1	1	1
T3			1	1
T4			1	1

b. Non-Decomposable with asymmetries

	T1	T2	T3	T4
T1	1	1	1	
T2	1	1		1
T3	1		1	1
T4		1	1	1

c. Non-Decomposable With symmetry

Figure 3.6 Task structure decomposability

tasks required to produce other papers, though the tasks involved in producing each paper may be interdependent among themselves and draw on similar inputs (assume negligible final assembly activities). Thus, there is no distinction between object- and activity-based division of labor in this case—each paper can represent either an intermediate object or a cluster of similar tasks.[5]

Next, consider the case where the task structure is not (or is only weakly) decomposable. There will now be dependencies across task clusters, whether the clusters are constructed based on activity or object. This situation can be further sub-divided into two cases: decomposable and non-decomposable products.

Case 2: Non-Decomposable Tasks and Products

In this case, only an activity-based division of labor is possible. This is true regardless of whether task structures feature asymmetry or symmetry. Asymmetric task structures are those in which tasks in one activity cluster are dependent on tasks in other activity clusters, but not the other way around. Symmetric task structures are those in which the tasks in one activity cluster are dependent on tasks in other activity clusters, and the other way around (see Figure 3.6).

Consider first asymmetric task structures (i.e. where task i is dependent on task j, but the converse is not true)—see Figure 3.6c. This is the case of production of soup or the continuous processing of oil (Woodward, 1958). Each step refines a single intermediate object (i.e. a stage of production), and the tasks at each stage are distinct but asymmetrically dependent across stages. The distinction between cases like the collected volume of papers (Case I) and the production of soup (Case II with asymmetric tasks) have been referred to as horizontal vs. vertical division of labor (Leijonhufvud, 1986) or heterogeneous vs. serial division of labor (Marx, 1906). However my further enumeration of cases below shows that these older categorizations do not exhaust the space of possible divisions of labor.

Next consider the case of symmetric task structures. Instances could include a string quartet or a surgical team performing a procedure: multiple activities are simultaneously involved in a single stage of production. Again, only activity-based division of labor is feasible—everyone plays a different instrument or exercises a distinct surgical skill.

Case 3: Non-Decomposable Task, Decomposable Product

In this case activity- and object-based division of labor are distinct options. First consider asymmetric tasks. One could choose to keep the tasks clustered based on similarity (i.e. activity-based) or in terms of the intermediate objects

---

[5] Such cases of perfect decomposability of task structures may be rare, if my difficulty in finding examples is any indicator.

being produced. For instance, producing a wooden chair requires several ordered tasks—such as cutting the wood, shaving the wood, painting it and varnishing it, and an activity-based division of labor would correspond exactly to these tasks. However, it is also possible to undertake an object-based division of labor, in which the legs, back and seat of the chair are each treated as intermediate objects, each of which requires the same ordered set of tasks.

Now consider symmetric tasks. An instance is the production of a report on the socio-economic development of two regions in a country. The two activity-based clusters could be tasks pertaining to analyzing economic indicators, and tasks pertaining to analyzing social indicators. These are symmetrically dependent activities. The report itself is decomposable into two sections, one for each region. Either an object (region)-based or an activity (data analysis for type of indicator)-based division of labor is feasible.

Thus, the choice between activity- and object-based division of labor as two distinct alternatives only emerges **when the task structure is non-decomposable, but the product is decomposable** (Case 3). If the product is not decomposable, no object-based division of labor is possible (Case 2). If the task structure is decomposable (Case 1), then object- and activity-based divisions of labor are identical. These arguments are summarized in Figure 3.7.

It is important to bear in mind that, unlike with Spin Master-like toys, typically we may guess but do not know the nature of the underlying task structure for new and unfamiliar tasks. Therefore, when I say decomposability of a task structure, I really mean decomposability of our representation of a task structure. Figure 3.7 thus shows the perceived opportunities for choosing one kind of division of labor or the other, given the representation I have of the task structure (Figure 3.6).

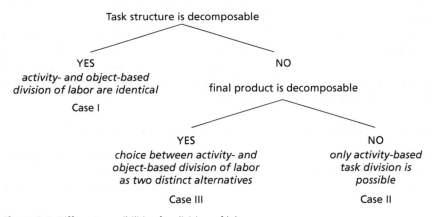

Figure 3.7 Different possibilities for division of labor

SPECIALIZATION VS. CUSTOMIZATION AS CRITERIA
FOR CHOOSING A DIVISION OF LABOR

Next we can turn to the question of what factors may shape the choice between activity- and object-based division of labor, if a choice exists between the two. In Smith's (1776) highly cited account, three benefits of the division of labor in the pin factory were described—the improved productivity of the worker, the saving in time lost in switching tasks, and the development of new methods of working (including mechanization) arising from specialization. Mintzberg noted that at the root of all three benefits cited by Smith is repetition (1979: 70)—in particular, repetition of a task cluster that requires similar inputs of skill and efforts, which consequently entails narrow cognitive scope, and allows rapid amortization of fixed costs. For a given scale of production, the potential for repetition by an individual is typically higher in an activity-based (rather than an object-based) division of labor, because of similarity of tasks within the cluster—that is after all the principle for clustering. Thus activity-based task division can enable skill-building (Simon, 1962: 102). Obviously, an increase in scale further enhances the gains from skill-building, an idea that is today strongly associated with Frederick Taylor (Taylor, 1911; but also see Smith, 1776; Stigler, 1951).

Another cornerstone of Taylor's ideas about scientific management was the match of the individual to the position (Taylor, 1911). In more recent times, through an extensive series of experiments, Argote, Moreland and colleagues (Liang, Moreland, and Argote, 1995; Moreland, 1999; Moreland, Argote, and Krishnan, 1996; Moreland and Myaskovsky, 2000) showed that joint assembly activities build "transactive memory"—knowledge of who is skilled at and knows what in a group—which is beneficial when the group approaches similar problems repeatedly. Skill (to task) matching is clearly a central feature of formal organizations that grow by recruitment, but in fact has been observed in division of labor patterns in insect societies as well, where no authoritative task allocation can occur (Anderson and Franks, 2001; Sendova-Franks and Franks, 1999). Skill-building and skill-matching are jointly referred to as gains from specialization, but they are analytically distinguishable. Common to both though is the fact that an activity-based task division allows them to be realized more easily than an object-based task division. The disadvantage of activity-based task clusters is that the interdependencies that exist between the tasks that together produce intermediate objects are de-emphasized, at the expense of increased focus on the interdependence between tasks in the same activity cluster.

However, the case for division of labor based on gains from specialization is not always clear. Primarily, object-based division of labor creates advantages through allowing more attention on the dependencies between the distinct tasks needed to produce an object (i.e. customization[6]), by allocating all such activities to one agent. Object-based clusters thus allow for local adaptation—in particular for exploitation of gains from customizing different tasks needed to produce an intermediate object, but at the expense of ignoring the inter-dependencies that exist between the tasks that are common to different intermediate objects. When there are no temporal dependencies between object-based clusters (or these can be ignored), parallelism is also feasible (i.e. one can save time by working on objects in parallel).

An important determinant of the choice between activity- and object-based division of labor thus is a comparison of the benefits of focusing on the interdependencies within a task cluster with the opportunity costs of de-emphasizing interdependencies that lie between the task clusters. When the cluster is an activity-based one, the benefits show up as specialization, and the opportunity costs as the missed opportunities for customizing across tasks that together produce an object. When the cluster is an object-based one, exactly the reverse is true.

A simple formalization may make this clearer. Assume a production process involving i different types of tasks results in a decomposable final product, so that it produces j intermediate objects. Each task T is of type i and contributes to product j, and so is written T_{ij}. Let V_k denote the value of output obtained when assigning a cluster of tasks to agent k, who can focus attention on managing the dependencies between the tasks in the cluster, and on the execution of the tasks themselves. Then the value of output with customization through an object (subscripted O) based division of labor with k agents is:

$$V_{O,k} = V_1(T_{11}, T_{21}...T_{i,1}) + V_2(T_{12}, T_{22}...T_{i,2})...V_k(T_{1j}, T_{2j}...T_{i,j}).$$

The value of output with specialization through an activity-based division of labor (subscripted A) with m agents is:

$$V_{A,m} = V_1(T_{11}, T_{12}...T_{1,j}) + V_2(T_{21}, T_{22}...T_{2,j})...V_m(T_{i1}, T_{i2}...T_{i,j}).$$

The value of output from one form of division labor is also the opportunity cost of the other, if it is impossible to coordinate between agents. However, we do not need such an extreme assumption. Let the parameters $\gamma_1, \gamma_2 \ \varepsilon \ (-1,1)$ capture the difficulties of coordination between agents under the two divisions of labor. Then the opportunity costs for an object-based division of labor will be $\gamma_1 V_{A,m}$ and $\gamma_2 V_{O,k}$ for an activity-based division of labor. For lower values

---

[6] We could also call this coordination (which is not precise enough) or co-specialization (but that could lead to confusion with specialization).

of γ, (arising for instance from improved communication technologies, shared history, physical collocation or specialized organizational mechanisms), the opportunity costs will be correspondingly lower. In theory, we could choose a division of labor simply by comparing the net quantities $[V_{O,k} - \gamma_1 V_{A,m}]$ and $[V_{A,m} - \gamma_2 V_{O,k}]$.

Yet, in a world of bounded rationality, none of the quantities above may be known, and it is seldom ex-ante obvious whether the gains from specialization within activity type (i.e. activity-based division of labor) outweigh the gains from coordinating across activities (i.e. object-based division of labor). In fact, the true extent of decomposability of the underlying task structure itself may be unknown (Eppinger, 2001; Ethiraj and Levinthal, 2004a; Gopkinar et al., 2010; Sosa, Eppinger, and Rowles, 2004), making it far from obvious what choices are even feasible.

It should therefore be clear that whether an activity- or object-based division of labor emerges is unlikely to be fully technologically determined. In part this is simply because of the subjective and limited nature of the understanding of the task structure T^R. Further, even within a given T^R, barring certain exceptionally obvious cases of decomposability of task structure and non-decomposability of product, there will typically exist a choice between activity- and object-based division of labor, and the relative magnitude of these gains may be very hard to determine. In addition, there may be many object and activity-based divisions of labor—since the decomposability of products as well as the similarity of underlying production tasks is a matter of degree. This may make the choice between activity- and object-based division of labor even more complicated.

Simple rules of thumb may nonetheless be useful to estimate when the gains from specialization may outweigh the gains from customization, and vice versa. For instance, if each intermediate object is distinct from others (i.e. it is a unique blend of activities, each of which might appear in some other objects, but not all together), then the gains from customization—i.e. managing the interdependencies between tasks within the object—may be significantly larger than the gains from specialization. Consider division of labor in the context of the design of complex technical systems, which has also been central to the growing literature on modularity in technology and organizations (e.g. Sanchez and Mahoney, 1996; Baldwin and Clark, 2000). If we consider the set of design decisions that define the specification of an object, as the task structure of T^R, task clusters correspond to sets of design decision that are clustered together in the sense that they are taken in a coordinated fashion (and effectively ignore design decisions being taken in other modules). In theory, the clustering can be by object (a component of the final artifact being designed) or by activity (similarity of underlying design skill, for instance), or some hybrid. However, because the objects being designed tend to be quite distinct from each other, and each design cycle is a one-shot project, in practice the object-based clustering typically dominates—and these are called design modules.

Conversely, if the scale (i.e. repeatability) of production is large, then the gains from specialization are correspondingly large. This was highlighted by Woodward in her description of mass and continuous process production (1958). Using hybrid structures that cluster simultaneously by object and activity (e.g. matrix organizations) or switching repeatedly between the two kinds of division of labor may also be solutions to the problem of distinguishing between comparable magnitudes of gains from activity- and object-based division of labor (Nickerson and Zenger, 2002; Gulati and Puranam, 2009).

OTHER CRITERIA THAT SHAPE DIVISION OF LABOR

An extensive body of work on job design (Herzberg, 1966; Hackman and Oldham 1976; Oldham and Hackman, 2010) has pointed out that the agents in an organization may not be agnostic about the type of division of labor. For instance, the intrinsic motivation among workers inspired by skill variety (the range of different skills required for carrying out an agent's cluster of tasks) and task identity (the extent to which the tasks performed produce a distinctly identifiable piece of work) seem to tip the balance towards object-based division of labor, particularly if each object-based cluster is assigned to one individual. However, the desirability of opportunities for interaction (Turner and Lawrence, 1965; Oldham and Hackman, 2010) may tip the scale back towards activity-based division of labor. This is because even in an activity-based division of labor, intermediate objects are produced; given non-decomposability of task structure the production of each of these intermediate objects will require the involvement of those performing very different tasks. In an object-based division of labor this is not the case, as the different kinds of tasks are all performed by the same individual.

There are other criteria that may influence the choice of division of labor besides the trade-off between customization and specialization. An important one is the measurability of the efforts of agents. Frederick Taylor's scientific management principles relied heavily on the idea of standardized sequence of actions, and the ease of observing whether the sequence was being conformed to. Such an assumption swiftly becomes untenable as the proportion of production that occurs in the worker's mind increases. Indeed, an object-based division of labor may be preferable to an activity-based one if intermediate objects are easier to observe and measure than activities. If so, then object-based division may enhance accountability and lower measurement costs (Barzel, 1982), enabling the use of sharp incentives that link rewards to outputs (Zenger and Hesterly, 1997).

The preference for equity (Adams, 1965; Fehr and Schmidt, 1999) is another factor that may influence the choice of the division of labor. To avoid perceptions of inequity, divisions of labor that result in unequal numbers of tasks across agents, or even leave certain agents unoccupied may be avoided, even if they represent highly modular clustering of tasks.

It is also possible that certain kinds of division of labor are just simpler to mentally represent and consider, when confronted with a novel production task. The advantages of Spin Master-like assembly toys for a student of division of labor are the explicit provision of the task structure, variation in decomposability of resulting products, and the opportunity for significant gains in manual dexterity through experience at assembly. Using these as experimental tasks, Marlo Raveendran, Massimo Warglien, and I (2015) have found that both individuals and groups show a greater propensity to perceive object-based task clusters rather than activity-based task clusters when engaging in task division. This tendency towards object-based task division seems to be reflected in their non-verbal behavior (what they pay attention to) as much as in their verbalized choices, and is manifested at the individual- as well as group-levels. Our data on attention allocation based on eye-tracking suggests that there is a bottom-up ("System 1"; see Chapter 2) processing aspect to this preference.

So far, I have assumed that the process of division of labor is conducted either by a single agent or by a group of agents whose interests are aligned with each other's. This need not always be the case; sometimes the division of labor must be agreed upon by agents whose interests diverge, such that each seeks to maximize his or her own gain, not joint value. Outsourcing relationships and strategic alliances between firms often feature agreements on division of labor between parties whose interests are not aligned (Inkpen and Tsang, 2007). Each party may have a private interest in developing or learning skills the other party currently possesses, or to hold on to skills they currently possess to avoid dependence. Consequently, task allocation may not occur based on skill matching, but instead either party may seek to do things the other may be better at doing. One or more parties may try to covertly learn the skills of the other through the relationship, resulting in so-called "learning races" (Hamel, 1991). The party that seeks to learn would in this case prefer a non-modular task division, whereas the party seeking to protect its skills would prefer a modular task division with minimal dependencies between partners. Finally, the division of design labor within a firm may also have implications for how easy it is easy for rivals to imitate the design (Ethiraj, Levinthal, and Roy, 2008). Modular designs may make it easier for rivals to copy the designs, as appears to have been the case in the PC industry once IBM modularized its design (Baldwin and Clark, 2000).

Thus, the specific choice of object- or activity-based division of labor in a situation must balance many factors (see Table 3.1).

Table 3.1 The distinctive features of activity- and object-based division of labor

	Individuals are assigned object-based task clusters	Individuals are assigned activity-based task clusters
Benefits	Customization—i.e. managing dependencies across dissimilar tasks needed to produce intermediate objects	Specialization—i.e. managing dependencies across similar tasks that may be present in multiple intermediate object-based clusters
Opportunity costs	Missed opportunities for specialization	Missed opportunities for customization
Other features	1. High skill variety 2. High task identity 3. Easier performance measurement 4. May be more intuitive to decompose task structure into object-based clusters	1. Low skill variety 2. Low task identity 3. May be harder to measure performance

Division of labor and interdependence between agents

Given an allocation of tasks to a dyad of agents A and B, symmetric interdependence between the agents exists when the returns to A from A's actions depend on B's actions, and vice versa. This conceptualization of interdependence between agents appears explicitly in the analysis of reward interdependence (Kelley and Thibaut, 1978), power (Emerson, 1962; Pfeffer and Salancik, 1978) and in game theory in general (e.g. von Neuman and Morgenstern, 1944).

In the theory of epistemic interdependence I developed jointly with Marlo Raveendran and Thorbjorn Knudsen (2012), we showed that interdependence between tasks is neither necessary nor sufficient for interdependence between the agents (that these tasks are allocated to) to arise. Unlike task interdependence, interdependence between agents depends entirely on a key feature of their reward structure—*incentive breadth.* This refers to the level of aggregation at which an agent's actions (or their results) are measured and rewarded. In the case of two agents, narrow incentives correspond to the reward of individual actions or their results in a manner that makes them independent of the other agent's actions. Broad incentives correspond to the reward of individual actions or their results in a manner that makes them at least partly dependent on the other agent's actions. For instance, if A provides a critical input to B and B is measured on the final output, then the reward structure is de facto broad for B unless B's actions can be measured and rewarded independently of whether A has provided the critical input. Agents are interdependent when they face broad incentives, but are independent when they face narrow incentives.

Put differently, interdependence between tasks is assessed by examining the *value function* that represents the combined system of tasks, while interdependence between agents depends on the *reward function* of the agents.

DIVISION OF LABOR **65**

Since in general these will not be identical, there will be a corresponding divergence between task and agent interdependence. Even if the tasks assigned to each agent are interdependent, the agents may be measured and rewarded narrowly for their own tasks.

Consider the pin factory example popularized by Smith (1776): as an example of independent tasks but interdependent agents, agents A and B are to produce 100 pins each (i.e. the value of A's task output does not change with B's output, and vice versa) but they are paid only if a total of 200 pins are produced. On the other hand, if this was a specialized production process, A and B could be tasked to produce a total of 300 pins, of which A produces the tails and B produces the heads. In this case, the tasks are clearly interdependent; however, if both A and B are rewarded on their individual output, respectively (i.e. A is rewarded if she produces 300 tails regardless of B's performance and vice versa), the agents are effectively independent. The differences between these cases arise from whether individual or joint production can be measured and rewarded.

A crucial consequence of this separation between task and agent interdependence is that by improving the ability to measure and reward individual performance, interdependence between agents can be endogenous to organization design, even if interdependence between tasks cannot be changed. Thus, the division of labor defines interdependence between task clusters assigned to each of the agents (while leaving T^R unchanged) as well as between the agents to whom the tasks are assigned, though these two patterns of interdependence may not be identical, and the latter may be modified even if the former cannot. Note that the same principles apply if we replace this two-task two-agent case, with the n-task m-agent case. Every dyad of agents can be rewarded with narrow or broad incentives, and their allocated tasks or clusters of tasks can be interdependent or independent with those allocated to other agents. This results in T^t, the matrix of interdependence between the agents themselves.

How interdependence between agents, given a division of labor, generates impediments to the integration of effort and how these impediments are resolved is the focus of the next chapter. To reiterate what I noted in Chapter 1, this sequential treatment of division of labor followed by integration of effort is for expositional convenience; choices about the former may often be influenced by the feasibility of the latter.

Conclusion

We have discussed three main themes in this chapter. First, division of labor involves task division and task allocation. For analytical purposes this requires a representation of the task structure and how it maps into agents. The matrix notation is a convenient and scalable one to go from microstructures to macro-structures.

Second, while there are many ways in which the task structure can be chunked and divided among agents, two important heuristic approaches involve division of labor by activity vs. object. A choice between these two forms of division of labor only arises when the task structure is non-decomposable, but the product itself is decomposable. There are multiple criteria for choosing between activity- vs. object-based division of labor (Table 3.1)—the gains from specialization is only one of them.

Third, an extremely important consequence of task division and allocation is the creation of interdependence between agents. In fact, division of labor is a process that converts interdependence between tasks into interdependence between agents.

Looking back at this list, it seems to me that we have only just begun the serious study of the phenomenon of intra-organizational division of labor. Much more remains to be discovered about how current division of labor shapes future choices, about how the process of division of labor unfolds when conducted by groups vs. individuals, by newly formed vs. existing groups, closed groups vs. open groups, through self-organization, either asynchronously (as in open-source software projects) or synchronously, through consensus (as in project teams). This can help bring our knowledge of these processes up to the same level as our understanding of the case of how division of labor unfolds in markets to promote specialization, catalyzed by the price mechanism.

4 Integration of effort

Many perspectives on organizations build on the premise that organization designs "solve" the problems relating to motivation and knowledge that arise when integrating the efforts of interdependent actors. The interdependence between actors is itself a consequence of division of labor (see Chapter 3). This premise is common to the analysis of organizational structures using diverse constructs such as information processing (e.g. Simon, 1947; Thompson, 1967), contingency and fit (e.g. Lawrence and Lorsch, 1967), complementarities (e.g. Milgrom and Roberts, 1990), epistatic interactions (e.g. Levinthal, 1997), power (e.g. Pfeffer and Salancik, 1978), reward interdependence (e.g. Kelley and Thibaut, 1978) and asset specificity (e.g. Williamson, 1975).

This chapter has three objectives.[1] The first is to consider in some detail the nature of the challenges to integration of efforts arising from motivational vs. knowledge-related causes. An important sub-topic of this theme relates to the conditions under which interdependence between agents gives rise to cooperation problems vs. coordination problems. Coordination failures occur when interacting individuals are unable to anticipate each other's actions and adjust their own accordingly (Schelling, 1960); evidence of coordination failures include misunderstandings, delays, and a lack of synchronization of activities. Often, no party benefits at the expense of the others from such failures. In contrast, cooperation failures occur when interdependent individuals lack the motivation to achieve the best collective outcome. Shirking, free-riding and reneging on agreements are the canonical instances of cooperation failures. Cooperation and coordination failures can occur independently of each other and are therefore individually sufficient reasons for the failure to achieve integration of effort (Heath and Staudenmayer, 2000; Holmstrom and Roberts, 1998).

A second objective for the chapter is to consider some ways in which the motivation and knowledge-related challenges arising from interdependence can be analyzed jointly, rather than separately as traditionally has been the case. I outline how we may bridge the gap between how interdependence is treated in these two conceptualizations of organizations—as systems that elicit motivated, cooperative action, or as systems that enable coordinated action.

Finally, a third objective is to develop the distinction between search and execution problems that arise in the integration of effort. An *execution* problem exists when either the designer or the agents know what the agents

---

[1] This and the next section draw extensively from Puranam, Raveendran, and Knudsen (2012) and Puranam and Raveendran (2014).

ought to do to produce integration of efforts; a *search* problem arises when neither the designer nor the agents know this. Understanding search problems is key to understanding organizational adaptation. In particular, this helps us comprehend organizations as "marvels but not miracles"—to see how design can be useful even when the designer is as boundedly rational as the agents in the system.

Impediments to the integration of effort and solutions

The integration of effort requires that the agents in an organization take actions that maximize the value of the organization for a given division of labor. Note that the actions in question may pertain to sharing information. This definition draws on the classic conceptualization of integration in a multi-unit organization, defined as the "quality of the state of collaboration that exists among departments that are required to achieve unity of effort by the demands of the environment" (Lawrence and Lorsch, 1967: 11).

There are several reasons why achieving integration of effort may be problematic, but it is helpful to think of these as falling broadly into two categories, relating to knowledge and motivation of the agents, respectively (Milgrom and Roberts, 1990; Hoopes and Postrel, 1999). Within each, we can also distinguish between situations where the agents are interdependent (or not), and when the tasks they perform are interdependent (or not). To clarify this, consider a simple dyadic microstructure. Given an allocation of task clusters to a dyad of agents A and B, interdependence between the agents exists when the returns to A from A's actions depend on B's actions and vice versa. Interdependence between the tasks performed by A and B exists if the value to the system of performing A's tasks changes when B's tasks are performed and vice versa (see Chapter 3).[2]

Building on these ideas, Table 4.1 organizes the causes of integration failures and their implications. A key argument embodied in Table 4.1 and developed below is that given interdependence between tasks, even individual

[2] A more general formulation can be given as follows: an organization can be considered a system that exists in an environment, whose components are agents, and their states represent the completion of tasks they undertake. If the fitness contribution (i.e. impact on system performance) of state 1 for component i depends on the state of component j, then there is *interdependence between the tasks* (states) of agents (components) i and j. If the private benefit of being in state 1 for agent i depends on the state of agent j, then there is *interdependence between agents* (components of the system). If the private benefit to each agent can be decoupled from everything except the fitness contribution of own state, then both kinds of interdependence are equivalent. For instance in inter-firm or inter-divisional relationships, where the profit (i.e. fitness contribution) of each unit can typically be measured separately, task and agent (i.e. firm or division) interdependence will be identical.

Table 4.1 Forms of integration failures

	Independent agents	Interdependent agents
Independent tasks	**Cell 1** Knowledge-related: Skill deficits	**Cell 3** Knowledge-related: Skill deficits and Coordination problems (when epistemic interdependence exists)
	Motivation-related: Agency problems	Motivation-related: Agency problems and Cooperation failures (when valence of interdependence is negative)
	Localized consequences	Systemic consequences
Interdependent tasks	**Cell 2** Knowledge-related: Skill deficits	**Cell 4** Knowledge-related: Skill deficits and Coordination problems (when epistemic interdependence exists)
	Motivation-related: Agency problems	Motivation-related: Agency problems and Cooperation failures (when valence of interdependence is negative)
	Systemic consequences	Systemic consequences

level knowledge and motivational gaps may nonetheless generate organizational level consequences. Further, given interdependence between agents (which can be endogenous to organization design, even if task interdependence is not), the consequences of integration failure will be felt at the organizational level, regardless of task interdependence.

In what follows, I illustrate arguments first using the simplest microstructure—a dyad, unless otherwise specified. Later, I show how matrix notation can be useful to scale to arbitrarily large numbers of agents.

INTEGRATION FAILURE THROUGH KNOWLEDGE GAPS

Bounded rationality implies that an agent's representation of a task environment is, at least to begin with, inaccurate and/or incomplete. In practical terms, this means that there are typically limits to an agent's knowledge, and that these limits prevent them undertaking the actions that produce integration at the organizational level. (For the moment, we will assume that these actions, if performed, generate rewards large enough to cover the agent's cost of effort—so that there are no motivation-related challenges). This inadequacy of knowledge may act as an impediment to the integration of effort in two ways.

Skill Problems

Consider first the case where in an organization, the agents are independent of each other, and are motivated to contribute efforts. There may yet be a failure of integration if the agents do not know enough to perform the task clusters assigned to them adequately. This is a *skill failure*: the sole impediment to an individual contributing to the integration of effort is the gap in an individual's knowledge about how to perform the tasks assigned to them.

Though the agents are independent of each other, the impact of this skill problem on the integration of effort in the system depends crucially on the interdependence of tasks in the system. In a system with highly interdependent tasks, skill failures at individual tasks may have substantial implications for system performance compared to that in a system with independent tasks (see Cell 2 vs. Cell 1 in Table 4.1). To see this, consider a pin factory operated by a dyad, with a division of labor between A and B in which each agent produces 100 pins each (i.e. no interdependence between tasks). A daily output of 100 fully functional pins is possible even if B (alone) lacked the necessary skill, in this case. However, with a division of labor where agents are specialized to produce heads and tails of pins, the 300 faulty heads produced by B due to a lack of skill will reduce the total value of the tasks to zero, even if A produces 300 perfect pin tails.

Coordination Problems

Next, we consider the case where the agents in the organization are inter-dependent, such that the value to A of his actions depends on B's actions (Cells 3 and 4 in Table 4.1). Interdependence between agents by itself does not generate coordination problems. We need one more condition: in addition, the interdependence must take the form that the action of each agent depends on a prediction of what the other agents will do. In the theory that Marlo Raveendran, Thorbjorn Knudsen and I developed (2012), we describe this as a situation of *epistemic interdependence*.

Epistemic interdependence theory proposes that the presence of agent interdependence is a necessary but not sufficient condition for the occurrence of coordination problems. A second necessary (and jointly sufficient with the first) condition relates to the timing of the actions—only if at least one of the interdependent agent's needs to act before knowing the other agent's actions will epistemic interdependence exist. For instance, if A provides an input to B and both are rewarded on final output, both agents are interdependent with each other; but only A is epistemically interdependent on B (this is the familiar backward induction problem in game theory).

To illustrate the concepts of epistemic interdependence, consider again the pin factory with independent tasks but interdependent agents (i.e. the agents are jointly rewarded only if 200 pins are produced at the end of the day and each agent is to produce 100 pins). A works the morning shift and B in the afternoon, and assume B can see A's total output before he starts his shift. B can therefore decide to take the rest of the day off if A has not reached her target. B need not make any predictions about A's actions because they are known before B acts. B is therefore not epistemically interdependent with A. However, A will have to make predictions regarding B's productivity since her final reward will be contingent on B producing his 100 pins once A has completed her part. A is therefore epistemically interdependent with B.

Given epistemic interdependence, for the agents to coordinate their actions requires predictive knowledge. A's predictive knowledge about B enables A to act *as if* he could accurately predict B's actions. The "as if" condition explicitly allows for agents to find coordinated patterns of action through mutual adjustment, rather than through forward-looking reasoning alone (e.g. Lave and March, 1993; Puranam and Swamy, 2010). In epistemic interdependence theory, a coordination failure thus occurs when there is epistemic interdependence but the agent(s) do not possess the necessary predictive knowledge. A pure *coordination failure* is thus one where the sole impediment to an individual contributing to the integration of effort in a situation of interdependence is the gap in an individual's knowledge about what actions others will take.

To illustrate how coordination failures arise given epistemic interdependence, consider two programmers, Ann and Bob, who together produce a computer program for a client. They decide to divide up the work into two code modules. Each module will require investment of effort by the assigned coder. When both modules are completed, the value to the client is V, and with one module only, it is v. When Ann puts in the effort to complete coding her module, but Bob does not complete his module, the client pays w_A units of utility to Ann and w_B to Bob. But if Bob completes his module, the client is willing to pay y_A units to Ann and y_B to Bob. The situation is symmetric from Bob's perspective: he gets x_A and Ann gets x_B if he delivers but she does not, and she gets y_A and Bob gets y_B if both deliver. If neither contributes effort, they get z_A and z_B respectively. The client's willingness to pay these amounts takes into account the net value to the client. These arrangements are summarized in Table 4.2.

Should Bob contribute to this project? There are two conditions to consider: 1) $y_B - w_B > 0$ and 2) $x_B - z_B > 0$. If both conditions are met, then Bob should contribute effort regardless of what Ann will do. If neither condition is met, Bob should not contribute effort regardless of what Ann will do. In neither case is Bob epistemically interdependent on Ann. However, if only one of these conditions is met, then what Bob should do depends on how certain he is of what Ann will do. If condition 1 is met but not 2, then Bob should not

Table 4.2 Coordination and cooperation failures illustrated

	Ann contributes effort	Ann does not contribute effort
Bob contributes effort	Net Value to client: $V-(y_A+y_B)$ Ann gets: y_A Bob gets: y_B	Net Value to client: $v-(x_A+x_B)$ Ann gets: x_A Bob gets: x_B
Bob does not contribute effort	Net Value to client: $v-(w_A+w_B)$ Ann gets: w_A Bob gets: w_B	Net Value to client: $0-(z_A+z_B)$ Ann gets: z_A Bob gets: z_B

contribute unless he is quite sure that Ann will contribute; if condition 2 is met but not 1, then Bob should not contribute unless he is quite sure Ann will *not* contribute. In both cases Bob is epistemically interdependent on Ann. If Ann is in fact going to contribute but Bob does not know this, and therefore does not contribute, this is a breakdown in integration arising from a coordination problem (a.k.a. a coordination failure).

Informally, we often equate coordination failures with communication and language-related challenges. This intuition is good but incomplete. It is good because a failure of communication can indeed prevent the formation of predictive knowledge, but incomplete because predictive knowledge can form without communication.[3] For instance, Kannan Srikanth and I (2011, 2014) in studying coordination in business process offshoring, documented the use of "tacit coordination mechanisms" that allow the formation of predictive knowledge across locations through enhancing observability of context, actions, and outcomes rather than through direct communication.[4]

Solutions to Skill and Coordination Problems

It has been a basic premise in the organization design literature that both individual competence (skill) as well as predictive knowledge for coordination can be formed through information-processing activities—communication, mutual observation, learning and (joint) decision making (e.g. Galbraith, 1973; March and Simon, 1958; Tushman and Nadler, 1976).

Epistemic interdependence theory points to a second channel: directly reducing (epistemic) interdependence between agents can also enhance integration. Let's consider again the microstructure consisting of two agents, A and B, in which each is epistemically interdependent with the

---

[3] In fact communication itself can be seen as a coordination problem, as the modern view of linguistics does: when communicating, I need to predict which among several possible meanings you chose to attach to the words you used. Talk, if it is to be understood, is seldom cheap—because communication is itself a coordination problem in the domain of meaning (Clark, 1996). We could for instance replace the action "contributes effort" for Ann and Bob in Table 4.2 with "chooses label 1," and "does not contribute effort" with "chooses label 2" when both see a signal. Set payoffs $y_A = z_A = y_B = z_B = 1$, and all other payoffs = 0. Table 4.2 now captures a matching coordination game in which Ann and Bob must agree on which label to assign a signal, and it does not matter which label they choose as long as both agree on it. Such a game is at the heart of language formation.

[4] Another subtlety about predictive knowledge involves the fact that it may but need not draw on shared knowledge among the agents. Precedents—actions used in the past that are psychologically prominent—and conventions—established principles of action that are not questioned—are forms of predictive knowledge that arise from shared knowledge (Camerer, 2003; Lewis, 1969; Schelling, 1960). The agenda of epistemic game theory (Aumann and Brandenburger, 1995) includes an investigation of the layers of iteratively shared knowledge necessary to produce coordinated action. On the other hand, mutual adaptation of agents may result in coordinated action with very little overlaps in knowledge, as each agent forms reinforced habits of action in response to the other. An important organizational instance is an interpersonal routine, which may be quite frugal in terms of shared knowledge requirements (Cohen and Bacdayan, 1994; Nelson and Winter, 1982; Aggarwal, Posen, and Workiewicz, 2016).

other (but whose interests are otherwise aligned). We can represent the degree of integration by the multiplication of the probabilities that A has predictive knowledge about B (p_{AB}) and B has predictive knowledge about A (p_{BA}). (We ignore skill problems for the moment—let's assume the agents are sufficiently skilled.)

The traditional approach to enhancing integration lies in specifying a pattern of information processing interactions among the agents that will improve predictive knowledge (i.e., increase the probabilities p_{AB} and p_{BA}). These could include communication, mutual observation, learning and (joint) decision-making by the agents. But a second approach consists of reducing epistemic interdependence between the agents so that only one or neither agent needs predictive knowledge about the other. This is equivalent to setting p_{AB} and/or p_{BA} equal to 1. Integration will then depend on only one probability or none so that reducing epistemic interdependence effectively increases the degree of integration (because probabilities are less than 1, they diminish further through multiplication).

But how exactly can epistemic interdependence be reduced (without necessarily being able to modify task interdependence—which may reflect physical or economic constraints)? The answer lies in the comprehension the designer of an organization has of its underlying task structure. With sufficient knowledge of the system, a designer can measure and sequence actions to reduce the need for predictive knowledge between agents.

For instance, it is possible to convert a simultaneous action schedule into a sequential action schedule using buffers and slack inventories, which no longer require the consumers of inputs to anticipate each other's consumption (Malone and Crowston, 1994). With no predictive knowledge needed, there is no possibility of a coordination failure.

Further, through superior measurement systems (Zenger and Hesterly, 1997) or the specification of interfaces and design rules (Baldwin and Clark, 2000), the designer can transform a broad measurement situation into a narrow measurement situation, because the performance requirements for different individuals can be specified in isolation from each other. This eliminates interdependence between agents (and therefore epistemic interdependence as well—the former is necessary but not sufficient for the latter).

Consider the practice of modularization, which is a strategy for managing complexity in partially decomposable systems with many and possibly unknown interdependencies (Sanchez and Mahoney, 1996; Baldwin and Clark, 2000; Ethiraj and Levinthal, 2004). By clustering elements into discrete clusters that de-emphasize interdependencies with other clusters, local improvements within clusters may be obtained, but possibly at the expense of overall system performance, because inter-module dependencies are ignored.

However, with a deeper understanding of the task interdependence structure, design rules and interfaces can be formulated that take into account what actions within one module are appropriate given interdependence with actions in other modules (Baldwin and Clark, 2000). When such rules exist and become the basis for measuring and rewarding performance, then agents working in different modules effectively become independent, because the returns to their actions no longer depend on the actions of others (even though task interdependencies may remain between them).

Besides improving measurement and converting simultaneous to sequential actions through task redesign, task allocation can also help to minimize the need for predictive knowledge. Even if the designer cannot sequence actions or measure actions or outputs narrowly, he or she can choose to allocate those tasks that would generate high epistemic interdependence between different agents, as clusters of tasks to individual agents. This allows the designer to create lower levels of epistemic interdependence between agents, possibly at the cost of raising the task and cognitive burden of individual agents (Baldwin and Clark, 2000).

Environmental Change as Change to Interdependence Structure

The macro-structural approach to organization design emphasized several environmental attributes such as environmental uncertainty (Donaldson, 2001: 22), velocity (Eisenhardt and Bourgeois, 1988), equivocality (Daft and Lengel, 1986: 567), and hostility (Burton and Obel, 1998: 171). The microstructural approach in this book follows the lead of scholars who have argued that the impact of environmental attributes can be ultimately traced through their impact on information processing within the organization (Burton and Obel, 1998; Galbraith, 1973, 1977; Mintzberg, 1979).

Specifically, these environmental attributes can ultimately be linked to their effect on the need vs. availability of skills and predictive knowledge (Puranam, Raveendran, and Knudsen, 2012). For instance, complex environments can be thought of as those characterized by limited architectural and predictive knowledge. The dynamism of the environment can be related to the frequency of shocks to the designer's architectural knowledge and/or the agents' predictive knowledge. Changes to the solutions to division of labor and integration of effort constitute the process of organizational adaptation to these environmental changes.

INTEGRATION FAILURES THROUGH MOTIVATION GAPS

Next, we consider a class of impediments to integration of effort that are traceable to the motivation of the agents. (For the moment, we assume that there are no knowledge-related impediments to the integration of efforts—there are no skill or coordination problems.) Just as bounded rationality is the key behavioral assumption when considering impediments to integration arising from knowledge-related issues (i.e. skill and coordination problems), the central behavioral assumption for understanding impediments to integration arising from the motives of the agents, is that agents have costly actions and that they do not undertake them unless their perceived rewards at least cover the costs.[5] Neither the rewards nor the costs are necessarily measured in cash they themselves receive or forgo (see Chapter 2).

A second assumption is that writing enforceable contracts is problematic. The problem of opportunism ("self-interest with guile"—Williamson, 1975) makes contracts harder to agree on between agents and designers because of opportunistic bargaining with misrepresentations, and harder to implement because of the possibility of reneging.[6] Absent such compulsions, we cannot take contribution of efforts for granted, but must examine whether the agents are sufficiently motivated.

The gap between the costs and benefits of efforts (i.e. gaps in motivation) can impede integration of effort in two ways.

Agency Problems

As before, first consider the case of independent agents in an organization (Cells 1 and 2 in Table 4.1). In the simplest case of integration failure, if the reward structure does not cover the agent's costs of efforts (and possible disutility from risk), then the agent will not contribute effort towards the task. This is known as an *agency failure*: the sole impediment to an individual contributing to the integration of effort is the gap between an individual's costs and benefits of contributing effort.

If the actions are not easy to contract on, and only noisy outcomes can be observed and rewarded, we have the canonical problem of principal–agent theory (Holmstrom and Milgrom, 1994; Jensen and Meckling, 1976). This theory proposes that an agent would put in only as much effort as he expects to be compensated for, after adjusting for the disutility of bearing risk (for instance, see Eisenhardt, 1988; Levinthal, 1988). Strategically anticipating this, a principal would design a contract with the optimal weight on the noisy measure of performance. The difference between the efforts the agent put in under this contract, and what they would have if the principal and agent together chose the agent's effort levels to maximize total surplus, is called "shirking."

In a system with interdependent tasks (Cell 2 in Table 4.1), agency failures will have implications for system performance, unlike the case of independent tasks (Cell 1). In general, task interdependence can exacerbate the effects of agency failures. Returning to the pin factory example, the impact of a poorly

---

[5] A stronger version would assume optimization of profits (rewards minus costs). We do not need such an assumption for our arguments below.

[6] See Hodgson (2004) for the argument that the challenges of creating enforceable contracts could remain in principle even without opportunism, due to bounded rationality alone.

designed reward structure for A will have more serious consequences with specialization and interdependence than without. Consider the case where A produces 300 faulty heads compared to A producing 100 faulty pins—in the former case the day's production will fall to zero, while in the latter, A's faulty output leaves B's output (of 100 pins) unaffected.

Cooperation Problems

In the case of interdependence between agents (Cells 3 and 4), it is still true that an agent will not take costly actions unless the rewards compensate these efforts sufficiently. The key question therefore is how interdependence between agents affects their rewards and costs of efforts. Interdependence between agents may be such that it either demotivates efforts or motivates them. In our work, Marlo Raveendran and I (2014) refer to this dimension as the *valence of interdependence*—whether the interdependence structure is such that it motivates (positive valence of interdependence) or demotivates (negative valence) the agent to contribute effort, given predictive knowledge of other agent's actions. Valence may be different for different agents in the same situation of interdependence. It answers the question "should I contribute effort, given I know what the other agent is going to do?"

When the valence of interdependence for all agents is positive, then cooperation will arise spontaneously (recall we assume predictive knowledge exists, so there are no coordination failures). When the valence is negative, we face a pure *cooperation failure*: the sole impediment to an individual contributing to the integration of effort in a situation of interdependence is the gap between an individual's costs and benefits of contributing effort.

The valence of interdependence depends both on the interdependence between the tasks that agents are assigned, and on the distribution of value between them via the reward system. To see this, we consider again our two coders, Ann and Bob, jointly developing a software program per the agreements set out in Table 4.2. We can again ask, should Bob contribute to this project? We have assumed that there is no doubt in Bob's mind as to what Ann will do (predictive knowledge is assured), and Bob is competent at his task (no skill problems either). Again, there are two conditions that are relevant: 1) $y_B - w_B > 0$ and 2) $x_B - z_B > 0$.

If Bob is *sure* Ann will complete her module, he should only contribute if condition 1 is met; if he is *sure* Ann will do nothing, Bob should only contribute his effort if condition 2 is met. The reasoning is similar for Ann. Each of these conditions makes the valence of interdependence positive for each agent, for each possible action of the other.

Note that both conditions depend on how the client is willing to divide the value created between himself and the two coders. Further, the conditions are unlikely to be met unless $V > v > 0$: the client must value the incomplete project less than a complete project, and no project less than an incomplete project. In turn, V is not the same as v (which is not the same as zero) because of task interdependence between the two modules. This illustrates how the valence of interdependence in this situation depends both on the impact of task inter-dependence *and* on the distribution of value via the reward structure.

If these conditions are both met, the valence of interdependence is positive for both possible actions of Ann, so that regardless of what Ann does, Bob will contribute effort towards an integrated outcome. In this situation, there is therefore no epistemic interdependence of Bob on Ann (and with symmetry, vice versa). More generally if the valence of interdependence is positive for both agents of the interdependent dyad A and B for all possible actions of the other, then there is no epistemic interdependence between them.

Nearly a century ago, a French agricultural engineer, Maximillian Ringelmann, observed that individual effort (sometimes) decreases as group size increases. This has been christened the Ringelmann effect (Forsyth, 2009). The valence of interdependence offers a simple explanation for why this should happen, as well as when it will not, given predictive knowledge.

If a fixed reward is split between more and more people drafted in to perform a group task (i.e. scaling), the valence of interdependence will even-tually become negative because adding agents dilutes the returns to actions for each agent (see Prendergast, 1999: 39–44, for a review of empirical tests of free riding). On the other hand, pooling tasks (and the agents performing them) need not produce free riding. B added to A's tasks would lower A's valence in that task because the reward must be split, whereas the cost of effort does not change. But at the same time adding A to B's task and splitting the reward for that task with A would increase valence in that task; with symmetry these must balance, *if* B and A are equally adept at each other's tasks.

Thus, how groups increase in size matters. Adding agents to a task can lower the valence of interdependence, but pooling tasks need not do so, if there is no specialization (i.e. every agent can contribute to every task equally well). With specialization, pooling tasks will lower the valence of interdependence, but conversely, synergies arising from task interdependence could increase the valence of interdependence. In other words, whether we observe the Ringelmann effect or not depends on the pattern of division of labor and its consequences—specialization and interdependence. Tobias Kretschmer and I showed these results formally in a model of incentive structure with division of labor (Kretschmer and Puranam, 2008).

Solutions to Agency and Cooperation Problems

There exists a large body of literature on incentives in the agency theory tradition that deal with both agency and cooperation problems (Prendergast, 1999; Gibbons, 2018). Formal models based on optimization by rational agents have also been formulated by students of organizations to understand the two key dimensions of optimal incentive structure (see Figure 4.1): *depth*—what fraction of an individual's pay depends on performance, and *breadth*—how many others contribute to the performance measure used to determine pay (e.g., Baker, 2002; Kretschmer and Puranam, 2008; Oxley and Pandher, 2015).

The depth dimension is expected to be conditioned by the agent's risk preferences, the extent of noise in the performance measure, and the agent's disutility from effort. Incentives must be deep enough to ensure the rewards exceed the costs. The empirical evidence on the role of risk-bearing in determining incentive depth is not supportive of this conjecture. However, the role of incentive depth in motivating costly efforts is less controversial (e.g., Prendergast, 1999, 2000). The evidence for the proposition that performance-related pay can cause agents to significantly increase their effort levels is strong. For instance, Lazear (2000) shows that the productivity of windshield installers in a large auto glass company increased 44 percent when the installers' pay scheme was changed from fixed wage to pay-for-performance, and Shearer (2004) shows similar increases in productivity through a randomized field experiment with Canadian tree-planters.

The breadth dimension depends on the synergy from collaboration between agents, and is optimally set to produce positive valence of interdependence between agents. For instance, both target rate incentives that only lead to rewards when a pre-defined performance target is met (Holmstrom, 1982; Petersen, 1992), or an expectation of an indefinite but large number of future interactions

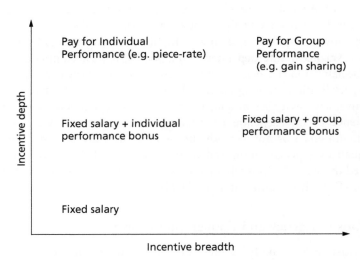

Figure 4.1 Two dimensions of incentives

("the shadow of the future") (Baker, Gibbons, and Murphy, 2002) effectively can make the valence of interdependence positive, motivating cooperation.

Solutions to agency and cooperation problems that do not rely on formal incentive design also exist. These include the creation of communication channels, which enable individuals to better understand the impact of their actions on individual and group outcomes through a process of discussion and learning (Dawes, 1980); social norms and peer monitoring that effectively change payoffs by encouraging cooperative behavior and sanction non-cooperative behavior (e.g., Ostrom, 1990); and the emergence of group identity, which modifies payoffs by inducing individuals to take the group interest into account when making their own decisions (Bouas and Komorita, 1996; Kollock, 1998). These are manifestations of framing and sorting (see Chapter 2).

A key fault-line between the agency theoretic and the social psychological views on incentive design lies in their distinctive views of the individual vs. social effects of incentives. By *individual effects*, I mean the ways in which incentives alter an individual A's compensation and therefore change A's behavior. By *social effects* of incentives, I mean the ways in which changing B's incentives may lead to a change in A's behavior or performance, even though A's compensation remains unchanged. Social effects assume the existence of other regarding preferences such as a sense of group identity and concerns with fairness (see Chapter 2), which agency theory rules out.

While this seems like a fairly clear and dramatic conceptual difference, individual and social effects can be easily confounded under conditions of team production with synergies (Shaw, Gupta, and Delery, 2002; Wageman and Baker, 1997). Teasing these apart empirically remains a challenge. Sunkee Lee and I (2017) attempted to tackle this using a natural experiment, in which an e-commerce company switched the incentives of employees from pay for performance to fixed pay, but in random (alphabetical) order. The staggered implementation gave us a randomized treatment and control group, and the change yielded competing predictions from the individual and social effects perspectives. We found strong evidence for the social effects of incentives, consistent with the idea that the switch may have shifted goal frames from gain to normative (see Chapter 2 on goal frames), resulting in greater cooperation within teams.

Our current state of knowledge certainly suggests that ignoring the social effects of incentives, such as concerns with fairness or the impact on group identity, can lead to bad design decisions. We may think of these social effects as constraints on the use of deep incentives that reward each agent for their own performance, but I believe this is rather narrow. An alternative is to think of these as mechanisms to increase the valence of interdependence by enhancing perceptions of fairness and group identity (Lee and Puranam, 2017).

An "integrated" approach to the integration of effort

It is well known that knowledge-related problems (skill and coordination) and motivation-related problems (agency and cooperation) are independently sufficient to create integration failures (Camerer and Knez, 1996, 1997; Heath and Staudenmayer, 2000; Foss, 2003).

For instance, consider a pure cooperation problem—the famous Prisoner's Dilemma. In a standard two-agent prisoner's dilemma, the valence of inter-dependence is negative. The rewards from acting cooperatively for either agent is never large enough relative to the rewards from defecting (see Table 4.3). However, there is no epistemic interdependence between them because each agent has a dominant strategy—their optimal actions do not depend on a prediction of the other agent's actions. The breakdown of integration here is purely due to motivational reasons.[7]

In contrast, in a pure coordination problem—such as matching (see Table 4.3)—the valence of interdependence encourages cooperation. Once the other player's actions are known, there is no reason for the focal player to withhold efforts to achieve an integrated outcome, but a lack of predictive knowledge may still deter its achievement. While both players prefer to take

Table 4.3 Some common two-player, two-choice game structures

Prisoner's Dilemma	
½, ½	0, 1
1, 0	¼, ¼
Stag Hunt	
1, 1	0, ½
½, 0	½, ½
Matching	
1, 1	0, 0
0, 0	1, 1
Battle of Sexes	
½, 1	0, 0
0, 0	1, ½

Note: The row player has two actions, Top and Bottom; the Column player has two actions, Left and Right. The four cells show the payoffs for combinations of actions (Top, Left), (Bottom, Right), etc. with the payoffs for Row player written first.

[7] If there were strong synergies from cooperating such that the temptation payoff should disappear, the game would cease to be a prisoner's dilemma (Camerer and Knez, 1996, 1997). The valence of interdependence would effectively become positive. Target rate incentive schemes, or the prospect of indefinitely repeated interactions can produce such an effect.

collaborative actions if they are sure of what the other is doing, they cannot be sure of this. The "battle of the sexes" is another instance where the valence of interdependence is positive (even though the players prefer different equilibria), but predictive knowledge is the constraint.

These game structures highlight the points that a) integration of effort can fail due to pure coordination or pure cooperation failures, and b) success at integration of effort requires both predictive knowledge and a positive valence of interdependence; neither alone is sufficient.[8]

These analytical distinctions notwithstanding, in the real world, problems of organization design do not come neatly and separately packaged into knowledge and motivation problems. Interdependence between agents may simultaneously have a valence that discourages the agents from investing effort towards integration, as well as make it necessary to predict other agent's actions to determine one's own. An exclusive focus on one or the other dimension is not only likely to lead to poor organization designs, but is also scientifically unjustified. Yet, selective focus on either motivation or knowledge problems in our theorizing about organizations and organization design is extremely common (Foss, 2003). As Dosi, Levinthal, and Marengo observed, tongue in cheek, alien social scientists visiting our planet might be stunned by the vastly different conceptualization of organizations that result from an exclusive focus on cooperation or coordination issues (2003). I believe there are two possible directions to explore further here.

INTERACTIONS BETWEEN KNOWLEDGE AND MOTIVATION-RELATED PROBLEMS (AND THEIR SOLUTIONS)

The first approach is to develop a deeper understanding of the interactions between knowledge and motivation problems. A natural partitioning of this space is into situations where the solutions to these problems are substitutes vs. complements. I give a thumbnail sketch below of the types of ideas in these categories that we may develop further.

It may sometimes be the case that organizational arrangements to improve coordination may lower the motivation to cooperate. Consider the problem of post-merger integration in technology acquisitions—the acquisitions of small entrepreneurial firms by larger firms for their technological capabilities (Puranam, Singh, and Zollo, 2006). In such acquisitions, unlike mega-mergers, there are no gains from eliminating redundancies and consolidating

---

[8] It is worth highlighting that with perfect predictive knowledge, it is still possible for the agents to arrive at a bad outcome from the perspective of integration of effort—as in the case of two employees who collude to shirk on the job, or two players of the Stag Hunt game (Table 4.3) who coordinate on the low equilibrium.

administrative overheads. Yet acquirers often structurally integrate such acquisitions—fold them into existing organizational units—despite the organizational disruptions and weakening of incentives this creates. Structural integration results in common procedures, common goals, and common authority between acquired and acquiring firms' technical employees, as they are located within common organizational units. This enhances predictive knowledge as all interacting parties adhere to the same procedures, are aware of a common goal, and are directed by the same source of authority. This strong "coordination effect," however, comes at the cost of disruption and de-motivation within the formerly autonomous acquired organization.

There is empirical evidence showing that following structural integration in technology acquisitions, the employees in the target organization may file fewer patents, though their work may be cited more often by the acquirer's employees (Puranam and Srikanth, 2007); initial products based on the target's technology may have lower hazards of being launched, but conditional on the first one being launched, future versions may appear more rapidly (Puranam et al., 2006). Tellingly, when acquirer and target have a significant pre-acquisition overlap in technical knowledge (a basis for predictive knowledge between them), then they are less likely to engage in structural integration in the first place (Puranam, Singh and Chaudhuri, 2009). These results support the existence of a tradeoff between coordination and motivation in post-merger integration. Another area in which a similar trade-off between coordination and motivation arises is in the problem of delegation within a managerial hierarchy, which I consider in Chapter 5.

One can also conceive of complementarities between solutions to coordination and cooperation problems. Consider a situation in which agents face a coordination problem (i.e. they face epistemic interdependence but lack predictive knowledge). Now, if the agents choose per expected utility, one can either enhance predictive knowledge (i.e. lower doubts about the other agent's actions) or increase the valence of interdependence (i.e. the gains from collaborating) to solve this problem. In fact, if the probability of an agent taking the action desired by the designer increases in its expected utility to the agent, then it is trivial to show that the designer's investments in increasing the agent's predictive knowledge or in increasing the valence of interdependence between them are complements in terms of improving the overall integration of effort.

In sum, it has been an analytical convenience to study mechanisms that produce integration of effort via knowledge and motivational channels separately. Given its aspirations to application, organization design as a field may be forced to pioneer the study of how these mechanisms act jointly and interact as complements and/or substitutes. We have barely scratched the surface of this topic, and I believe the opportunities to study "crossover" effects—when mechanisms for changing motivation impact coordination and vice versa—is a fruitful area for further research.

Another approach is to bundle knowledge and motivation-related problems into the construct of integration, and focus on that for the purposes of organization design. Put simply, "interdependence between agents must be matched by integrative influence"—if agents in an organization are inter-dependent, there must be mechanisms in place to help integrate their efforts by ensuring predictive knowledge and positive valence. This formulation has the status of a "folk theorem" in the field of organization design—it is very widely accepted, but there are no obvious claimants to being the first to articulate it, despite it being present in implicit form in many classics (March and Simon, 1958; Thompson, 1967; Laurence and Lorsch, 1967; Tushman and Nadler, 1976; Galbraith, 1973).

One obvious advantage to treating integration at the dyadic level in this somewhat coarse manner (i.e. without further distinction between knowledge and motivation-related challenges to integration) is that it allows for easier analysis of macro-structures. The Technical Appendix to this chapter shows how the folk theorem can be expressed for the m-agent case using matrix algebra. In essence, we represent interdependence and integrative influence between agents as two different networks on the same set of agents, and look for isomorphism between the two.

A second advantage is that this formulation is framed in terms of a match between interdependence between agents and the integrative influences linking them—leaving open a very important role for organization design in terms of shaping both the former and the latter. Variations in the ability to adjust interdependence between agents through changes to task allocation, scheduling, and measurement reflect differences in architectural knowledge—or knowledge of the underlying task structure—across organ-ization designers (Baldwin and Clark, 2000; Henderson and Clark, 1990; von Hippel, 1990).

ARCHITECTURAL KNOWLEDGE AND INTEGRATION OF EFFORTS

There are several important implications of the proposition that interdepend-ence between agents can be modified based on architectural knowledge, even if task interdependence remains unchanged.

First, consider the phenomenon of *equifinality* in organizational designs (Gresov and Drazin, 1997). Organization design can be seen as the interplay between the existence of designer's knowledge of how to divide and allocate tasks (architectural knowledge) and the existence of mechanisms for integrat-ing the efforts of interdependent agents (i.e. to create predictive knowledge and generate positive valence). A functional equivalence in terms of integration of various combinations of architectural knowledge and mechanisms for integra-tion thus naturally arises as shown in Figure 4.2. There are many different combinations of architectural knowledge and integrative mechanisms that can

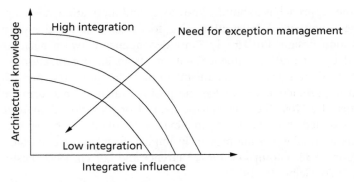

Figure 4.2 Equifinality in organization design

produce the same level of integration. For a given division of labor, this functional equivalence also translates into equifinal performance outcomes—organizations designed on the basis of superior architectural knowledge and those that contain agents with effective integrative influences may function equally well. Highly decoupled and highly interactive groups of individuals may do equally well on an interdependent set of tasks.

Second, we can explain why *mirroring* between the structure of task clusters and organizational structures may therefore occur only under some conditions, rather than what we would expect by default (Colfer and Baldwin, 2010). A key hypothesis in the literature on modularity has been that of correspondence between the structure of tasks (i.e. the pattern of interdependencies within and between task clusters) and the structure of organization (i.e. in the pattern of interactions between individuals working on tasks). This conjecture has been known as the "mirroring hypothesis" in the literature on organizations, and as Conway's Law in computer science. Note that this is almost but not quite the same as our folk theorem about interdependence needing integrative influence, which states that the mirroring is between agent (not task) interdependence and integrative influence (of which formal structures are only a subset).

Colfer and Baldwin (2010) reviewed 102 studies from both within and between firm contexts and found that over two-thirds of the studies they analyzed found some support for the mirroring hypothesis. Two key classes of exceptions were also found: situations in which integrated organizations produced modular technologies, and in which distributed non-integrated organizations worked on highly integrated products.

They suggested that the first category of exceptions represented the process of coming up with modular designs. Uncovering a good modular partitioning of tasks is neither easy nor unique, and may paradoxically require an integrated, non-modular organization (also see Cabigiosu and Camuffo, 2012). Put differently, to form architectural knowledge may require deep exposure to the interdependencies in the task structure. The second category of exceptions showed that there were alternatives to traditional formal organizational structures to accomplish integration (including the visibility of actions and alignment of goals—as in open source software development communities). With high levels of pre-existing predictive knowledge and positive valence of interdependence, the formal organizational structure need not mirror the task structure. Thus, either the need to form architectural knowledge, or the pre-existence of predictive knowledge may "break the mirror."

Third, a novel explanation is possible for the frequently observed relationship between organizational size and the bureaucratization of work (e.g. Mintzberg, 1979). Interdependence minimizing strategies (i.e. using architectural knowledge to reduce interdependence by improving measurement, buffering and allocating clusters of tasks) will increasingly dominate "integrative influence raising" strategies such as communication, incentives and mutual observation as organizational size increases (see Figure 4.3). This dominance of top-down design that atomizes and standardizes work, over active lateral collaboration with increasing scale is a straightforward consequence of the multiplication of probabilities that arises in the measure of integration.

Finally, there are some implications for the conditions under which authority and slack are useful in organizations. One manifestation of authority is in the design choices around division of labor (task division and allocation) and integrative influences (e.g. incentives, communication channels). But with imperfect integration (i.e., the joint probability that the agents will achieve the required degree of integration is less than 1), exceptions and errors will arise. Therefore, additional provision to manage the exceptions that inevitably occur must be made separately.

A common solution is to add a third agent, C, with authority to resolve disputes between A and B. Investing an agent with the authority to monitor and reward, or sanction other agents who shirk or free-ride may mitigate

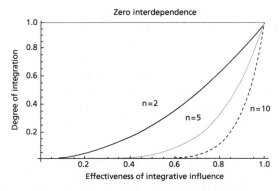

Figure 4.3 The advantages of architectural knowledge with scale (n = number of agents)

agency and cooperation problems (Alchian and Demsetz, 1972), as well as coordination failures between agents.[9] The next chapter (5) on Authority develops the idea that the dispute and exception resolution function of authority may be one of its most important roles in organizations, and one that may continue to be relevant even in an egalitarian ethos.

A second approach to managing exceptions is the provision of slack (Galbraith, 1977; Tushman and Nadler, 1976; Lecuona and Reitzig, 2013). Slack or increased fault tolerance is a means by which organizations may be able to cope with low levels of integration arising from skill or coordination problems. Thus, as shown in Figure 4.2, the need for exception management (in the form of authoritative dispute resolution or slack) should decrease as either architectural or predictive knowledge increases.

Integration of effort: execution vs. search problems

Having argued for the need to think in an integrated fashion about the challenges to integration of effort from motivation and knowledge-related factors, let me now argue for thinking in a more differentiated manner along a different dimension: search vs. execution.

Generating integration of effort when the designer or the agents know what the agents ought to do, may be seen as an *execution* problem. The basic agency theoretic model is a good illustration: the designer knows the technology of production and the problem is one of motivating the agent to take the appropriate action. The literature on mechanism design takes the opposite perspective: the agents know things about themselves the designer needs to find out, and incentive contracts can be designed such that agents are forced to reveal this information through self-selection.

A more complicated situation arises when neither the designer nor the agents know what the ideal actions for the agents are, so that we confront a *search* problem. Since bounded rationality is a property of human agents, there is no obvious reason why the designers of human organizations should be any more exempt from this property than its constituting agents. A profoundly interesting question, for me at least, has been why organization design can still be useful even if the designer has no particular insight into what the agents ideally should do to meet organizational goals. The development of organizational (i.e. multi-agent) search models has been one of the vibrant areas of

[9] Relatedly, Demsetz (1988) offered an interesting argument about how investing a single skilled agent with authority could economize on the need to train the unskilled—the more skilled agent would simply order the less skilled agent to act based on their instructions without the need for costly communication and knowledge transfer, thus solving skill-related integration problems.

development in organization science in the recent past, with models outlining the roles that organizational structure—even if designed by a bounded rational agent—can play in integrating effort in search situations (e.g. Rivkin and Siggelkow, 2003; 2005; Ethiraj and Levinthal, 2004; Lee and Puranam, 2015; Knudsen and Srikanth, 2014). These models help to explain how organizational adaptation can be a marvel without being a miracle.

To explain the intuition behind such models, let's take a canonical instance of an organizational search problem—one in which specialists from different domains search for optimal interdependent actions. For instance, managers within a multi-business company, despite incentives to pursue synergies, may have limited knowledge of the complementarities in production or the cross-elasticities of demand across divisions. Teams of engineers developing sub-systems may know that certain design choices in each sub-system could lead to dramatically enhanced performance of the system as a whole, but do not know which ones. Because the boundaries of specialization often constitute barriers to interpretation, these joint search problems are characterized by communication constraints arising from differences in perspectives, jargon, languages and technical backgrounds in addition to ignorance about how the key actors are interdependent (Lawrence and Lorsch, 1967; Dougherty, 1992; Heath and Staudenmayer, 2000).

The challenges to effective organizational search in situations of interdependence and communication constraints are so widespread (e.g., Alexander, 1964; Eppinger, 2001; Thomke, 1997; Thompson, 1967) that they have now acquired their own name—*coupled learning* (Puranam and Swamy, 2016; Knudsen and Srikanth, 2014). Effective learning requires being able to form valid connections between one's actions and observed outcomes. Interdependence obscures the links between individual actions and outcomes, because the observed outcomes may be the result of the actions of many interdependent actors (Levinthal and March, 1993; March and Simon, 1958). When the nature of these interdependencies is well understood, then it is possible to account for the impacts of other's actions on the observed outcome; but when it is not, a serious challenge to organizational learning is posed. The dangers of learning superstitiously—of drawing misleading conclusions from performance feedback—are high in such situations because the feedback contains information not only on the value of one's own actions, but also the unobserved actions taken by others (Levinthal and March, 1993).

A toy example may help to see more transparently the core issues that make coupled learning such a challenge. Let's say that our hard-working students Ann and Bob now participate as a team in a joint code-breaking game. Each has at hand a set of three colored flags each—red, blue and green. In each round of the game, Ann and Bob each choose independently one of their flags to hold up. They each stand on either side of a screen and can't see each other or the flags they are holding up (i.e. communication is constrained), but the judge of the game can see both their flags. There is a combination of colors—say Ann holding up red and Bob holding up green, that is the winning answer, and the judge will announce a win (i.e. interdependence). For all other combinations of colors held up by the two, the judge tells them they don't have the right combination yet.

Now the chances of Ann and Bob getting the combination right the first time are slim indeed ($1/3*1/3 = 1/9$). Suppose, as is more likely, they fail to get it right the first time, and the judge declares they don't have the right combination (yet). Both will learn from this feedback and will adjust their actions, by trying other colors. Herein lies the problem: there is a $2*(1/3*2/3) = 4/9$ chance of a "false negative," where either Ann or Bob picked the right color, but the disappointing outcome led them to discard their choice. In fact, the chance of this happening is as large as that of a "true negative" in this case ($2/3*2/3 = 4/9$). Worse, the more responsive that Ann and Bob are to feedback—the more likely they are to adjust their choices to feedback—the worse the impact of the false negative is likely to be on them. "Good" individual learners may nonetheless lead to poor organizational learning!

UNINTELLIGENT DESIGN AND SECOND-ORDER COORDINATION PROBLEMS

Coupled learning problems are not like typical coordination problems in Table 4.3, in which there are multiple equilibria in a game, and the challenge for interacting individuals is to jointly select the same equilibrium under communication constraints (e.g. matching, stag-hunt or battle of sexes). However, we can think of coupled learning as a second-order coordination problem—a kind of higher-order matching game—in which one agent must stay still and the other must search. Either allocation of roles is an equilibrium and acceptable to the agents but difficult to coordinate on (Puranam and Swamy, 2016).

A boundedly rational designer may still be able to enable integration of effort in at least three ways in such second-order coordination situations. First, some structural solutions may facilitate communication between specialists, thus improving more effective joint search (see also Foss, 2007 for a review of the knowledge governance perspective on such mechanisms); for instance, the creation of task forces or overlapping production and development teams or formal integrator roles function in this way (Clark and Fujimoto, 1991).

Second, merely sensitizing the agents to the fact of their interdependence (without being able to tell them how to act) may still be a major contribution that an organization designer can make towards the integration of effort. Heath and Staudenmayer (2000) present a fascinating series of examples of "partition focus"—a tendency by individuals to place more emphasis on the task division process and less on the process of achieving the integration of efforts, as well as "component focus"—a tendency to focus exclusively on the component tasks so created. This is equivalent to Ann and Bob not even being aware that they are playing a game in which the right answer is a combination of colors they hold up, not a single color. It seems reasonable to assume that the existence of interdependence can only be discovered as the agents perform their individual actions and an exogenously generated change in the value of their action is noticed. Thus, one way in which a designer may be useful is to help highlight such surprises for the agents, and rule out incorrect alternative explanations (such as bad luck) and improve the cross-visibility of the actions of one set of agents to another (Srikanth and Puranam, 2011, 2014).

Third, even if the designer cannot improve communication or cross-visibility of actions, the designer can provide a common (possibly faulty) prior to the agents rather than let the agents work with a mix of good and bad priors—and this can be advantageous when the agents adapt rapidly to feedback. Murali Swamy and I (Puranam and Swamy, 2016) developed a formal model to illustrate this "common prior" advantage.

In the model, agents engage in coupled learning through a trial and error (reinforcement learning) process in a set up much like the joint code-breaking game, in which specialists from different domains learn how to make interdependent choices. We showed that when learning is rapid but communication is restricted, faulty initial mental representations held by all agents can suppress superstitious learning and promote valid learning, relative to situations where no agent has a representation, or a mix of correct and incorrect representations exists among the agents.

The intuition for the "common prior advantage" can be expressed as follows in the context of the joint code breaking game: if both Ann and Bob are led to believe (erroneously) that the right code is (blue, red), then while their probability of getting it right is now smaller (= 0 vs. 1/9), the probability of a true negative is now much higher (= 1 vs. 4/9) and a false negative is smaller (= 0 vs. 4/9). This improves the chances of their being able to learn the right choices eventually. Thus, while maintaining the assumption that the designer faces the same ignorance about the nature of interdependence as the agents, our results suggest that a designer who can influence initial representations of the agents (even if only to coordinate their state of error, rather than allow differential knowledge), can be valuable.

Even if a designer does not know what actions are optimal for interdependent agents, knowing they are interdependent and designing opportunities for interaction and the build-up of predictive knowledge, or ensuring common (even if inaccurate) initial beliefs may be useful in the process of achieving integration of efforts through search. Organization design, as this example shows, need not be particularly intelligent design to be useful. We are not forced to choose between assuming the Olympian rationality of an omniscient designer, or the relegation of design to a completely ritualistic endeavor (Meyer and Rowan, 1978). We will return to the theme of the surprising effectiveness of un-intelligent design in subsequent chapters.

Conclusion

This chapter has outlined three major sets of ideas. First, the arguments in this chapter emphasize that for a given division of labor, (potential) breakdowns of integration can be traced to either motivational or knowledge-related sources (or both). The consequences of integration failure are difficult to localize unless both agents and the tasks they perform are independent of each other. Integration failures arising from coordination problems require managing the need for and/or the extent of predictive knowledge; those arising from cooperation problems require managing the valence of interdependence.

Second, I have argued that a holistic approach to studying integration breakdowns arising from knowledge and motivation is yet to be developed in any great depth. A fruitful area for further enquiry awaits the student of organization design at the intersection of these sources of integration failure. I outlined two possible approaches: a closer look at the interactions between knowledge and motivation-related issues, or a coarser bundling of both into the construct of integration.

Third, given the behavioral assumptions of adaptive rationality (Chapter 2), thinking of integration of effort as a search problem may be an area of high research potential. While we are accumulating models in this domain, the empirical evidence base has yet to be built up, and the theorizing has still to grapple with the existence of more complex and changing goals. The agenda for research into effective organizational adaptation using the concepts we have been discussing seems promising.

■ APPENDIX TO CHAPTER 4: THE FOLK THEOREM IN MATRIX NOTATION

To generalize the idea that "interdependence between agents requires integrative influence" for the m-agent case, we can use the matrix notation developed in Chapter 3 (see Puranam, Raveendran, and Knudsen, 2012 for more details). We require two binary matrices as below.

1. Let the pattern of interdependence between agents—the *interdependence structure*—be represented by an $m \times m$ binary matrix E, the elements of which are denoted by e_{ij}. Here $e_{ij} = 1$ if agent j is interdependent with agent i, or else $e_{ij} = 0$, and $e_{ii} = 1$ (each agent is interdependent with himself).

2. Define the ***integration influence structure*** I_t at time t as an $m \times m$ matrix, the elements of which $p_{i,j,t}$ represent the probability that agent j has predictive knowledge and positive valence of interdependence w.r.t agent i at time t. When $p_{i,j,t} = 1$ for the corresponding nonzero elements in E (i.e. if $p_{i,j,t} = 1$ for $e_{i,j} = 1$), we can say with certainty that the efforts of agents j and i are integrated.

How effective an organization design has been at enabling the integration of efforts can be gauged through its degree of integration (ρ_t), defined as the product of the $L_t \leq m^2$ elements from I_t for which the corresponding elements in E ($e_{i,j}$) = 1. The degree of integration of the organization at time t can thus be written as:

$$\rho_t = \prod_{i=1}^{m} \prod_{j=1}^{m} \delta p_{i,j,t}$$

where $\delta = 1$ if $e_{i,j} = 1$ (there will be L_t such terms in E).

The goal of organization design can be restated as enhancing ρ_t as efficiently as possible. There are two paths towards this goal. The fist involves avoiding both omission errors ($p_{i,j,t} < 1$ for $e_{i,j} = 1$) as well as commission errors ($p_{i,j,t} > 0$ for $e_{i,j} = 0$) in terms of integrative influence. One can construct objective functions for design that penalize these errors according to different weights (see Clement and Puranam, 2017). The second is to reduce the number of cases in E where $\delta = 1$ (i.e. to reduce interdependence between agents). The first approach involves enhancing integrative influence where necessary, the second relies on architectural knowledge. They can produce equifinal outcomes (see Figure 4.2).

5   The exercise of authority

Authority is a prominent feature in human organizations. It might be embedded within the framework of a formal employment contract, legitimized by tradition, or may depend purely on the personal attributes of the individual who wields it (such as charisma, prestige, or dominance). Authority is exalted for its role in an organization's functioning, but also reviled for its conflict with the individual's need for autonomy (not to mention the sycophantic responses it too often seems to elicit).

Ronald Coase set up authority in contrast to the price mechanism, when he famously noted that "If a workman moves from department Y to department X, he does not go because of a change in relative prices, but because he is ordered to do so" (Coase, 1937). This contrast has since dominated economic thinking about organizations. An extensive literature has also developed around the construct of authority in the study of organizations and related disciplines. The aim of this chapter is to provide a conceptualization of authority and a framework to think about how it is exercised, which is specifically useful to study organization design.

Authority refers to the legitimate ability of A to demand obedient behavior from B within a specified realm of actions. Thus, authority exists if B accepts the decisions of A in a domain, without independently examining the merits of that decision (Weber, 1922; Barnard, 1938; Simon, 1947). Four features of authority are implicit in this definition. First, it is a form of asymmetric influence.[1] Second, it is a legitimate form of influence. The legitimacy of authority could arise from considerations of moral appropriateness and legality, but also from the belief that others subject to authority besides oneself are also likely to accept it. Third, it is domain-specific: A may have authority over B in a particular decision domain, but not in another (Simon, 1951). Fourth, it is a relational construct between agents: one agent has authority over another.

From an organization design perspective, authority has three very specific roles. First, authority can be the basis on which solutions to any of the universal problems of organizing are selected and enforced (even if these solutions themselves do not involve authority at all). For instance, an authoritative superior may decide whether subordinates should be compensated in cash, task autonomy, or opportunities for career progression, or how tasks should be

---

[1] To be precise, it is anti-symmetric, because authority can be interpreted as reflexive (I have authority over myself). Asymmetry requires both anti-symmetry and irreflexivity.

divided up among which employees. This is the authority to *design*. Second, authority can be a solution to one or more of the fundamental problems underlying the integration of effort. An authority figure may monitor, hold accountable, sanction, and instruct employees to ensure their efforts are integrated. This is the authority to *direct* subordinates. Third, authority is used to resolve exceptions arising from imperfections in the solutions to the fundamental problems of organizing. They may arise from challenges to cooperation, coordination, or the individual competence of the agents (Chapter 4). For instance, when colleagues disagree on their roles and responsibilities (a sign of possible imperfections in task division and task allocation), the disputes may be referred to an authoritative superior. This is authority as *dispute resolution*. These three facets of authority are often bundled together in organizations, though it is not obvious if this must universally be so.

Understanding how authority is exercised within organizations is in part challenging because of the profusion of terminology that has crept up around the topic, independent of the fact that authority is itself manifested in the three main ways noted above. To minimize confusion, I consciously eschew the use of authority in the sense of pure expertise (e.g. "she is an authority on how social media work"). We often accept, without verification, the opinions of experts, but we could in theory overturn or reject their recommendation. Further, since I adopt a definition of authority as a relational construct between individuals, I will refrain from using it to describe the distribution of tasks (e.g. "he has authority over these decisions or tasks").

To discuss the multiple aspects of authority as well as several related constructs in a reasonably simple manner, I use the triadic microstructure shown in Figure 5.1. This is a small multiplex network, in which the solid lines indicate authority and communication relationships, whereas the dashed lines indicate communication alone. In this microstructure, S has authority over s_1 and s_2 within a particular decision domain, D_i.

Figure 5.1 A triadic microstructure

The delegation of authority

Authority is often, either by intention or despite it, delegated. Two apparently similar reporting structures where a superior has authority over subordinates, may nonetheless translate into very distinct experiences for the superiors and subordinates, depending on how and to what extent the superior's authority is delegated. To understand exactly what this means, and the different ways this can happen, I find it helpful to think of *ex ante* (before implementation) vs. *ex post* (after implementation) intervention probabilities (see Figure 5.2).

These are:

- the probability, p^a that S will exercise her right to overturn the decisions of s_1 and s_2 ex ante (before these decisions are implemented). A high value amounts to S effectively ordering the subordinates to take certain actions.
- the probability, p^p that S will hold the subordinates accountable for decisions ex post (after their decisions have been implemented). A high value indicates that the subordinates must make their decisions knowing they will be asked to account for them later (possibly with reference to obtained outcomes, or even simply on whether a particular action was taken).

Delegation of authority by S to the subordinates s_1 and s_2 can be thought of as a reduction in the probabilities p^a, p^p such that they are less than 1. Figure 5.3 shows the space of possibilities in terms of these two probabilities. When both probabilities are equal to one, we are in a regime that has *centralization* of authority. S will direct the subordinates s_1 and s_2 ex ante as well as evaluate ex post. It may seem odd that the superior both approves the subordinate's actions as well as evaluates the subordinate afterwards, but note that the evaluation need not be on the performance consequences; it may be a verification that the subordinate indeed acted as ordered, because this is not apparent until the action has been taken.

In contrast, when both intervention probabilities are zero, the subordinate's decisions are neither subject to reversal by S, nor are they accountable for them. I will refer to this as a case of *decentralization* of authority—where the relevant decision rights in this domain have effectively been transferred from S to the subordinates. For instance, in the public administration literature,

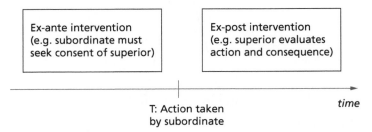

Figure 5.2 Authority as the right to intervene

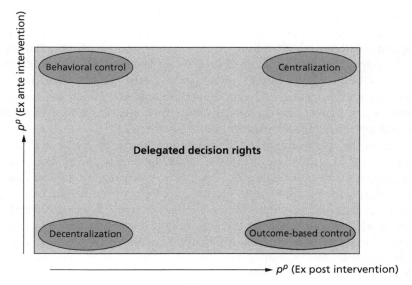

Figure 5.3 The space of delegation possibilities

decentralization refers to "any act in which a central government formally cedes powers to actors and institutions at lower levels in a political-administrative and territorial hierarchy" (Ribot, 2001: citing Mawhood, 1983).

If only ex-ante intervention is certain ($p^a = 1$, $p^p = 0$), then the superior is effectively controlling the subordinate by ordering particular actions. If only ex-post intervention is certain ($p^a = 0$, $p^p = 1$), the superior is controlling the subordinate purely through evaluation of actions and/or outcomes.[2] All other intermediate cases where $0 < (p^a, p^p) < 1$ fall broadly under the rubric of "delegated authority." It seems natural to me to think of delegation as including not only the cases where I let my subordinate choose actions, but also the cases where I fully specify what my subordinates should do, but then do not check to see if they have done it or hold them accountable for performance.

In most legal regimes, decision rights within a firm may not be transferred internally via contract, so that the chief executive officer is always legally responsible. Authority in a corporate hierarchy is therefore delegated everywhere except at the very apex, and true decentralization is impossible. Further, delegation is not restricted to firms; whenever ultimate accountability lies at the top of an authority hierarchy, delegation must be present beneath.

---

[2] Interestingly, ex-post intervention policies can produce emergent strategies. When a subordinate expects with high probability to be evaluated ex post on the decisions taken, it is not surprising that they decide in a way that they believe will meet the approval of the superior. Of course, they may not be able to guess this correctly; there can be a failure of coordination of expectations. Therefore, if the intervention by the superior only occurs ex post, the organization may make decisions that are not consistent with the preferences of either the superior or the subordinate.

Note that Figure 5.1 features authority in a traditional "top down" manner—implying that authority flows down from above in the form of a sequential filtering of decision rights. However, it is possible for the flow to be in the opposite direction. In democracies, for instance, delegation is "from below" with the voters (who have ultimate authority) jointly delegating it to their elected representatives, who are accountable ex post. In self-managed teams, team leaders may be elected who are subject both to ex-ante and ex-post authority of their teammates (see Chapter 8).

Within the space of Figure 5.2, the region where p^a is high but p^p is low corresponds to a situation of *ex-ante control* by S of s_1 and s_2. Conversely, the region where p^p is high but p^a is low is a situation of *ex-post control* by S of s_1 and s_2. Control via evaluation of performance outcomes can impose greater risk on subordinates, whereas control via ex-ante specification of actions can diminish the subordinate's sense of autonomy. This distinction corresponds to the difference between incentives that reward appropriate actions vs. appropriate outcomes (where outcome could be the observability of the subordinate's action and/or its performance consequences). In the literature on corporate strategy, for instance, these are well-known as two distinct models of headquarters influence on subsidiaries/divisions within a multi-business organization (e.g. see Puranam and Vanneste, 2016: chapter 11).

One may also have rules for switching regimes (i.e. moving within the space of delegation possibilities) based on some conditions, rather than fixed intervention probabilities. For instance, S may impose a veto only if s_1 and s_2 propose actions that S disagrees with. This is equivalent to a conditional switch between centralization and decentralization regimes. To see this, assume that the expected number of times that a superior can veto the subordinate's decision is "k," and that the cost to the subordinates of being vetoed each time is "c." Then if the gains from selecting their preferred actions are greater for the subordinates than the expected cost of being vetoed (i.e. E[kc]), this is equivalent to a case of decentralization, else it is equivalent to a case of centralization. Clearly, if k goes to infinity, then this is the same as centralization (and will be seen through as such by all but the most naïve subordinates). But at lower values of k, c can determine the regime.

Another possibility is conditional decentralization, a form of "authority by exception," which is pertinent when the actions of s_1 and s_2 are interdependent. This describes a situation in which the supervisor has delegated decision-making to the subordinates, and subordinates are tasked with finding an agreement on their own, but failing to do so results in the supervisor taking the final decision. In this juxtaposition of the decentralized and centralized scenarios, supervisors effectively act as they would in the centralized regime if subordinates do not agree; otherwise, their behavior is the same as in the decentralization regime.

Yet another form of conditional decentralization is that the superior only intervenes when the subordinate's decisions are of a particular type (e.g. second-guess all proposals the subordinate accepts, but do nothing about those they reject, as in a sequential screening process, e.g. Sah and Stiglitz, 1986).

A key property of the large space of possibilities bounded by the corners in Figure 5.2 is that the intervention probabilities (p^a, p^p) cannot be contracted upon.[3] Decision rights under delegation are "loaned, not owned" (Baker, Gibbons, and Murphy, 1999); delegation is typically contingent, as in principle, S could with some probability overturn the decisions of subordinates even after delegating these decisions to them (possibly at some cost to herself—see Aghion and Tirole, 1997). In such instances, it makes sense to say that S is the "formal" authority holder, while the subordinates are the "real" holders of authority (Aghion and Tirole, 1997) (though as students often point out, exactly the opposite nomenclature also seems plausible).

This difficulty of contracting on delegation raises a question of the conditions under which delegation is *credible*—i.e. the conditions under which s_1 and s_2 perceive the intervention probabilities to be low. Baker et al. (1999) provide a model in which under some conditions it is a dominant strategy for S to abstain from overruling the subordinates' decisions even if the choices of the subordinates appear poor. With common knowledge of these conditions across superior and subordinates, delegation becomes highly credible. Stea, Foss, and Foss (2015) generalize the argument to say that organization design features that make intervention by the superior more expensive to the superior (such as division of responsibilities, public commitments, organizational culture), or less necessary in the first place, can serve to enhance credible delegation.

But moving past the question of how to delegate (credibly), the more fundamental question is—why delegate at all? To answer this, we must look closer at why authority is useful in the first place: then, why sometimes sharing it with subordinates can be useful will become obvious.

What authority does: direction, dispute resolution and design

THE AUTHORITY TO DIRECT

As we noted in Chapter 4, agency and cooperation problems impede integration of effort because of insufficient motivation for agents. Giving one agent the

---

[3] In typical principal–agent models (e.g. Holmstrom, 1979; Holmstrom and Milgrom, 1991), the partition of decision rights is contractible, with ex-post performance based control being the typical response to not being able to observe efforts; then the probability of ex-ante intervention is contractually stipulated to be zero.

authority to monitor and reward (or sanction) other agents who may be tempted to shirk or free-ride can mitigate agency and cooperation problems (Alchian and Demsetz 1972; Williamson, 1975). In Figure 5.1, S monitors the efforts and actions of s_1 and s_2, holds them accountable for these, and allocates rewards or punishments as appropriate if any deviations from the integrative actions are observed. Consequently, the subordinates' actions are effectively integrated. This, in a nutshell, is how vertical integration and the bringing together of interdependent value chain segments under a common authority framework is supposed to work in transaction cost economics (Williamson, 1975, 1985).

As we know, integration of effort is also impeded by skill and coordination problems. In this case, authority can be used to exploit differences in knowledge while economizing on the costs of transferring this knowledge. By making the knowledgeable individual in a domain the decision-maker for that domain (Demsetz, 1988), and letting this individual direct the actions of others, the agent's efforts will be effectively integrated. For instance, as s_1 and s_2 follow the orders of the knowledgeable S, their actions can be expected to aggregate usefully, as well as draw on the superior skill of S. A subtle variant of this is an idea that is canonical in the Carnegie school: authority allows control of decision premises (Simon, 1947; March and Simon, 1958). By imposing the same decision premises or assumptions on multiple agents, their actions can effectively be coordinated without the need for them to communicate directly with each other. Simon (1981) elaborated on this idea to note that the centralization of beliefs (rather than actions) may be the distinguishing and useful feature of administrative hierarchies. When uncertainty is likely to affect many parts of an organization in the same way, he noted, "it may be advantageous to centralize the making of assumptions about the future and to require the decentralized units to use these assumptions in their decisions" (1981: 43).

The authority to direct, whether in the form of policing to deal with motivation related impediments to the integration of effort, or in the form of wise leadership, to deal with knowledge-related obstacles, is thus a fundamental way in which authority is exercised in organizations. Authority as direction can therefore be seen as an alternative to either a) skilled, motivated action by autonomous individuals, or b) peer-to-peer cooperation and coordination (see Table 4.1 in Chapter 4).

THE AUTHORITY TO RESOLVE DISPUTES

Authority also manifests itself as the right to resolve exceptions arising from imperfect solutions to the fundamental problems of organizing—task divisions, task allocation, reward and information provision (see Chapter 1). The solutions that designers come up with are imperfect, as they are the products of limitedly rational problem solving. For an organization to continue to exist, it is therefore useful to have in place some mechanism for resolving these problems on an ongoing basis as exceptions arise.

Dispute resolution based on authority is an important instance of such a mechanism (Galbraith, 1977; Tushman and Nadler, 1978). In this case, authority acts as a "stopping rule" that ensures a resolution (and possibly a speedy one) to a failure of integration arising either from motivation or knowledge-related impediments. The resolution may occur through an evaluation of the relative merits of the espoused positions of the subordinates, or through a clarification/ interpretation of the design decisions regarding division of labor and integration of effort (e.g. "this falls within the task allocation of subordinate A, who therefore prevails over B").

Another way to see this is to think of the counterfactual: how would peers resolve disagreements? As the number of interacting peers, n, increases, the number of dyadic interactions, and therefore the number of dyadic interactions that lead to disputes which cannot be resolved bilaterally, increases as a quadratic function $n.(n-1)/2$. Disputes that cannot be resolved bilaterally may yet be resolved through peer pressure. One can imagine the primary disputants recruiting others to their respective causes, and the one who can build the significantly larger sub-group of supporters prevails. However, the same size-conflict quadratic relationship should also make it harder to build a large conflict free sub-group of supporters. This *"quadratic explosion"* effectively means that as n increases, the possibility of dispute resolution through peer-to-peer interactions in general declines. It may then be useful to authorize an individual to decide on behalf of the group. This role of authority as "referee" is an alternative to peer-to-peer consensus among agents to resolve disputes when they arise.

THE AUTHORITY TO DESIGN

Even when authority plays no direct role in solving the fundamental problems of organizing, it may nevertheless be critical in selecting from among a multiplicity of possible solutions, and enforcing the solution. This is true for both division of labor and integration of effort. For instance, of the many possible ways to conduct task division and task allocation, one must eventually be selected and adopted (Raveendran, Puranam, and Warglien, 2015). Of the many possible ways to reward agents (including primarily through intrinsic motivation), or coordinate them (including through lateral communication), some must be chosen. Once chosen, the solution may be self-enforcing (i.e. it is an equilibrium from which agents see no reasons deviate), or may require active enforcement by an authoritative individual, capable of issuing sanctions against non-conformers. By investing particular agents with the authority to make and enforce these decisions, the resulting solutions will be stable and speedily determined.

The authority to design is a relatively understudied phenomenon, relative to the authority to direct or resolve disputes. It also appears less likely to be delegated than other forms of authority; the overall design of a complex organization is typically determined near the apex, even though the authority to direct or resolve disputes between subordinates may often be delegated to the lowest layers of the administrative hierarchy. At most, some decisions on task allocation (e.g. staffing) may be delegated, but it is rare to see managers who are lower in a hierarchy enjoying the freedom to design their organizations. However, that this is the typical pattern should not lull us into the confidence that it is the only possible one. A careful investigation into the costs and benefits of delegating design rights remains on the agenda for future research in organization design.

Why delegate?

If authority can be useful in all these ways, why (and when) should it be delegated rather than kept centralized? Indeed, the benefits of authority appear immediately as the opportunity costs of delegation—poorer integration of effort and interminable conflicts between s_1 and s_2 (Galbraith, 1977; Tushman and Nadler, 1978; see also Jensen and Meckling, 1992 on the loss of control of S).

There are three well-known benefits to delegation. First, delegation can allow decision-making to reside closer to the locus of knowledge (Lawrence and Lorsch, 1967; Galbraith, 1974), economizing on the costs of information transfer (Aghion and Tirole, 1997). If authority is delegated to s_1 and s_2 they can act immediately on available information, rather than incur the time and cost of moving the information to S. Relatedly, if s_1 and s_2 are just better at making certain decisions than S, then it is sensible to delegate more decisions to subordinates (i.e. a vertical division of labor). Dobrajska, Billinger, and Karim (2015) conduct a detailed examination of delegation patterns within organizations by examining responsibility charts, which specify which agents are responsible for vs. execute tasks. They find evidence strongly consistent with the idea that delegation of tasks by an agent responsible for them is more likely when the agent is overloaded or lacks specialist expertise in the relevant tasks. Further, tasks that require coordination across agents are less likely to be delegated to multiple subordinates.

Second, delegation is a "quick-fix" to the problem of an S who is overloaded because of a large span of control (i.e. too many subordinates to supervise effectively). A better approach may be to re-evaluate the span of control. Of course, a large span may also be a subtly designed source of pressure on S to delegate.

Third, delegation has motivational consequences. It empowers those who receive enhanced authority, but also impoverishes those who give it away. Fehr, Herz, and Wilkening (2013) show experimental evidence for systematic under-delegation within a framework in which it is easy to specify the optimal level of delegation, because the power to make decisions appears to be prized for its own sake. Those with the strongest tendencies towards loss aversion delegate the least, showing that they treat power as they would any other resource subject to an endowment effect. On the other hand, delegation has positive motivational effects on subordinates (Ryan and Deci, 2000). The perception of discretion and autonomy of choice is a source of motivation in itself, and organization designs may differ in the extent to which they produce this effect (Stea, Foss and Foss, 2015). Thus, if authority is valued for its own sake, moving it even partially towards the subordinates (i.e. delegation) may improve their motivation, ideally resulting in productivity gains that S can capture in excess of the pain of giving up authority.[4]

Authority beyond the firm

In the business organization we call a firm, authority plays a very prominent role in solving each of the four universal problems of organizing. The employment contract, which defines the zone of acceptance of employees, and provides immunity from adjudication by a court of law in most situations (Williamson, 1975) is the basis for authority in traditional business organization—it is created implicitly through the terms of entry into the organization. This authority is the basis for decisions about task division and allocation, the set-up of reward and information structures, as well as recursively solving the problems that arise when any of the solutions prove less than perfect (Coase, 1937; Galbraith, 1973; Simon, 1947).

Alternatives to formal authority (derived from an employment contract) as a basis for organizing are of course quite well known. These include informal authority based on expertise, reputation and status (e.g. the role of Linus Torvalds in the Linux community) as well as bargaining power (e.g. Toyota in its supplier network). These can result in fairly large and legitimized asymmetries in influence, even without any formal authority at work (for instance see Gulati, Puranam, and Tushman, 2012 on stratification in meta-organizations).[5]

---

[4] One can think of other secondary reasons for delegation, such as training subordinates, or of discovering the skills and preferences of the subordinates.

[5] We could treat a market as a special kind of organization (e.g. Milgrom and Roberts, 1992), whose goal is to maximize the utilities of buyers and sellers using prices as the key mechanism through which

However, if the reader is willing to engage in an adventurous foray into less charted territories, we will discover that some of the benefits of authority in organizing are known to exist even in the animal kingdom. In a fascinating review of "leadership behavior" (essentially, asymmetric influence) in a variety of mammalian species, Smith et al. (2016) compared its manifestation and exercise across both animal and small-scale human organizations. These included lions, meerkats, zebras and chimpanzees, as well as several modern hunter-gatherer societies (see Table 1 in Smith et al., 2016). The important role of asymmetric influence in within-group conflict resolution and inter-group relationships appears to be a universal feature that cuts across a startling variety of species (2016: 10).[6]

Yet uniquely in human societies, authority is heavily circumscribed by its perceived legitimacy among those who are subject to it; subordinates can and often do form coalitions to limit the exercise of authority by superiors (also see Boehm, 1997 for an interesting account of the evolutionary origins of egalitarianism). As Freeland (1996) expresses it, authority typically operates with *consent*. Further there is also no analogue to authority as the right to design in non-human societies (presumably, this role is fulfilled by natural selection; in the ant colony, natural selection writes the design into genetic material, which produces interlocking patterns of behavior that further the organization's goals). Both these differences are very likely due to the greater cognitive sophistication of humans. This exercise in "comparative organization science" across species suggests at least two directions in which our knowledge of authority as a component of organization design can be extended.

First, the results from animal societies strongly suggest that not all the benefits of authority necessarily depend on it being wielded by the wise; a mere structure of asymmetric influence may already confer certain advantages, independent of the properties of the occupants of roles in that structure. Some of us in the organizational modeling community have been particularly interested in understanding the extent to which authority can usefully perform one or more of its functions even when it is not married to superior wisdom. This is not out of any sympathy for the witless boss in the Dilbert cartoons. Rather we believe this helps to tackle a fundamental puzzle in the study of organization design as a normative field (Ethiraj and Levinthal, 2004; Lee and

---

task division, task allocation, reward and information distribution occur; the conditions under which markets can achieve this goal are very well known. Evolution through natural selection represents another approach to finding solutions to the basic problems of organizing.

[6] Levi-Martin (2009) reaches a similar conclusion. As he notes, "Among chimpanzees, the alpha may keep order by breaking up fights according to the simple but effective principle, 'hit anyone who hits.' . . . Such a sense of the social structure is seen, first of all, in the fact that in many primates and some birds the highest status animal is not merely able to dominate all others, but seems to fulfill some qualitatively different role" (2009: chapter 4).

Puranam, 2015; Simon, 1955): how should we reconcile the bounded rationality of the constituents of an organization—which makes design necessary in the first place—with that of the designer?

The spirit of the results we have obtained so far is that in a world of bounded rationality and imperfect decomposability of task structures, the architects of complex organizations may function as "blind watchmakers," to borrow an analogy from evolutionary biology (Dawkins, 1986). Through a series of models in the adaptive rationality tradition, which focus on the integration of effort as a search problem (see Chapter 4), we have come to learn that authority can aid effective organizational adaptation even if it is unaccompanied by any superior insight.

Authority can create differential adjustment, which is useful in coordination problems (e.g. Lave and March, 1993; Lounama and March, 1984); enhance stability and exploration (Rivkin and Siggelkow, 2003; 2005; Ethiraj and Levinthal, 2004; Lee and Puranam, 2015); and provide common (even if inaccurate) priors for the search for actions (Knudsen and Srikanth, 2014; Puranam and Swamy, 2016) and for structure itself (Clement and Puranam, 2017) in coupled learning processes. The results from this approach represent a fundamentally different answer to the question of why authority is such a pervasive feature of organizations, compared to say that offered by agency theory or Marxian ideology.

Second, the fact that authority seems to be systematically weaker in human organizations than in animal society points to important forces that seem to underlie our somewhat uneasy relationship with authority. While military, church and empire have often provided implicit or explicit models for modern human organizing, the nature of authority in these systems has a level of domain generality and strength that most would find unacceptable in a modern corporation or government.[7] Evolutionary psychologists claim that extreme authoritarianism is quite alien to the way authority manifested itself in the social organizations our remote ancestors evolved in (Nicholson, 1997; van Vugt, 2006). It is generally accepted today that a large stretch of human evolutionary history has seen us organized in hunter-gatherer communities (Cosmides and Tooby, 1997).[8] While the implicit organizational goal of such communities is to enhance the reproductive success of its individuals, explicitly articulated (sub-)goals such as locating food sources, patrolling the group's territory, warfare, infant care, and the maintenance of religion also

---

[7] For instance, in traditional (historical) military organizations, the requirement for consent was low, the domain of decisions within which authority operated was very large, the punishment for non-compliance was draconian, and there was little scope for voluntary exit.

[8] A hunter-gatherer society is one that subsists primarily on direct procurement of edible plants and animals from the wild, without domesticating either.

exist (Boehm, 1999; Megarry, 1995). They thus fulfill the criteria of being organizations.

Researchers who study hunter-gatherer societies report that they are typically egalitarian in nature (Boehm, 1999: 37), possibly because of the strong need for resource-sharing, given the variability of hunting/gathering success. This egalitarianism is achieved through coalitions of the weak, which impose a "reverse dominance hierarchy" on those who would otherwise have been dominant. Leaders in hunter-gatherer communities must build consensus rather than give orders, and it is rare to see multiple layers of delegated authority in such societies. Viewed from the perspective of organization design, group size seems restricted in hunter-gatherer communities by the limits of peer-to-peer dispute resolution (i.e. the quadratic explosion) without strong authoritative intervention. Put differently, the scale and complexity of the modern business firm may have come at the sacrifice of egalitarianism and the acceptance of multi-layered authority hierarchies. At the same time, an interesting conjecture that arises is that if the hunter-gatherer social structure is the one we are adapted to, then perhaps the enthusiasm for flat self-managed organizations, independent of their ability to deliver organizational goals, may reflect this instinct. I return to these issues in Chapters 6 and 8.

Conclusion

In this chapter, I outlined three roles for authority—design, direction and dispute resolution. I argued that authority could be delegated in two fundamentally different ways—in terms of a commitment to refrain from ex-ante or ex-post intervention. Sequential delegation produces hierarchies of authority, the topic of the next chapter.

I have favored a discussion of authority over power in general, because the former is the basis for organization design choices. Other forms of power arise in organizations, but as Pfeffer observed, power comes from position in the social structure (1981), and organization design choices affect the internal social structure of an organization. I have also ignored the question of where authority comes from (i.e. employment contract, tradition, charisma, expertise) in favor of focusing on what it does. The former is also important for organization design, but I have little to add to what we already know about it.

In an influential article, Robert Michels propounded the "Iron Law of Oligarchy"—the view that regardless of the reigning political ideology, the control and exploitation of the many by the few was inevitable (1966). The reason is that "the majority is...permanently incapable of self-government." Put differently, Michels was implicitly arguing that the concentration of power in the hands of the few was necessary to govern the many. An organization designer would paraphrase the claim as "organizing requires authority."

While on theoretical grounds, the existence of authority is not a necessary condition for an organization to exist, it is undoubtedly very common to see it feature as a solution to the universal problems of organizing. In fact, it is such an effective solution that the blind forces of natural selection appear to have discovered it as well, as the evidence from animal behavior suggests. Authority may be useful for effective organizational adaptation even when divorced from superior insight or ability. This may make it particularly challenging to find a substitute.

6 Hierarchies of authority

"Hierarchy" as a concept is both central and ambiguous in the literature on organizations. In this chapter, my focus is on hierarchies of authority. I begin by describing a formal set theoretic definition, and distinguish authority hierarchies from other social structures that exist within and between organizations. Some such structures may look like hierarchies but are not, some that do not appear like hierarchies in fact are, and not all hierarchies found in organizations are authority hierarchies.

With the language to describe hierarchies established, I turn to substantive issues. First, we know surprisingly little about how hierarchies of authority emerge. I outline a process model of hierarchical growth through sequential delegation as a first cut at the problem. Second, I consider the consequences of the growth of layers in an authority hierarchy. Control and information losses in multi-layered authority hierarchies may act as a limit on organizational size. However, they may also serve as a valuable source of exploration by the organization as a whole, aiding effective organizational adaptation. Third, I discuss re-organizations and how they re-shape existing hierarchies. Fourth, I conclude with some thoughts on the unpopularity of authority hierarchies, despite their obvious success as a form of organizing.

What hierarchies are (and what they are not)

A hierarchy can be thought of as a set of objects grouped into sub-sets, with some special restrictions on the kinds of relationships that exist within the sub-sets, as well as between objects in different subsets (the Appendix gives a formal set theoretic definition).

Within the sub-sets, the relationship between pairs of objects must satisfy two properties: symmetry and transitivity. For instance, the relation "has the same height as" is symmetric. If A has the same height as B, it must be true that B has the same height as A. It is also transitive. If A is the same height as B, and B has the same height as C, it must be true that A has the same height as C. An equivalence class is a sub-set within which the relationships between objects have these properties.

For objects taken from different equivalence classes in a hierarchy, the relationship between these objects must also satisfy two properties, asymmetry and transitivity. The relationship "is taller than" is asymmetric, because if A is taller than B is true, then B is taller than A must be false. It is also transitive (e.g. if A is taller than B, and B is taller than C, then A is taller than C). In a hierarchy, there is thus a relationship *between* objects in different equivalence classes that is asymmetric and transitive, whereas the relationship between objects *within* equivalence classes is symmetric and transitive (Simon, 1962; Levi Martin, 2009; Ahl and Allen; 1996).

A particular kind of hierarchy of relevance to us is a nested or containment hierarchy, such that equivalence classes of lower order are proper subsets of classes of higher order. The asymmetric, transitive relationship between objects in different classes in this case is *inclusion*. Within classes, the symmetric, transitive relationship can be defined as "is a co-member of." Taxonomies and classifications are instances of nested hierarchies (e.g. all cats are mammals, all mammals are animals). In fact, one of the most influential conceptions of a hierarchy in the organizational sciences is that of a nested hierarchy (Simon, 1962, 1996: 184): "By a hierarchic system or hierarchy, I mean a system that is composed of inter-related sub-systems, each of the latter being in turn hierarchic in structure until we reach some lowest level of elementary sub-system." This is the "boxes within boxes" metaphor; A has two sub-boxes, B and C, each of which has two sub-boxes each, and so on.

This nesting structure can evolve, Simon argued, because of near-decomposability—because interactions within a sub-system are greater than those between sub-systems nested within the same parent system (also see Chapter 3). Simon's core argument about hierarchies is that simple systems will evolve towards complex systems more easily if there are stable intermediate forms; stable intermediate forms are more likely with near-decomposability; and the resulting complex structures will be hierarchic—specifically will be containment hierarchies (1996: 196). For this reason, he argued, (containment) hierarchies occur in many aspects of Nature where evolutionary processes are at play. Organizations and the competitive environments they inhabit are plausibly in this category (Nelson and Winter, 1982).

While containment hierarchies are important, they do not exhaust the kinds of hierarchies we encounter in organizations. Note that the relationship between objects in a containment hierarchy—inclusion—need not be the same as influence. One group may be contained in another larger group, but this does not automatically mean that the larger group exerts asymmetric, transitive influence on the smaller one (e.g. a community of practice within a company), unless explicitly specified as such (e.g. a department within a division).

In many applications, we find it useful to represent hierarchies using graphs (networks), in which each node is an object, and the links represent binary relations (see Krackhardt, 1994 for a very useful introduction to graph theoretic representation of hierarchical structures).[1] Figure 6.1 is a graphical representation

---

[1] Multiplex graphs can be used to display multiple binary relations between nodes (e.g. asymmetric and symmetric relations, establishing orders and equivalence classes, respectively).

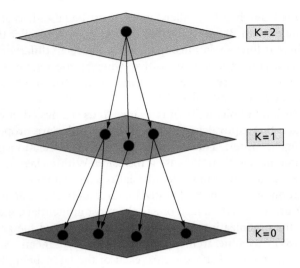

Figure 6.1 A three layered hierarchy

of a hierarchy. Graphical representation allows us to describe many analytically useful properties of hierarchies.

- The *span* of a node is the number of "child" nodes (i.e. nodes that are at the receiving end of a directed link) that are connected to the focal node through the asymmetric relationship that defines the hierarchy. Since nodes may vary in their span, a hierarchy is often characterized by its *maximum span*. When the maximum span in a hierarchy is equal to one, we obtain a linear hierarchy. When the maximum span is infinity, the result is a two-layered structure called a flat hierarchy.[2]
- The *rank* of a node in a hierarchy is the shortest distance of that node to the apex node (i.e. a node that has no parent).
- A layer is a set of equivalence classes whose members have the same rank. For reasons that will become clear, I will follow the convention of counting layers from the bottom–up, even though rank is counted from the apex. For a fixed number of nodes, an increase in span necessarily implies a reduction in layers, and vice versa.

These formal definitions provide the precision to allow us to appreciate several points about hierarchies in the context of organizations.

First, on the same set of individuals, it is possible to define multiple relationships and therefore multiple hierarchies (if the relationships meet the requirements for hierarchy). Hierarchies of wealth and power may coexist

---

[2] The usage is ambiguous. In a two-layered structure transitivity is not evident. I will use multi-layered hierarchy to refer to hierarchies that have at least three layers.

in an organization (and indeed also of skills, salary and title; these are not necessarily identical). Not all of these imply an influence relationship, as they may simply be rankings. The most obvious example is that hierarchies of skill and pay may not coincide with hierarchies of authority.

In fact, hierarchies within organizations need not involve individuals at all; one can produce a task hierarchy from the relationship among tasks defined as "must be completed before." Such a relationship is both asymmetric and transitive. Sub-sets of tasks may at the same time be in an equivalence class, defined by the relationship "must be completed at the same time as." Task structures, which show the pattern of interdependence between tasks (see Chapter 3) may thus be represented as task hierarchies, when the interdependence is expressed in the form of an asymmetric, transitive relationship such as "must be completed before," or "provides inputs to."

Later in this chapter, I discuss the importance of maintaining a clear conceptual separation between task and authority hierarchies (or more generally between interdependence and influence hierarchies), and what happens when they overlap or do not. For many applications, it will be necessary to think about both as distinct but inter-related. But my main point here is simply that if we mean to discuss authority hierarchies, much confusion can be avoided by simply saying so.

Second, authority as a binary relation does not automatically produce a multi-layered hierarchy. Authority is the legitimate ability of A to demand obedient behavior from B within a specified realm of actions (see Chapter 5). Such a relation is asymmetric, but not necessarily transitive. **Delegation produces transitivity.** When authority can be delegated, a multi-layered authority hierarchy arises.[3]

As we noted in Chapter 5, within most legal regimes, decision rights within a firm may not be transferred internally via contract so that the CEO is always ultimately legally responsible. Authority in a corporation is therefore delegated everywhere except at the very apex, producing the multi-layered authority hierarchy. More generally, forms of authority around which commonly understood norms of delegation exist, can produce hierarchies. Such norms could be anchored in legal institutions like contracts, but need not be; tradition may serve the same function. Authority structures in religious

---

[3] Another way in which it can be created is if a formerly independent individual accepts the authority of another. Client kings who were conquered by the armies of the Roman Republic were evidently often allowed to retain their kingdoms, but under the condition that they accepted the ultimate authority of the Roman senate. The hierarchy of Roman authority thus grew by this concatenation. It could lead to a member of royalty having to defer to a civil servant with a limited term of office. While this is a different path to the creation of a hierarchy, the end result is the same: a transitive influence relationship is established, with higher-level agents capable in theory of overruling the decisions ex ante or ex post of lower-layer agents. With what probability they do so is the extent of delegation, and may have been negotiated at the time of the king accepting client status.

orders have the same property of widely shared norms of delegation and can thus produce multi-layered hierarchies (see Levi Martin, 2009: chapter 7 for a fascinating discussion of transitivity in influence structures across cultures and historical eras).

A corollary to this point is that informal authority may not produce multi-layered hierarchies. Prestige, status and dominance are relationships that are asymmetric, but do not automatically possess transitivity, because at least to some extent these properties lie in the different eyes of different beholders. A may think that B is more prestigious than A, C may think A is more prestigious than C, but may think B is less prestigious than C. A discussion among a cross-disciplinary group of organizational scholars (preferably fueled by a little alcohol) about the relative prestige of various journals and departments can be an entertaining demonstration of this idea. Absent a shared understanding of a transitive structure of relations, these remain asymmetric relationships, not necessarily multi-layered hierarchies.

Third, in interpreting graphs, it is extremely important to consider both the topology (the overall pattern of linkages between nodes), as well as the ties (the binary relation being depicted by the links in the graph). While the graph that has a tree structure (i.e. each node has at most one parent) is the one that most of us intuitively identify with a hierarchy, this can be misleading. **A tree structure is neither necessary nor sufficient for a graph to represent a hierarchy.**

A multi-layered tree is an undirected graph in which any in which any two nodes are connected by at most one path. Regardless of how "tree-like" the structure looks, it is not an influence hierarchy unless the binary relationship between layers has the property of asymmetry, the relationship within layers is symmetric, and both are transitive. In formal terms, the graph must be a *directed acyclic graph* (or DAG) to be a hierarchy. In such a graph, the property of asymmetry is captured by the directed ties. Transitivity is captured by acyclicality—it should *not* be possible to "cycle" in the sense of going from node A to B, B to C and back from C to A.

Figure 6.2a is a tree, but it is not a hierarchy, because all links are symmetric. On the other hand, non-tree like graphs may in fact be hierarchies of influence (see Figure 6.2b, which makes transitivity explicit instead of implicit through mediated influence). In fact, Figure 6.1 is also a hierarchy that is not a tree, for the same reason.

Trees are rather restrictive models of hierarchies, their popularity in this role notwithstanding (Radner, 1993; Krackhardt, 1994). Nothing in the definition of a hierarchy prevents a node from having multiple parents (as in Figures 6.1 or 6.2b). Authority hierarchies are often shown as tree structures with directed ties because of the heuristic that "unity of command" or the "scalar principle" are effective ways of organizing. But matrix organizations routinely violate such principles and are increasingly common, with many employees having more than one boss, even in the same domain (Galbraith, 2012; Levinthal and Workiewicz, 2017).

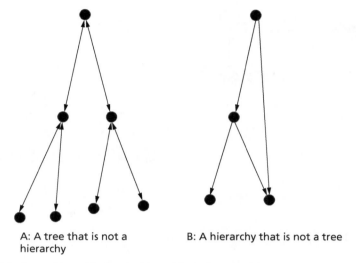

A: A tree that is not a
hierarchy

B: A hierarchy that is not a tree

Figure 6.2 A non-hierarchical and a hierarchical micro-structure

The emergence of authority hierarchies

The tree-shaped authority hierarchies we commonly observe in organizations are not constructed by assembling the entire workforce and then deciding simultaneously on the span and layers of the hierarchical structure to manage them, nor were they primarily concatenated from smaller organizations, as very few organizations have grown solely through merger with or acquisition of smaller organizations. Rather, the primary process that generates the authority hierarchy is very likely the same as that which enlarges the organization: growth. Indeed, one could say that the growth of formal organization is the growth of its administrative hierarchy.

Systematic longitudinal observations of entrepreneurial ventures and how they scale have been surprisingly rare (see Mintzberg, 1979 for an excellent synthesis of prior work in this area, as well as William F. Whyte's fascinating discussion of the growth of Tom Jones' short-order kitchen). What little we know does suggest some common patterns, which I have tried to summarize into a process model, represented in Figure 6.3.

At t = 0, there exists an entrepreneur (for simplicity, let's start with one; it doesn't change the story qualitatively if we had a founding team). This entrepreneur single-handedly produces and distributes goods or services. For this single producer, it makes little sense to distinguish division of labor from integration of effort. These are organizational constructs, and there isn't an organization yet, since there is a single agent.

At some point $t = T_1$ we reach the first significant milestone on the path to the development of the administrative hierarchy—the separation of the

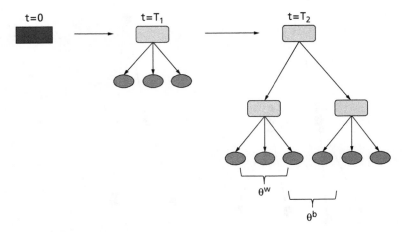

Figure 6.3 The growth of authority hierarchies

entrepreneur's function into the distinct tasks of production and integration (see Mintzberg, 1979: 18–34). We will refer to this as a *separation point*, as it represents the point in time at which the authority and task hierarchies diverge. This is necessitated by capacity constraints of the entrepreneur, either in terms of scale (i.e. the entrepreneur alone can no longer produce at the scale that is needed) or specialized skills (i.e. production now requires skills that the entrepreneur does not possess).[4] How quickly the limits of the entrepreneur are encountered will depend on demand conditions, and how quickly these limits can be offset through hiring will depend on the labor supply conditions for production workers. In either case, more production workers enter the organization, and their efforts need to be integrated. This gives rise to an opportunity for a division of labor between integration and production; the organization is now stratified along production (layer 0) and integration (layer 1). This creates a micro-structure of one supervisor and several subordinates, which we refer to as a *segment*.

At some further point t = T_2 we reach a second significant milestone. This is the point at which we hit a *span of control* constraint *in the production layer* for the first specialized integrator (perhaps the entrepreneur himself, who now takes on this role). More integrators (managers) thus become necessary to take on the supervision of more producers in layer 0.

What determines the span of control in an authority hierarchy? To answer this question, one must go back to the basic functions of authority we discussed in Chapter 5—direction, dispute resolution and design. Span of

---

[4] The emergence of a line/staff distinction is an instance of this process.

control constraints arise when the number of subordinates exceeds the number over which a superior can exercise authority along one or more of these dimensions in a manner that seems satisfactory (Tushman and Nadler, 1978).

In general, as the number of direct subordinates (n) for a supervisor in layer 1 rises, the difficulty of directing them effectively should increase linearly in n. The slope of this linear function may depend on employee skill, motivation and need for autonomy. The difficulty of managing disputes among them, and how it depends on n, requires a bit more elaboration. First, the number of possible interactions should increase quadratically with n, as it is n^* $(n-1)/2$.[5] However, the probability with which any interaction turns into a dispute that cannot be resolved bilaterally can vary with factors such as the extent of interdependence between subordinates, and how aligned their interests and representations are. We use θ as a parameter that captures this, and it can vary significantly with the underlying decomposability of the task structure, and the modularization implicit in a selected division of labor. Thus, the burden of direction and dispute resolution on an individual in the hierarchy can be written as a function increasing in both arguments, $f(\theta,n)$ and we can safely say that it will increase in a non-linear manner in n, but at rates that depend on θ.

We can thus re-describe the second milestone in the growth of the hierarchy (namely hitting the production layer *span of control constraint*) more formally: it is the point in time when the first layer 1 supervisor's capacity for direction and dispute resolution, denoted by C, falls below $f(\theta,n)$. At this point, more supervisors will be hired, with new segments being created. This also requires us to now distinguish θ^w (within segment) from θ^b (between segment). The first (theta *within*) captures the likelihood of disputes and need for direction within each segment comprising a layer 1 superior and her direct subordinates in layer zero. The second scales the likelihood of interdependence *between* segments in layer zero. These parameters reflect the selected division of labor and the underlying decomposability of the task structure, with low values indicating an effective modularization.

The last qualitatively distinct milestone arises at some further point $t = T_3$ when the integrators in layer 2 hit a *span of control constraint* for the integration layer. This span of control constraint may be different from that of the production layer, but the basic logic is the same. The ease of monitoring and the infrequency of disputes among subordinates in layer 1 enhance the span of control in the integration layer 2, just as they did with supervisors in layer 1 for subordinates in the production layer. But what determines the frequency of disputes to be resolved that would arrive at the desk of a manager in layer 2?

---

[5] I assume the difficulty of designing their interactions increases at some rate between the linear rate for direction and the quadratic rate for dispute resolution, and therefore ignore this dimension of the exercise of authority.

Consider the growing authority hierarchy in Figure 6.3. Assume an organization adopts a functional grouping of production tasks in layer 0—i.e. the key interdependencies are between the tasks that make up functions, but are minimal between functions. Under this assumption θ^w will be high but θ^b will be low (on average, assuming each segment at layers 0–1 is a functional grouping). To keep things simple, assume further that every supervisor is empowered to resolve any issues (pertaining to direction or disputes) arising within their segment, and within their segment only. They have no interactions or disputes with their peer managers in the same layer. Further, they pass on upwards, unfiltered, any disputes that fall outside their jurisdiction (i.e. outside their own segments of direct and indirect reports). Both these assumptions would be relaxed in a more formal treatment, and this can have interesting implications.

Given these assumptions, the only issues that reach supervisors at layer 2 are those that cut across segments in layer 0, and their expected frequency will therefore increase with θ^b. Since the increase in the actual number of subordinates for a layer 2 supervisor as production scales, will be faster with higher θ^w (because that reduces span for layer 1 supervisors), it follows that layer 2 supervisors span of control constraint will depend on both θ^w and θ^b. The argument can be applied recursively above layer 2, so that θ^w and θ^b influence the shape of the entire hierarchical structure.

The key implication of this process model, which Eucman Lee and I have been working to formalize, is that the resulting shape of the hierarchical authority tree should vary systematically not only with the sheer number of producers in layer 0 (the scale of operation), but also the principle of division of labor among them. We believe that this is one of the mechanisms through which organizational imprinting could arise, in which conditions at time of founding have long term implications (see Simsek et al., 2014 for a review of the imprinting literature).

This approach to understanding the shape of the hierarchy differs from past work in that it accounts explicitly for imprinting and path dependence, links hierarchy shape to underlying task structure and division of labor choices, and predicts that there will be systematic variation of span across layers in a hierarchy. At the same time, it also makes predictions consistent with what is observed in prior empirical work. For instance, if the feasible span of control at all levels increases due to better technologies for monitoring or better modularization of the production layer, for instance, then for a fixed number of employees, we would expect fewer layers in the organization (Colombo and Delmastro, 2007; Bloom et al., 2009). If the span of control increases exogenously, the pressures to delegate decision making to subordinates or formalize (i.e. rely more on rules to coordinate subordinates) increases due to the limits of supervisory capacity (Gittell, 2001; Mintzberg, 1979).

To be clear, this stylized account of growth of administrative hierarchy is a hypothesis rather than a confirmed theory, though it does seem to capture key aspects of the spirit of the process. It also has the possibly odd feature that all production takes place only in layer 0. The rest of the organization simply manages the producers, and manages the managers, and so on. There is a tradition of treating organizational hierarchies in this way, going back at least to Williamson (1967). Besides precedent, one may also remark that this is after all consistent with Peter Drucker's vision of the post-industrial society, in which organizations are primarily concerned with decision-making, not production.

But a more precise way of thinking about this model is to interpret it as depicting the case where there is a sharp separation between *the (production) task hierarchy and the authority hierarchy*. For simplicity, and indeed to highlight this point, I have assumed in my description above that these are fully orthogonal—the sequence of tasks needed to produce (even if the production is knowledge-based) all lie within layer zero.

However, consider the other extreme, when production involves the sequential flow of work through increasingly powerful actors (e.g. in a consulting firm, a research team, or in a craftsman's shop).[6] A common feature of such situations is that the selection, oversight and filtering of inputs from subordinates is an integral part of the production process, rather than merely being processes that achieve the integration of their efforts. Here, the authority and production task hierarchy are not separated, with the individual with ultimate authority contributing to the production process; this is in contrast to say an automobile manufacturing firm in which the divisional general manager clearly does not slap on the last lick of paint on the car before shipping it off to customers.

GROWTH OF THE TASK HIERARCHY

We can revisit the process model of hierarchy growth, with a new condition that the separation point does not arise; production and authority hierarchies grow together. Growth would still involve scaling and span constraints, but the factors and processes that drive the span constraint could indeed be different. I will refer to this as a *non-separated hierarchy* (i.e. task and authority hierarchies coincide) to distinguish it from a *separated hierarchy* (i.e. task and authority hierarchies do not coincide).

To understand the growth process of a non-separated hierarchy, it is useful to recall from Chapter 3 that sequential task decomposition results in a

---

[6] Knowledge hierarchies (e.g. Garicano, 2000) and hierarchies that enable parallel information processing (e.g. Radner, 1993) are task hierarchies but not necessarily authority hierarchies.

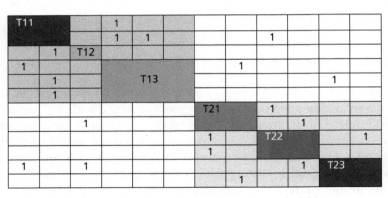

Figure 6.4 The growth of task hierarchies through recursive task division

hierarchy of tasks, in which layers arise if the right to decompose tasks further is delegated downwards (see Figure 6.4). Each individual at layer k in a non-separated hierarchy thus has the authority to decompose her task into sub-tasks (i.e. authority as design), as well as the authority to direct, and resolve disputes among the subordinates who perform the new sub-tasks. The growth, or to be precise, elaboration of a non-separated hierarchy, should occur in the reverse direction (i.e. top-down) to that of a separated hierarchy (bottom-up) discussed in the previous section.

At any layer in a task hierarchy, the potential span is the number of sub-tasks it can be partitioned into. First, this should reflect the architectural knowledge of those doing the task decomposition. The better the task structure is understood, the finer it can be partitioned. Second, the finer tasks are partitioned, the greater the interdependencies will be between the sub-tasks. Thus, the number of sub-tasks will also be determined by the trade-off between the gains from specialization (which can be exploited by a fine decomposition of tasks) and the costs of managing interdependencies between sub-tasks (which increase with number of sub-tasks). The span of the task hierarchy should thus reflect the extent of architectural knowledge available—which may enable finer or coarser partitioning of tasks, as well as the opportunities for economies of scale—which can lead to finer and finer task partitions (Stigler, 1951).

The elaboration of a task hierarchy through sequential decomposition is also likely to produce a gradation of architectural knowledge: at the uppermost layer, perception of the task structure can be of broad scope but quite coarse. An individual in layer k only needs to perceive a subset of more-fine-grained task structure but of reduced scope in layer k-1 (e.g. the architectural knowledge needs be relatively high only for the sub-tasks that lie within the designer's task structure). Travelling down the layers of a task hierarchy, we can expect that the grain of architectural knowledge will become finer, but the scope more restricted.

Time scales may also differ as we travel down a task hierarchy. Elliot Jaques (1990) has observed that the time spans for task completion are typically much higher at the apex than at the base of a task hierarchy. This may reflect the importance of continued organizational existence as part of the overall organizational goal; its sequential decomposition could then also lead to shorter time scales as task partitioning grows finer.

Because sequential task decomposition involves sequential modularization, the costs of managing interdependencies should escalate rapidly as layers are added, because it should get harder and harder to find good modularizations within clusters. Once the costs of coordination exceed the gains from specialization, we have reached the limit of productivity gains from the growth of the task hierarchy via task decomposition.[7] In a non-separated hierarchy, this also translates into smaller spans the deeper down we go (in contrast to a separated hierarchy, where the opposite should be true).

---

[7] This is why it is conventional to assume that economies from specialization are exhausted rapidly as scale increases, see Williamson (1967).

Once we have exhausted these productivity gains, further scaling can only arise by the reproduction of the entire non-separated hierarchy. But in that case, we can replace a production worker in our model of growth for a separated hierarchy by an entire non-separated hierarchy (see Figure 6.3). In other words, we can interpret our model of hierarchical growth for a separated hierarchy as unfolding after the limits of elaboration of the task hierarchy have been reached. This also implies that a) non-separated hierarchies are likely to be constrained in their scale of production compared to separated hierarchies, and b) as production scale increases, they will be overlaid by a separated hierarchy. Empirical analysis that is sensitive to these distinct properties of separated and non-separated hierarchies of tasks and authority may do better at identifying the antecedents of the span of control in organizations (Dewar and Simit, 1981; Puranam et al., 2012).

To reiterate, what I present here is still mostly speculation, and much empirical and theoretical work remains to be done on these issues. The implications of different degrees of alignment between the production task and authority hierarchy in an organization certainly seems a fascinating topic to study both as an antecedent, as well as a consequence in itself.

Control and information loss in authority hierarchies

CONTROL AND INFORMATION LOSSES AS LIMITS TO GROWTH

The basic model of hierarchy growth I have proposed above assumes that effectiveness of delegation of authority is unchanged as layers in the hierarchy expand. I now relax this assumption and consider what happens to the exercise of authority as the layers in an authority hierarchy increase. There are two kinds of "transmission loss" effects arising from the sheer number of layers—control loss and information loss. These are conceptually distinct, though may also reinforce each other. When these transmission losses become severe enough, the key property of transitivity of authority is undermined, threatening the very existence of the hierarchy of authority.

Consider the right to direct subordinate's actions (the discussion may be easier to follow in the three-layered hierarchy of Figure 6.1). In principle, the agent i at apex node in layer 2, may have the authority to direct all subordinate nodes. However, through delegation, this right may be delegated to subordinate j in layer 1 by i. This means that the ex-ante and ex-post intervention probabilities by i to intervene in how j directs subordinate k in layer 0 are lower than 1. It follows that i necessarily has less control over k in this three-layered structure, than he would have had in a two-layered structure. There is also the sheer cognitive burden on a superior in a hierarchical structure faced with the prospect of observing many direct and indirect subordinates. It is a structural property of a multi-layered branching hierarchy that as one approaches the apex, the total number of subordinates increases at an increasing rate. This phenomenon of control loss through an increase in layers in a delegated authority hierarchy is well known (Williamson, 1967; Galbraith, 1973; Jensen and Meckling, 1979).

Lower control may also imply lower ability to extract relevant information. But even if that were not true, to the extent that information cannot simply be broadcast but must pass through nodes in the network, increasing layers in an authority hierarchy necessarily implies information losses (Williamson, 1967). The limits to human information processing that we discussed in Chapter 2 virtually guarantee this. Increasing layers thus makes it harder for the same information to be held across layers in a hierarchy. This works in both directions: higher-layer agents cannot observe or process everything that lower-layer agents are saying, and lower-layer agents may not understand what the higher-layer agents expect of them. This in turn may stimulate additional delegation, to move decision-making closer to where the information is, implying further control loss.

Control loss and information loss also interact to shape how authority as dispute resolution operates in multi-layered hierarchies. An escalation of a dispute between two subordinates beyond their immediate superior represents, in a sense, the inverse of delegation: it is an appeal for ex-post intervention, so that the decision rights in this case are being "handed back up." Yet even when the decision rights may flow smoothly if slowly back up the authority hierarchy in an escalation process, the information need not do so. Thus, the more the layers needed to climb before two disputants encounter a common source of authority whose decision will be binding on them, the longer it will take and the less informed the decision might be. This is often seen as a weakness peculiar to matrix organizations, but in fact is also generally a problem in traditional authority hierarchies when the disputants report to different bosses (with the dispute itself possibly signaling a non-modular division of tasks between them).

The increase in control and information losses with hierarchical layers also suggest an explanation for why design decisions might not be delegated very far down the hierarchy. Perhaps design decisions are viewed as more consequential than operational ones, or it may be the need for maintaining comparability and equity perceptions across different parts of the organization that create pressures towards avoiding the delegation of design rights. We do not really know. But independent of the motivations to delegate design, it does seem highly likely that design decisions taken at the apex of the authority hierarchy will typically be based on limited information about the conditions at the bottom.

Transmission losses appear to limit the number of layers in a hierarchy (and therefore its size, unless span can be expanded). However, it is worth noting that neither control loss nor information loss is universally "bad" for organizational performance and effective adaptation. Let's take each separately.

HIERARCHIES AS FILTERS: DESIGNED INFORMATION LOSS

If the transmission loss at each node in the network represents perfect screening, then the quality of information may improve as it moves through a hierarchy, even as the quantity is lost. Information loss in hierarchies may thus nevertheless lead to higher information quality.

Superiors could get error-free reports and ideas by filtering the reports through a large funnel of subordinates, and subordinates may receive precise operational instructions after middle managers have filtered out the fluff from vision statements. However, the nature of human rationality does not automatically grant us such a convenient outcome. Screening is typically imperfect, because the representations that agents hold (in this case, about what makes an alternative worthy of positive evaluation) may be flawed (see Chapter 2).

Consider a binary evaluation process—whether to accept or reject a proposal based on some information one has about it. In general, fallible decision-makers could make two types of error: they may reject an acceptable alternative (omission error) or accept an unacceptable one (commission error). All hope is not yet lost though, as the layers in an authority hierarchy and the pattern of delegation in it may nonetheless help to improve the aggregate screening of the organization. This idea was first proposed by Sah and Stiglitz (1985, 1988) with subsequent elaboration by others (Christensen and Knudsen, 2010; Csaszar, 2013).

For example, in a three-member linear hierarchy, imagine that a new project is first evaluated by k, the lowest-level manager. Only if she accepts the project does it get passed on to middle manager j. Otherwise, the project is rejected and not evaluated further. Middle manager j, in turn, then also decides to reject it or accept it to send it on to the senior manager i for final approval.

Readers will recognize that this represents a particular pattern of conditional delegation (see Chapter 5). The superior in each case intervenes ex ante, with probability 1 for an "accept" decision by a subordinate, and may overturn it based on her own screening. However, the intervention probability on a "reject" decision by a subordinate is zero. It should be obvious that this kind of authority structure should do well at avoiding errors of commission, but is quite prone to errors of omission. One could also imagine other patterns of delegation in this authority hierarchy, of course, though in the literature this structure is often identified uniquely with "hierarchy."

In contrast, imagine a situation in which all three managers would evaluate the project and acceptance by one is sufficient for project approval. This is referred to as a "decentralized polyarchy." It should be clear that such a structure should be good at avoiding omission errors, but will do poorly in terms of commission errors. These building blocks can be used to describe a wide range of possible decision architectures, with many hybrid forms such as committee-voting and averaging opinions, falling between the extreme forms (Csaszar and Eggers, 2013). By combining these structures, one can in theory build an aggregate screening function that can approach perfect screening (Christiansen and Knudsen, 2010).

Hierarchies as Instruments of Search: Control Loss and Exploration

Some degree of control loss can lead to adaptive outcomes for a hierarchy, by serving as a valuable source of bottom-up exploration for better strategies (Burgelman, 1983; March, 1991; Levinthal and March, 1993).

"Bootleg innovation" refers to situations in which individuals ignore top-down management directives, to make their own choices on how to invest company resources to pursue innovation. Well-documented instances exist in which such deviations from strategy have been beneficial to the firm (Augsdorfer, 2005). Delegation in resource allocation decisions to functional and middle managers can produce a similarly useful divergence between intended and realized strategy in complex multi-layered organizations (Bower, 1970; Burgelman, 1983).

Variations between directives and actions, and even outright errors, can lead to improvements in organizational knowledge. As I noted in Chapter 2, erroneous variation between an erroneous representation and action can be a useful avenue for discovering better representations (March, 1991). High levels of control may curtail such useful variation. For instance, Benner and Tushman (2002) have documented the adverse consequences for exploratory innovation of process management techniques (such as total quality management) that are explicitly meant to reduce variation and improve alignment between strategy and employee actions (also see Benner and Tushman, 2003; Slater, Hult, and Olson, 2010).

Eucman Lee and I studied the conditions under which control and information losses were useful for the revision of representations at the top of the hierarchy, using a computational model of strategy implementation with delegation in a multi-layered hierarchy (Lee and Puranam, 2015). We concluded that control and information losses between layers i and j in a hierarchy could generate exploration that acts as a substitute to exploration induced by similar losses between j and the next layer k. Thus, an emphasis on precise implementation at the bottom of the hierarchy (the "implementation imperative") may be quite sensible, given inevitable control and information losses in the rest of the hierarchy. We also found that information losses can be more harmful than control losses in terms of effective organizational adaptation, as the former can induce biases in the learning process, not merely noise.

Another recent model by Levinthal and Workiewicz (2017) studies matrix reporting as a mechanism that can produce useful control losses. When the two bosses of an employee in a matrix cannot agree, often the employee has discretion to do what they prefer. This is control loss for the superiors, but it can be a useful way to produce exploratory search in certain kinds of task environments. In fact, it may do so precisely when it is most needed (i.e. when interdependencies in the task structure make it harder for the bosses to agree, and less useful to simply compromise by picking at random).

In sum, while control and information losses in multi-layered hierarchies are inevitable, they may also create some adaptive advantages, besides setting a limit on the size of the organization (Williamson, 1967).

Re-shaping hierarchies: grouping and re-grouping

Besides the layers and span of authority hierarchy, the other important attribute of its shape is the basis on which subordinates are grouped under the common authority of a superior. So important is this attribute that for most non-experts in the field, organization design is (erroneously) synonymous with the boxes on organization charts that show grouping.

Which roles are grouped together into organizational sub-units, and why, were important questions for early organizational scholars (Gulick and Urwick, 1937; Simon, 1947; Fayol, 1949; March and Simon, 1958). Later elaborations by Thompson (1967), Galbraith (1977), Tushman and Nadler (1978, 1990), have given us the basic form of the arguments that we still use today.

In this received view, the primary purpose of grouping positions under common authority is to enhance the integration of effort among them (or equivalently, to reduce coordination costs among them). The trade-offs created are a) that grouping boundaries act as barriers to integration between groups, and b) increasing group size weakens the effectiveness of integration within group. Accordingly, prioritizing which activities/roles need to be integrated is a precursor to grouping decisions—whether by activity (e.g. functional departments), or by object (e.g. product or customer centric divisions).

As we noted in Chapter 4, the integration of effort occurs through several mechanisms, and many of these are involved in grouping. Organizational boundaries serve to focus attention by limiting the number of interdependent activities that decision makers need to consider. In doing so, boundaries serve to increase the available attention and cognitive capacity for a given set of interdependent tasks by shielding the decision makers from all other tasks.[8] Another advantage of placing interdependent activities within the same organizational unit with common objectives is the effect on incentives. If the objectives are well defined and measurable, then performance at the level of the organizational unit can be observed, measured, and rewarded, thereby creating motivation to cooperate (Barzel, 1982; Zenger, 1994; Zenger and Hesterley, 1997; Baker, 2002).

Grouping also influences motivation for individuals through identification and interaction with the set of peers so defined (see Chapter 2 for the role of structuring in shaping individual goals). Over time, groupings influence the emergence of a shared communication system. The effect of accumulation of shared experience and continuity of association is likely to be strong within organizational boundaries, as boundaries dictate who interacts with whom on a regular basis and often imply spatial collocation (Arrow, 1974).

Complementary to these mechanisms that underlie grouping, but perhaps more fundamental than any of them, is the fact that grouping within the formal structure is first and foremost a mechanism to bring interdependent agents under the shadow of common authority. The power to direct and resolve disputes and exceptions is valuable in ensuring the integration of effort. The same idea in the context of a multi-layered hierarchy of authority can be expressed as follows: grouping can enable integration though authority by minimizing the distance to the first common boss for interdependent individuals. In fact, this is just a particular instance of the "folk theorem" of organization design that I discussed in Chapter 4—interdependence between agents requires integrative influences.

As Nadler and Tushman noted (1997), what cannot be grouped, but must still be coordinated, can be linked (e.g. through committees and taskforces). Linking mechanisms are however necessarily weaker than grouping, because they cannot bundle common authority, incentives, and objectives (and often collocation) as powerfully as the grouping structures do. Grouping is therefore a first-order design concern.

THREE LEVELS OF RE-ORGANIZATION

It is useful to distinguish three different levels of re-design or re-organization (Lee and Puranam, 2015). A Level 2 re-design leaves both task division and task allocation unchanged, but alters the pattern of information provision and reward distribution (typically through changes in administrative grouping structures; March and Simon, 1958; Nadler and Tushman, 1997).

---

[8] It is interesting to note that Parnas (1972) articulated this advantage of self-containment in his discussion of the information encapsulation principle in software design and development.

Of particular interest is how close to layer 0 does the re-grouping take effect. Viewed from the apex, the difference between a divisional and functional structure is that the layer zero workers in the former will be from more than one functional background. But divisional structures can vary in the layer at which layer 0 workers from different functional backgrounds encounter their first common boss.

Level 1 re-designs leave the task division unchanged, but may involve a change in task allocation (e.g. job rotation, or the rotation of responsibilities—for instance for seminar series, recruitment and PhD admissions within an academic department), and consequently also in the patterns of information provision and reward distribution across individuals. Level 0 re-designs involve a fundamental change in the solutions to the basic problems of organizing—the pattern of both task division and task allocation may change, and consequently also the pattern of information provision and reward distribution. It is therefore equivalent to a "greenfield" or blank slate design problem. Re-designs can be in principle of any level, though we would rarely expect them to be of level 0, given gains from specialization and learning, which would have to be abandoned when undertaking such a fundamental re-organization.

While improving integrative influence may be the design objective in re-organizations, its realization is hampered by the imperfect understanding of task structures (which may be compounded by the distance in the hierarchy between the production layers and the layers where design decisions are being made). Accordingly, in a world of imperfectly decomposable (and poorly understood) task structures, grouping decisions can be neither perfect nor permanent.

Further, authority is not the only mechanism for integration, as we have noted above. To the extent that group identity, communication networks and the ability to coordinate based on mutual familiarity or self-selection serve as substitutes, then bringing interdependent actors under the shadow of common authority is less useful. For both these reasons, periodic re-groupings or re-organizations are inevitable. Changes in technology, competition, strategic priorities and emergent patterns of informal internal organization can all be instances of triggers for reorganization (Chandler, 1962; Nickerson and Zenger, 2002; Gulati and Puranam, 2009).

What we do not like about authority hierarchies

Independent of whether authority hierarchies are an effective means of organizing in terms of accomplishing organizational goals, it is interesting to consider why the inhabitants of these structures are sometimes quite critical of them. My reading of the popular literature suggests at least four distinct kinds of arguments.

First, there is an irrefutable concentration of power (even if it is legal) at the apex of the authority hierarchy, which the denizens of an egalitarian ethos naturally dislike. Power at the top necessarily implies less autonomy for subordinates over their own actions. Autonomy is a fundamental human need (Chapter 2). As egalitarian values become more widespread and entrenched, the willingness and ability to express this need more strongly increases, as does the expressed dislike for authority hierarchies.

Second, when hierarchies arise because of task decomposition (i.e. in non-separated hierarchies), it is inevitable that sub-tasks are defined more and more narrowly as one travels down the hierarchy, producing ever-greater specialization. To the extent that variety in work is also valued for itself (see Chapter 2), extensive task hierarchies may give rise to dissatisfaction on this account, particularly towards the bottom of the hierarchy.

Third, because delegation necessarily involves some loss of control, those at the top of formal authority hierarchies also tend to use standardization of work and procedures as an additional means of control. To those at the receiving end of standardization, the local costs tend to be more visible in the form of red tape and rigid bureaucracy than the global benefits of coordination and control (quite independent of their relative magnitudes). Somewhat relatedly, when communication becomes isomorphic with the authority hierarchy, bottlenecks and delays become common. But there is no obvious reason why the communication network must necessarily reflect the authority hierarchy.

Fourth, the results of purely managerial work—such as the role of middle managers in an authority hierarchy who exist as a reflection of span of control constraints (and not of the task hierarchy) are less easy to see, compared to the tangible outputs of employees engaged in production activity. Thus, independent of their relative value, the ease of perceiving their value is not identical. This can lead to angst about the "bloat" introduced by middle management layers, and concerns with politics supplanting competence as the basis for career progression. "Excessive layers" is a common complaint about hierarchies by their inhabitants, yet it does not seem to be widely recognized that the only ways in which layers can be reduced are a reduction in overall size of the organization, or an expansion in average span of control. Note that these dissatisfactions with hierarchy could exist independent of whether an organization design featuring authority is in fact useful in furthering the attainment of the organization's goals.

I believe it is useful to distinguish between the first two arguments, which have to do with what people want, and the second two, which deal with what they (don't) know. If human nature comes equipped with a preference for autonomy and task variety, then addressing the dissatisfaction with hierarchies because they currently do not allow expression of these preferences, will require us to think of new ways of organizing **equally** large numbers of people.

This is a hard problem, and Chapter 8 examines some of the experiments that are currently being undertaken to solve it.

A second, possibly easier problem to solve is one of better informing people about how hierarchies work. More generally, how and why certain parts of the organization work the way they do is not transparent to others in a hierarchy. This compartmentalization, both vertical and horizontal, conserves valuable mental resources. It also gives rise to concerns about fairness and bureaucratic rigidity that may not always be justified. A thorough understanding of concepts like control loss, span of control constraints, the relative costs of omission and commission errors and the limits of delegation can productively sharpen critiques of hierarchies towards their real, rather than their imagined failings.

Conclusion

Multi-layered authority hierarchies are ubiquitous today in organizations. They provide what has been an exceptionally successful template for organizing large groups of people. Hierarchy has its discontents, as it seems to violate basic human preferences for egalitarianism, autonomy and task variety (see Chapter 2). For this reason, non-hierarchical forms of organization may sometimes enjoy a popularity that exceeds their direct economic significance.

Yet others see hierarchy as inevitable. For instance, in an influential article, Elliott Jaques (1990) argued that "The hierarchical kind of organization we call bureaucracy did not emerge accidentally. It is the only form of organization that can enable a company to employ large numbers of people and yet preserve unambiguous accountability for the work they do. And that is why, despite its problems, it has so doggedly persisted."

From the perspective of the universal problems of organizing, authority is an extremely important, but not the only, solution concept. It follows that authority hierarchies are not inevitable. Further, there is no reason why as organization designers we should not place the satisfaction of fundamental human preferences onto our list of design criteria. Put differently, if we do not like multi-layered authority hierarchies, we must either find good substitutes for authority, find ways to increase spans of control within existing authority hierarchies, or manage the negative perceptions surrounding hierarchy more effectively. I will return to this topic in Chapter 8, which tackles novelty in forms of organizing.

■ APPENDIX TO CHAPTER 6: FORMAL DEFINITION OF HIERARCHY

A hierarchy is a partially ordered set whose elements can be grouped into equivalence classes.

An **order** is said to exist among a set of elements {a, b, c . . . , z} when there is a binary relation between any two elements (which we can denote by "R") that has the following four properties:

- It is *complete* (for any distinct a and b, either a R b is true or b R a is true)
- It is *antisymmetric* (for any distinct a and b, if a R b is true, then b R a must be false. Alternately, if a R b and b R a are both true, it must be true that a = b)
- It is *transitive* (if a R b is true and b R c is true, then a R c must be true)
- It is *reflexive* (a R a must be true)

For instance, consider the binary relationship "is not taller than." This relation is complete, because the heights of any two individuals can be compared (i.e. either a*b or b*a must be true). It is antisymmetric, since if Ann is not taller than Bob, the converse cannot be true unless their heights a and b are exactly equal. It is transitive, since if Ann is not taller than Bob, and Bob is not taller than Charlie, then Ann must not be taller than Charlie. Finally, no individual can be taller than himself.

Relaxing the first condition, completeness, yields a partially ordered set (sometimes abbreviated to "poset"). In a partial order, the binary relationship in question is not defined for every pair of elements—not all pairs can be compared. For instance, on the set of domestic pets, the binary relationship "barks louder than" can be used to compare within the subset of dogs, but not across dogs and cats. Every ordered set, by definition also meets the weaker requirements of a partially ordered set.

An **equivalence** is said to exist among a set of elements {a, b, c,} when there is a binary relation between any two elements (which we can continue to denote by "R") that has two of the same properties as a partial order—transitivity and reflexivity—but a distinct third one: symmetry. This implies that if aRb is true, then bRa must also be true. Consider the binary relationship "is as tall as." If Ann is as tall as Bob, the converse must be true (symmetry). It is a transitive relationship, because if Ann is as tall as Bob and Bob is as tall as Charlie, Ann must be as tall as Charlie. Finally, Ann must be as tall as herself (reflexivity). Equivalence relations partition sets into "equivalence classes."

In the interests of simplicity, in the text I do not distinguish between asymmetry (which requires both anti-symmetry and irreflexivity) and anti-symmetry. The loss in precision does not seem very consequential in most organizational applications.

7 Formal and informal structure of organization

The *formal structure* of an organization constitutes a desired pattern of behavior and interactions between agents, specified by those with the formal authority to do so. It encompasses both an interdependence structure and an influence structure. The former is primarily the result of choices about the division of labor (Chapter 3), whereas the latter primarily reflects choices about integration of effort (Chapters 4–6).[1]

Bounded rationality is a property of the designers as well as the inhabitants of organizations. The architects of the organization's structure are not guaranteed the ability to perceive precisely the optimal patterns of behavior and interactions between individuals given the organization's goals. Nor can they perfectly enforce the formal structure which they design according to their own possibly faulty perception of the ideal structure. The result is therefore an actual pattern of interactions—the *realized* organizational structure—that may diverge significantly from the specified formal structure. The divergent elements of the realized structure constitute the *informal structure*—and these are the result of emergent patterns of individual behavior and interactions between individuals, as well as the norms, values, and beliefs that underlie such behaviors and interactions (Roethlisberger and Dickson, 1939; Smith-Doerr and Powell, 2005).

Given the reality of the distinct existence of the formal and informal structure in organizations (and the limits to design of the former), some scholars have argued that it would be naïve to think of formal structure as a complete template for successful organizational behavior (Fligstein and Dauber, 1989) or to mistake it for an accurate description of organizational behavior (Granovetter, 1985: 487). But if the design and enforcement of formal structure are both so limited, then why have we bothered talking about it for so many chapters in this book? For some theorists, the formal structure has at best symbolic value, useful for invoking legitimacy, signaling an ideology, or as itself being the result of the pressures of conformity. At worst, it may be fully decoupled from the actual workings of the organization (Meyer and Rowan, 1977; DiMaggio and Powell, 1983).

There are undoubtedly symbolic effects of the formal structure of this sort that it would be incorrect to ignore (among the more important, I think, being

---

[1] This chapter draws on Gulati and Puranam (2009) as well as Clement and Puranam (2017).

a mechanism for enabling self-selection into the organization by signaling the preferred stakeholder type). But it is also incorrect, I argue, to assume that this is all that formal structure does, or to equate realized structure entirely to informal structure. This is for two reasons. First, the influence of the formal structure on the informal structure is critical. As Blau and Scott (1962) recognized, "The fact that an organization has been formally established however does not mean that all activities and interactions of its members conform strictly to the official blueprint... The roots of these informal systems are embedded in the formal organization itself and nurtured by the very formality of its arrangements." Second, the former is amenable to direct managerial intervention, the latter is not. Ignoring the formal structure would be akin to ignoring the temperature control on the air conditioning unit in a room, on the grounds that actual room temperature is affected by many other things we cannot fully understand or control.

In this chapter, my aim is to describe the links between the formal and informal structure of organizations, and propose a systematic approach to analyzing these links. I first discuss how the two are related and influence each other. Next, revisiting the theme of organizations as "marvels but not miracles" (see Chapters 4 and 5) I argue that formal design can be useful even when it not predicated on high levels of comprehension or intelligence. This is because it can compensate for aspects of the informal organization, as well as shape the emergence of the informal organization. I discuss an instance of a micro-structural approach to such issues in some detail, and conclude by offering a multiplex network formulation that can help us make progress in studying the complex interactions between formal and informal organizational structures.

How formal and informal structure are related

In a recent review of the literature, McEvily and colleagues noted a fairly dramatic change in organizations research from a focus on formal structure (as seen in the iconic work in the structural contingency tradition), to a near-complete rejection of it and an emphasis on the informal (McEvily, et al., 2014). They noted that it has become common in contemporary research on intra-organizational social networks to portray the positions of agents solely as the results of their own free choices, without explicit consideration of how the formal design may have shaped these (2014: 312).

A few researchers who have carefully examined both mandated and realized patterns of interactions in organizations have noticed significant variations in the extent to which the two appear to converge or diverge, as well as in the performance consequences of this (Sosa, et al., 2004; Sosa, 2008; Gokpinar, et al., 2010; Soda and Zaheer, 2012). This suggests that assuming away the links between formal and informal structures is not only bad science, it is also bad for practice. A good starting point for correcting this lacuna is to develop an understanding of the relationship between formal and informal structure. I believe this can be usefully done by considering, separately, a) the influence of one on the other, and b) their joint influence on organizational performance.

FORMAL, REALIZED AND INFORMAL STRUCTURES

Let me begin with an analogy from statistics: if we regress the realized structure (i.e. the actual stable pattern of interactions between the individuals in an organization) on the formal structure, we should not expect the (standardized) coefficient on the formal structure to be one. The error term in this regression is the informal structure. It may be decomposed into a component that is correlated with the formal structure because of the influence of the formal on the informal structure, and another that is independent of it. **Thus informal structure can be seen as a "correlated error term" in the regression of realized on formal structure.** Put differently, the data generation process is one where realized structure is the result of the formal structure and the informal structure (which is itself partly the function of the formal structure).

What causes the correlation between the formal structure and informal structure? To understand the influence of formal organizational structure on the emergence of the informal organizational structure, I find it helpful to think in terms of "roles."[2] A role is a delineation of the set of recurrent behaviors appropriate to a particular position in a social system. Roles can be usefully viewed as containing both non-relational and relational aspects—who does what as well as who interacts with whom (Barley, 1990).

Formal organizational structure can thus be seen to comprise a set of prescribed roles and linkages between roles, for instance as set forth in job descriptions and reporting relationships (Scott, 1998). The right to design roles is one of the attributes of authority (Chapter 5). Informal organizational structure then refers to the emergent patterns of individual behavior and interactions between individuals that are not present in the specified formal structure (Roethlisberger and Dickson, 1939; Smith-Doerr and Powell, 2005). Using the construct of roles, we can understand how formal structure affects the emergence of a related informal structure in three ways.

Formal Structure Shapes the Emergence of Expertise

First, let's consider the purely non-relational aspects of roles. Repetitive performance of role-related activity as specified in job descriptions leads to

---

[2] This section draws on Gulati and Puranam (2009).

enhanced competence and expertise at carrying out the specified activities (Mintzberg, 1980). This expertise may be embodied in skills, mental models and heuristics. Such expertise is an important component of the informal structure as it is manifested in an emergent pattern of behavior (i.e. better methods of working) that is not reflected in the official job-description; yet the existence of the latter depended on the former.

Formal Structure Prioritizes Some Interactions Over Others

Second, formal structures can affect the emergent relational aspects of roles by emphasizing some interactions over others. This occurs through two basic mechanisms of organization design—grouping and linking, which occur at all levels within organizations (Nadler and Tushman, 1997).

Grouping collects formal roles together within organizational unit boundaries, in order to manage interdependence among agents. Grouping can pull together roles involving similar activities (e.g. R&D), outputs produced (e.g. soaps and detergents division) or the kind of markets served (e.g. the emerging markets division) (Daft, 2001). The purpose of grouping is to prioritize integrative influence for interdependent agents (March and Simon, 1958; Thompson, 1967; Nadler and Tushman, 1997). For instance, grouping all individuals involved in product development is equivalent to prioritizing their interactions with each other over their interactions with individuals in other organizational groups (such as in marketing or manufacturing). Linking mechanisms specify vertical and horizontal interactions between (groupings of) roles. These include reporting and workflow-related relationships and mandated periodic communication. Grouping and linking mechanisms may often be reinforced by collocation, and interdependent rewards (Wageman, 1995).

By emphasizing some interactions over others, grouping and linking mechanisms can strongly influence the shape of the emergent informal structure. This is because the likelihood of informal tie formation between individuals increases with propinquity and the frequency of contact (Smith-Doerr and Powell, 2005). Thus, an employee formally assigned to a group to be coordinated by a common boss is more likely to build friendship and advice ties to others within the same group, than to individuals in other groups (also see Smith-Doerr and Powell, 2005: 384–5). While the reporting relationship was part of the mandated formal structure, the friendships are not; yet a correlation between the two exists.

Formal Structure Defines The Social Reference Group

Third, formal groupings and linking mechanisms are organizational structures with their own identifiable boundaries, and membership within such boundaries results in internalization of values, norms, and beliefs specific to that membership (Lawrence and Lorsch, 1967). As we noted in Chapter 2, there is a tendency for the goals of these reference groups to be internalized and preferred when they conflict with those of other groups and the organization at large. This group is also the one within which social comparisons processes operate and considerations of equity matter most strongly.

Following Schein (1985), if we think of organizational culture as shared beliefs acquired through learning, grouping provides the natural foci for the formation of sub-cultures. Thus, members of a product development unit may be socialized into an informal engineering subculture with its own values (e.g., technical novelty), beliefs (e.g., about the relative effectiveness of technical solutions) and norms (e.g., assisting colleagues with technical problems) as a consequence of their membership in a unit that engages in product development activity. Again these elements are correlated with, but not specified in the formal structure.

FORMAL STRUCTURE AS A NON-DETERMINISTIC INFLUENCE

These three mechanisms—namely i. influences on what experience can be accumulated, ii. where to seek interaction partners, and iii. which sub-group is the social reference group—link a choice of formal structure to an emergent informal structure. This is not to say that these effects of formal structure are deterministic. In Chapter 6, we have encountered the problem of control loss in hierarchies, which is but a particular manifestation of the general point that the behavior of agents deviates from that prescribed through formal authority in their organization. This can arise because of preference and/or cognitive misalignments which cannot be contractually mitigated (Williamson, 1991). Private interests and private understanding may limit the extent to which a designer's intentions are reflected in the behavior of the individuals who comprise the organization. Therefore, rather than assume that the relationship between formal and informal structure is all or nothing, I believe it is useful to think in terms of a *non-deterministic influence*.

Of all the things prescribed in the formal structure, many will not find a place in the realized structure; and others that exist in the realized structure may not be specified in the formal structure (though some may be indirectly influenced by it). Again, the regression analogy, in which the informal structure is the correlated error term in the regression of realized structure on formal structure, is worth keeping in mind.

Gerald Salancik gave an evocative analogy between organization designers and architects trying to predict pedestrian traffic on a university campus. "They [the architects] lay their cement, install fences and other obstacles, but inevitably the flows of people and classes carve bare spots in the grass where the sidewalks need to be." (Salancik, 1995: 347). The campus architect may not be able to stop students finding the shortest path through the grass, but can erect fences and build attractive paths with flower-beds on the side. These will neither deter the time-constrained sophomore who is willing to clamber over the fence, nor direct the distracted professor who has no eyes for anything around her. But many others will be more susceptible to these design influences, though none may order their entire behavior on campus in accordance with the architect's desires.

The non-deterministic influence that the formal structure may have on the informal structure may also take time to unfold. This is most evident when we consider re-organizations (Nickerson and Zenger, 2002; Gulati and Puranam, 2009). While the formal organization can be changed relatively rapidly, the informal organization may be subject to limits and lags in its adjustment to the new formal organization (Lamont and Williams, 1994; Miller and Friesen, 1984; Nickerson and Zenger, 2002). Prescribed roles may be changed instantaneously by administrative sanction, but the surrounding web of informal organizational elements that comes to be associated with the role may persist for some time.

For instance, as individuals adjust to the new formal organization in which they find themselves, pre-existing informal networks will weaken as individuals prioritize building new relationships rather than maintaining old ones. It takes time and effort for individuals to generate new social interactions, while existing ties are strengthened over time through familiarity and reciprocal commitments (Gargiulo and Benassi, 2000). This restricts the ability of individuals to quickly adapt their network of relationships to the mandates of the formal structure (Barley, 1990: 99; Kleinbaum and Stuart, 2014b: 42). Lags in the adjustment of the informal organization after a change in the formal structure can result in a reflection of past formal roles that lingers in the current formal organization. By its existence, such a residual effect makes individuals behave in a manner inconsistent with the current formal blueprint of organizational interactions (Staw and Boettger, 1990).

Culture (defined by a set of values, norms, and beliefs) changes through exposure to new organizational members and organizational tasks, but also not instantaneously (Becker and Geer, 1960; March, 1991). These gradual changes to the informal organization may be a consequence of the fact that the processes underlying the emergence of informal organization—socialization, tie-formation, learning, and preference transformation—are themselves gradual. The analogy between reorganizations and a thermostat switch that Nickerson and Zenger (2002) provide is an apt one—one can flick the switch instantaneously, but it takes time for the effects to be completely realized.

Reverse influence

An influence in the opposite direction of the informal structure on formal structure is also possible, in the sense that a designer might choose formal structure in recognition of her understanding of the informal structure (and the constraints that may create in terms of what formal structures are even worth attempting to institute). For instance, given a certain culture (e.g. an egalitarian one), it may be simply impossible to enforce certain formal structures (e.g. high formalization, or low delegation). The informal structure may also be a clue as to what the formal structure must look like. In Salancik's metaphor, if there appears a well-beaten track through the campus lawns, perhaps it signals the existence of a heavily used shortest path that the architect was formerly unaware of; but it can now be formalized with paving and signposts. At a minimum, one would take the existence of this path into account when adding new features to the campus terrain. This idea of the "reverse influence" of informal on formal structure is yet to be developed in detail in the study of organizational structure, but we have some useful clues from related literatures.

For instance, in the study of technology-driven mergers and acquisitions, Harbir Singh, Saikat Chaudhuri, and I (2009) found that technical interdependencies between acquirer and target technologies makes post-merger integration more likely, but pre-existing shared knowledge of the technologies offers acquirers an alternate informal path to achieving coordination, and so lowers the likelihood of integration. Another domain where this reverse influence relationship arises is that between contracts and informal governance arrangements in inter-firm relationships. Drawing on concepts such as substitution, complementarity and crowding out, scholars have variously argued for (and found evidence consistent with) both positive and negative relationships between trust and governance complexity. Bart Vanneste and I (Puranam and Vanneste, 2009) used a simple formalization to state the conditions under which one might expect a negative or a positive relationship between pre-existing trust and optimal governance complexity, and whether crowding out or complementarity arguments are necessary for such outcomes. In a related empirical paper (Vanneste and Puranam, 2010), we investigated how repeated interactions may both encourage and discourage reliance on complex formal contracts between parties, and the conditions under which each effect may prevail.

The realized structure and organizational influence

Ultimately, organizational performance does not depend on either the formal or informal structure, but the realized structure. What people actually do, whom they interact with, and to what extent these actions contribute towards the goal of the organization is what matters. The formal and informal structure matter to the extent they jointly shape the realized structure. They may do

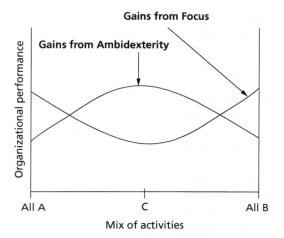

Figure 7.1 Interactions between activity-types and organizational performance

this in a manner that is consistent (i.e. both formal and informal structure shape employee behavior towards pursuit of the same goal) or inconsistent (i.e. pursuit of different goals). To illustrate, let's consider the case where there are only two distinct types of activity that the employees can undertake, A and B (see Figure 7.1). The realized structure produces a particular mix of these activities (the split between A- and B-type efforts). The formal and informal structures are consistent if they both push in the same direction (towards all A or all B); otherwise they are inconsistent.

Is consistency always good? (Conversely, is inconsistency always bad?) It has of course been well known since the work of Chester Barnard (1939: 169) that the informal organization can augment the formal organization by legitimizing its authority and enabling the performance of tasks that can be only partially specified through formal organizations (Child and McGrath, 2001). It therefore does seem intuitive that inconsistency detracts from internal fit between organizational elements. Internal fit refers to a pattern of reinforcing interactions between organizational elements such that one element enhances the impact on organizational performance of another element (Drazin and Van de Ven, 1985; Milgrom and Roberts, 1990; Van de Ven and Drazin, 1985).

Ranjay Gulati and I however argued against this assumption that reinforcing effects between organizational elements can only arise when they are consistent[3] (Gulati and Puranam, 2009). Organizational performance depends on the

---

[3] For instance, the "McKinsey 7S" is a popular practitioner framework that embodies the belief in the importance of the formal and informal organization being consistent with each other in motivating the same kind of employee behavior.

mix of activities that the employees engage in, *as well as* the manner in which performance depends on the mix of activities (see Figure 7.1). We can therefore distinguish two situations. First, consider the case when the performance of the organization is *higher* at point A or B than at any intermediate point between them. This arises because the two activity types have strong substitution effects (doing more of one activity *decreases* the marginal product of the other activity) between them so that the greater the extent of activity A, the less valuable it is to engage in activity B (and vice versa) (Milgrom and Roberts, 1990, 1995). We call this situation one in which there are "gains from focus."

In contrast, the second situation is one in which the performance of the organization is *lower* at points A and B than at any other point along the curve connecting A to B. This means that any combination of the two activities always dominates "pure A" or "pure B" type activity. This arises because the two activity types are strongly complementary (doing more of one activity *increases* the marginal product of the other activity), so that the greater the extent of activity A, the more valuable it is to engage in activity B (and vice versa) (Milgrom and Roberts, 1990, 1995). This is a situation of "gains from ambidexterity" (Tushman and O'Reilly, 1996). Thus the joint effects of formal and informal structure on organizational performance depend on the nature of the relationships between the activities supported by each—whether they are substitutes or complements.

Why formal structure is important even when it is imperfect

In order to design a formal organizational structure which enables successful collaboration between agents, a designer must understand the interdependences between agents which were created through the allocation of tasks. However, individuals differ in their ability to perceive such interdependences (Heath and Staudenmayer, 2000) and different task environments generate different levels of difficulty in developing such an understanding (Gavetti and Levinthal, 2000: 121). The designed structure is thus a hypothesis, at best, which may vary significantly in its accuracy.[4]

---

[4] In fact, limits on enforcement of the formal design imply that this hypothesis cannot typically be perfectly tested. The designer may have a structure in mind, but because the realized structure is likely to deviate, possibly in ways unknown to the designer, even learning from feedback to improve design is challenging. This problem occurs whenever a separation between beliefs and actions occurs: B imperfectly implements A's suggested actions based on A's beliefs. Is a poor outcome because of A's imperfect beliefs or B's imperfect execution of A's wise beliefs? While recognized in the context of strategy implementation (e.g. Lee and Puranam, 2015), this attribution problem also plays a role in the re-design of formal organizational structure.

If the formal structure is an imperfect hypothesis, and enforceable only imperfectly within limits and with lags, why is it of use to the organization designer? In keeping with the theme that organizations can be marvels without being miracles (also see Chapter 4), I outline some reasons why formal organization designs can be useful even if they are not particularly intelligent designs.

The first reason is that the comprehension of design requirements and implementation of the resulting design may both be far from perfect, but this does not mean they are useless. In fact, even if both design comprehension and implementation are poor, they may still be better than the alternative to designed formal structure: self-managed organization. This involves individuals in an organization themselves discovering how to interact and collaborate in order to accomplish the organization's goals, without guidance from a formal structure. Despite the periodic appearance of iconic examples of organizations that seem to succeed without (extensive) formal structure, they have yet to be shown to be broadly workable (e.g. Foss, 2003; Puranam and Hakkanson, 2015) (also see Chapter 8). I do not mean to imply here that they will never be found to be broadly viable; we simply do not know yet.

A subtler, and perhaps more interesting answer, is that the weaknesses of formal structure—limited comprehension of design criteria and imperfect enforcement—may interact to compensate for each other, or even produce surprisingly useful outcomes. This strand of thinking has been developed in a series of theory papers that I briefly describe below.

In one of the first formal treatments of the links between formal and informal structure, Nickerson and Zenger (2002) built a dynamic simulation model to explain why companies seem to undergo frequent reorganizations and move in a pendulum-like fashion between discrete organizational structures that embody centralization and decentralization respectively. Nickerson and Zenger's argument turns the limited enforceability of formal structure into a strength, because it produces continuousness of the informal organization: informal relationships and organizational culture may motivate a full range of behaviors and produce many combinations of organizational functionality, rather than emphasizing a unique ideal that discrete structures (such as functional or divisional groupings) point to. This continuous aspect of informal organization creates value by overcoming the discreteness of the more rigid formal structures. (They assume that realized structure is the same as informal structure.) By switching between discrete formal organizations, and allowing the informal organization to adjust gradually to these changes, the authors argue that discreteness can be overcome. The analogy is to discrete settings of a thermostat that nonetheless allow setting all possible intermediate temperatures. Thus lags in the influence of formal design on the informal organization can be useful, precisely because of the limits of being able to implement formal designs that are not discrete.

Ranjay Gulati and I (Gulati and Puranam, 2009) argued that reorganizations produce inconsistencies between formal and informal structure, and these can be the basis for the pursuit of "dualities"—jointly desirable, but organizationally incompatible objectives (Evans and Doz, 1989). Instances of dualities abound in the literature on organizations and strategy—exploration-exploitation, cost reduction-product differentiation, organizational differentiation-integration and static-dynamic efficiency, to note a few. Even when they are jointly desirable, the organizational attributes that underlie one pole of the duality are typically seen as being incompatible with those that underlie the other.

Inconsistencies can help solve the problem of organizational incompatibility and allow the pursuit of jointly desirable dualities when the resulting formal organization and the informal organization each emphasize opposing poles of a duality. We term this an instance of "compensatory" fit between the formal and informal organization, in which they compensate for each other by motivating dissimilar but jointly valuable employee behaviors. This is distinct from what one might call "supplementary fit," the more familiar instance of superior performance through the formal and informal organization emphasizing the same set of employee behaviors.

The informal structure can thus enhance the effectiveness of the formal structure either by supplementing it—in effect acting as "the last mile" that connects the formal structure to employee actions—or by compensating for it by motivating behaviors that are valuable but inadequately emphasized by the formal structure. We formalized this argument in a dynamic game between designers and employees, in which we treat the formal and informal structure symmetrically, and focus on how they jointly serve to adjust the mix of employee behaviors. In this model, the limits to enforcement of the formal structure can create a condition in which the formal and informal structure enable the pursuit of distinct activities both of which are necessary for organizational success.

Formal design and the search for structure: a micro-structural model

In both the Nickerson and Zenger, and Gulati and Puranam models, imperfect enforcement is shown to be useful in certain (different) conditions, but both assume the designer is in no doubt as to what the optimal structure is; the challenge only lies in not being able to implement it. These are typical execution problems (see Chapter 4). In a more recent project, Julien Clement and I have extended the analysis to a search problem. We considered the question of what (if any) the value of formal structure might be when the designer simply does not know (any better than random chance) what the optimal structure should be, in addition to being unable to enforce it perfectly (Clement and Puranam, 2016). Our analysis based on an agent-based computational model shows that a lightly enforced formal structure regenerates the network of interactions between agents who are searching for useful connections and learning which interactions to keep or discard, because in the absence of the formal structure, the network decays rapidly, leading to isolated agents.

While our model had networks of many agents, to see the intuition for the key results, consider a triadic micro-structure, where S is the organizational designer, and s_1 and s_2 are members of the organization. Let's simplify the designer's task down to a simple question: should s_1 and s_2 be connected by an integrative influence? (We can assume social interaction can provide this.) For the designer, this depends on whether he believes interdependence exists between these agents (i.e. the folk theorem). Let's say he is not sure, and thinks that the probability is q that an interdependence exists between them. Let the probability that s_1 and s_2 each attempt to interact with each other even in the absence of any formal structure be p. Interaction occurs only under the double coincidence of such attempts with probability $p^*p = p^2$. The question we investigated is should the designer attempt to enforce a formal structure that increases p even if q = 1/2?

Let's start by considering the possible outcomes in this situation: match or mismatch between social interaction and interdependence structure (see Table 7.1). There are two different kinds of match (Cases I and IV), which may generate two different payoffs: where both interaction and interdependence are jointly present or jointly absent. Mismatch can also occur in two ways (Cases II and III): forgone interaction when interdependence is present (an omission error) vs. the cost of interacting when no interdependence is present (a commission error). To keep things simple, let's assume that the opportunity costs are equal in magnitude to the benefit if realized, and that either kind of match provides the same benefit. This allows us to write all payoffs in terms of a single variable, w, signed appropriately. The expected value of this organization, obtained by taking the value of all four cells in Table 7.1 weighted by the probabilities is $(1-2p^2)(1-2q)w$. It then follows that to design a single period of interaction, it is a good idea for the designer to invest in increasing p

Table 7.1 The designer's perspective

	Interdependence present with probability q	Interdependence absent with probability 1–q
Interaction occurs with probability (p^*p)	Case I: Match (value = +w)	Case II: Mismatch (value = −w) (Commission error)
Interaction does not occur with probability $1-(p^*p)$	Case III: Mismatch (value = −w) (Omission error)	Case IV: Match (value = +w)

only if q>1/2, and to decrease p when q<1/2. If the designer's knowledge is no better than chance (q=1/2), he should do nothing.

Now suppose that this process unfolds over multiple periods, with the subordinates updating their respective values of p (now denoted $p_{i,t}$ where i denotes the subordinate) in response to feedback. Keeping with the behavioral assumptions outlined in Chapter 2, assume they increase the likelihood of their action taken (i.e. whether to attempt to interact, if they had interacted, or to avoid interacting if they had not interacted) if the payoff is positive, or else reduce it (i.e. the Law of Effect). Then, from the designer's perspective, it would be ideal if the subordinates could increase $p_{i,t}$ in Cases I and III, and decrease it in Cases II and IV.

The challenge however is that the subordinates typically only know their own choices and payoffs, not the state the dyad is in. From their perspective, the world appears as shown in Table 7.2. The possibility of misleading feedback exists. Consider for instance the case where a subordinate attempts to interact, and receives a payoff of −w. This could be either because the organization is in Case II or Case III. A decrease in $p_{i,t}$ by this subordinate is inevitable, but only helps the organization in Case II, and harms it in Case III. Conversely, if this subordinate received +w, the situation could be either Case I or Case IV. The subordinate will increase $p_{i,t}$, but this only helps the organization in Case I, and harms it in Case IV.

From the first subordinate's perspective, Cell B produces misleading feedback—false negatives and false positives—whereas from the second subordinate's perspective Cell C does the same. Therefore, moving both agents to Cell A or Cell D avoids misleading feedback. Clement and I showed that the superior, S, can play a useful role in this multi-period situation by coordinating the search of the subordinates even if S was maximally uncertain about the existence of an interdependence (q=1/2); a formal structure will increase the chances that both subordinates fall into Cell A or Cell D, and as long as it is not too strongly enforced (p is not too high or low), will allow them to learn rapidly from the feedback, which will be less likely to mislead.

Another way to express this intuition is that the formal structure can shift the error distribution in Table 7.1 towards commission errors (Case II), which the agents can then easily correct as it takes only one agent to break an

Table 7.2 The subordinate's perspective

	Subordinate 2 Attempts to interact	Subordinate 2 Does not attempt to interact
Subordinate 1 Attempts to Interact	Cell A: Interaction occurs Case I (+w) or Case II (−w)	Cell B: Interaction does not occur Case III (−w) or Case IV (+w)
Subordinate 1 Does not attempt to Interact	Cell C: Interaction does not occur Case III (−w) or Case IV (+w)	Cell D: Interaction does not occur Case III (−w) or Case IV (+w)

interaction; this is an improvement over a situation with omission errors (Case III), which takes both agents to correct. And the designer of the formal structure can accomplish this even when he has no idea if the structure is correct. What I want to emphasize here is the hurdle—however low—set by formal structure, that self-managed organizations must beat to replace formal structures in our organizational landscapes.

A way forward: the multiplex network approach

The links between formal and informal structure, and their implications for performance can be quite complicated. But without a representation to tackle these constructs jointly, it seems hard to see how we can make progress. An approach that seems promising is the multiplex network approach I first described in my work with Marlo Raveendran and Thorbjorn Knudsen (Puranam, Raveendran, and Knudsen, 2012). I think of it as the "sandwich" approach—in which we add a network layer above the realized structure—the formal structure; and a layer below it—the underlying task structure. We are thus dealing with at least three networks on the same set of agents. Studying the relationships across layers of this multiplex network allows us to give precise interpretations to concepts such as enforcement of formal structure, informal structure, the designer's architectural knowledge and organizational performance. To elaborate on these ideas, let's consider each layer of this multiplex "sandwich," and what overlap between layers mean.

INTERDEPENDENCE LAYER (T^T)

At the bottom of this three-layered multiplex network is the interdependence layer, which captures interdependencies between agents. In a world of imperfect decomposability and bounded rationality, it is inevitable that organizations often give different agents tasks which are interdependent, i.e. whose values affect one another. For instance, an agent's task may constitute the input to another agent's task, or two agents may work jointly on the same input. In Chapter 3, we described how T^t the m × m matrix of interdependence between m agents arises through the division of labor. In this matrix, if agent i is allocated a set of tasks whose value is affected by the tasks allocated to agent j, i is considered to be dependent on j in this task environment, and entry (i,j) is non-zero. The existence of this underlying interdependence layer is a matter of ontological realism: nobody needs to understand it, nor does it need to be constant over time (which makes it harder to understand), but its material consequences cannot be escaped.

INTERACTION LAYER (R)

The interaction layer captures the pattern of realized interactions between agents. These provide the integrative influences necessitated by interdependence (i.e. the folk theorem). We can represent the interaction structure as a symmetric m × m matrix R where cells filled with 0 indicate that two agents do not interact, while non-zero cells indicate interaction. An interaction can be a transfer of information or material. The information transfer can take the form of communication, command, being jointly commanded by common superior, advice, solutions to a problem, etc. Each of these can provide integrative influence. In specific applications, we may want to distinguish these forms of interaction.

FORMAL STRUCTURE LAYER (F)

In this multiplex network representation, we abstract from the multiplicity of antecedents and variants to formal structure, and model it through its consequences: a *mandated* pattern of interactions (i.e. integrative influences) between agents. We thus assume that ultimately all elements of the organizational structure that are mandated through formal authority, such as grouping decisions and linking mechanisms, reporting relationships, systems, incentives, allocation of design rights, locus of activities or even hiring decisions translate into a specified pattern of interactions. For instance, the designer may reduce the probability of interaction between two agents by placing them in different units or locations (Hansen, 1999; Doz, et al., 2001; Hinds and Kiesler, 2002), or by hiring agents whose personal traits are different enough to preclude homophily-based interaction (McPherson et al., 2001). That is, the formal structure encourages interactions between agents who are perceived by the designer to depend on each other and implicitly discourages interactions between those who are not

The formal structure can therefore be represented as a matrix F of dimensions m×m, with each cell containing either a zero (i.e. interaction is restricted) or a non-zero value (i.e. it is encouraged to varying degrees). It should be apparent that F is equivalent to the grouping structure in an organizational chart. To see this, consider that a clustering algorithm applied to F will produce clusters that then correspond to organizational units, where ties in clusters are within-unit ties, and bridging ties are committees or cross-functional teams. Differences and asymmetries in tie strength can represent authority and control relationships.

Assume we can construct a measure of similarity between any two matrices S{matrix1, matrix2} that is bounded between 0 and 1. When the matrices are binary, these can be the proportion of cells with identical entries; when the entries are continuous, pairwise Pearson correlations (e.g. Mollgaard et al.,

2016: 6) can be used. Given this measure, various constructs can be intuitively generated across the layers of this multiplex network.

The folk theorem—that interdependence requires integrative influence—tells us that *organizational performance* should be an increasing function of S $\{T^t, R\}$. If an organization is a system for aggregating the fruits of the division of labor, then managing interdependence between the divided tasks will naturally play a central role in achieving the goals of the organization. In aggregate, the performance of the organization increases with correspondence between the interdependence structure T^t and the interaction structure R. This is because interdependence creates a requirement for interactions (i.e. integrative influences) between agents (Thompson, 1967; Tushman and Nadler, 1978); conversely mismatches between the matrices T^t and R create a potential for coordination and/or cooperation failures (Puranam et al., 2012: 425).

As noted in Table 7.1, mismatches can arise either from omission errors—when an agent fails to interact with another agent whom it depends on (i.e. $T^t_{ij} = 1$ and $R_{ij} = 0$) or from commission errors, which arise when an agent interacts with another agent whom it does not depend on (i.e. $T^t_{ij} = 0$ and $R_{ij} = 1$). These errors need not have the same cost, and not even all commission (or omission) errors need to be equally costly (e.g. there may be a power law distribution whereby a few agents are extremely important to interact with while typical interactions yield only a small contribution to the focal agent).

The designer's *architectural knowledge*—knowledge of the underlying task structure (Baldwin and Clark, 2000; Henderson and Clark, 1990; von Hippel, 1990) should be correlated with S$\{T^t,F\}$. It must be reflected in the formal structure if the formal structure is designed to encourage interactions between agents who are perceived by the designer to depend on each other, and discourages interactions between those who are not. The extent of *enforcement* of the formal structure should be an increasing function of S$\{F,R\}$. Finally, the *informal structure* is R−F.[5]

The key empirical challenge to the application of the multiplex network formulation lies in the fact that T^t is rarely observable, and we may at best see a sub-set of R. However, this is in principle no different from the challenge faced by any theories of organization that invoke properties of the task environment as parameters, and observe some but not all organizational features. First, at least sometimes, we understand the task environment well enough because it is relatively stable and has been around for a while. Second, a weaker form of knowledge is in comparative terms across task environments; we may know that interdependence structures in some task environments are more or less decomposable, or that the relative costs of omission and commission errors vary systematically across them. Third, to the extent that performance-based

---

[5] Unlike F and R, the informal structure can have negative ties which produce no ties in R when combined with ties in F.

selection operates at either the individual or the organizational level, R is informative about T^t. As in Salancik's story, there may be a useful signal in where the paths through the grass lie.

Conclusion

Continuing to study informal structure in isolation is clearly not a useful way forward either for understanding how organizations work or designing organizations (McEvily et al., 2014; Hunter, 2015). This chapter offered three key ideas that may be useful in the more fruitful journey that combines both.

First, the informal structure can be understood as a correlated error term in the regression of realized structure on formal structure. It explains the discrepancy between the two, but is not independent of the formal structure. Second, I argued that the effect of the formal structure on the realized structure reflects a non-deterministic influence, and traced the mechanisms to properties of roles and how they interact. Third, I suggested that a joint analysis of the formal and informal structure can be accomplished using the multiplex network ("sandwich") formulation.

8 New forms of organizing

Novelty in forms of organizing is a topic of great interest to organizational scientists.[1] In fact, key milestones in the theoretical development of organization science can be linked to the arrival of innovative forms of organizing, which unleashed bursts of academic analysis and writing. We need only think back to the assembly line, the common stock company, the use of information technology in administration, the M-form, the transnational corporation, the matrix form, and today non-hierarchical, network forms of organization—and to the volumes of academic writing dedicated to each of these, and the careers built upon them.

Before we can turn to the sources of novelty in organizing, and the theoretical implications of this novelty, we must first agree on what it means. In this chapter, I give a definition of novelty in forms of organizing, discuss different kinds of novelty, and reflect on what this novelty means for our theories.

Novelty in forms of organizing

To understand novelty in organizing, I will rely on the Universal Problems of Organizing framework (see Chapter 1). Oliver Alexy, Markus Reitzig, and I (2014) argued that any functioning organization comprising goal-oriented agents must have solved two fundamental and interlinked problems: the division of labor and the integration of effort. The problem of division of labor is constituted of two related sub-problems: *task division* and *task allocation*. Integration of effort also involves solving two related sub-problems: *distributing rewards* (both monetary and non-monetary) and creating *information flows* that motivate and enable agents to execute and coordinate their actions. Since no set of solutions to these problems is likely to be either perfect or permanent, there must be in place some mechanism for re-solving these problems on an ongoing basis as exceptions arise.

A "form of organizing" is a set of solutions to these universal problems. An organization design is a specific sub-set of these solutions (Chapter 1). The reliance on formal authority to design the structure of tasks, allocate tasks, motivate, coordinate and manage exceptions is thus *a* form of organizing (and it is currently a widespread one). It follows that novelty in forms of organizing

---

[1] This chapter draws primarily on three articles: Puranam (2017), Puranam, Alexy, and Reitzig (2014), and Lee and Puranam (2015).

can only arise in the form of novel solutions to one or more of these problems. Put simply, **a new form of organizing solves the problems of division of labor and/or integration of effort in a novel manner.** But novel compared to what? While we need not insist that the standard of novelty of the solution requires it to be new to the world, there must be novelty relative to a comparison group.

We argued that to establish the comparison group, it is useful to consider organizations with comparable goals. Thus, one may observe a new form of organizing to contract out R&D services, to develop software, to develop video games or to generate encyclopedic content, but in each case the novelty can only be appreciated with respect to existing forms of organizing that aspire to the same goals. For this reason, we argued that the more similar the goals of two organizations, the more insightful will be a comparison of their under-lying forms of organizing. This also implies that comparisons of organizations which share similar goals at high levels of generality (e.g. "be profitable," or "survive") are less likely to be useful than a comparison featuring organiza-tions that share goals at high levels of specificity (e.g. "develop an operating system" or "provide encyclopedic content").

This way of thinking about novelty also implies that what we call a "form of organizing" is not necessarily the same as an "organizational form." The latter is used in the sociological literature on the processes by which audiences confer legitimacy on novel categories of organizations. An organizational form is treated as a bundle of attributes, and the presence or absence of these attributes influences the process of legitimation by the relevant audience (Hannan and Freeman, 1977; Hsu and Hannan, 2005). These features could also include the goals of the organization, and indeed in empirical practice that is how organizational forms are often distinguished. The conception of an organizational form is primarily in terms of an object of social evaluation; how the organization works is of secondary, if any, importance. When assessing novelty in organizational forms, the goals are not necessarily held constant; in contrast assessing novelty in forms of organizing would be impossible without holding the goals constant.

New forms of organizing may or may not involve new organizational forms. To take one instance, a plethora of new organizational forms emerged in response to a change towards market-based logics in the U.S. financial sector, as documented by Lounsbury (2002). While these differed in their business models, they did not seem to display novelty in forms of organizing. Con-versely, if the novelty within new forms of organizing remains invisible to the audience of evaluators, then it may not qualify as a new organizational form (Hsu and Hannan, 2005).

Below, I consider instances of novelty in terms of each of the universal problems of organizing. I take as the baseline category a hypothetical "trad-itional" form of organizing, in which authority plays a key role in task division, task allocation, and exception management; monetary rewards are the primary

Table 8.1 Novelty in forms of organizing

Universal problems of Organizing	Forms of Organizing	
	Traditional forms	Possible novel forms
Task division	Organization designer selects structure of tasks; only visible to (selected) members of firm	Emergent through self-selection; transparently visible to everyone
Task allocation	By authoritative superior, primarily on skill-match	Self-selection
Reward distribution	Salaries and bonuses as determined by the authoritative superior; combination of extrinsic incentives and monitoring	Use needs; intrinsic motivation; managing excludability
Information flows	Documentation, physical collocation and grouping, mediated by authoritative coordinator	Virtual collaboration infrastructure; task modularization
Exception management	Based on formal authority resulting from employment contracts	Based on informal authority; slack; self-governance norms

means of motivating effort, and information exchange between agents when needed can occur face-to-face. This is admittedly a caricature of a physically collocated formal authority-based organization, closer in spirit to the factory shop floor than a Fortune 500 boardroom or consulting or coding team. However, it serves as a useful common baseline against which to compare different forms of novelty in organizing (see Table 8.1 for an overview).

I should also note that my consideration of examples below is not meant to be comprehensive, but rather to be illustrative. It samples heavily from the research on open source communities—such as Linux or Wikipedia, problem-solving contests such as those organized by Top Coder or Innocentive (Harhoff and Lakhani, 2016)—and "boss-less" organizations such as W. L. Gore and Valve (Puranam and Hakkanson, 2015). These have dominated researchers' attention at the time of writing. However, I believe the basic approach to thinking about novelty we proposed will survive turnover in this crop of iconic examples.

NOVELTY IN TASK ALLOCATION

Across a range of sectors and industries, formal organizations tend to feature task allocation by an authoritative superior. While individuals may apply for roles, once they get the job, in most organizations the boss assigns them tasks. Indeed, classic conceptions of the employment relationship assumed employee indifference to a set of tasks, from among which the superior could select what the employee must accomplish in return for a salary (Simon, 1951). In contrast, self-selection into tasks is a feature of novelty in many new forms of organizing. Open source software development (von Hippel and von Krogh, 2003), boss-less organizations (Puranam and Hakkanson, 2015), holacracies (Roberston, 2015) and problem-solving contests (Jeppesen and Lakhani, 2010) all incorporate this element, at least to some degree.

Situations where individuals select from a menu of options are of course staple fare in any theory of decision-making, so by itself it may not seem to point to any theoretically interesting form of novelty. However, the criteria by which individuals choose tasks when self-selecting have consequences for organization design. The criteria include skill-match, the fulfillment of use-needs, intrinsic motivation and extrinsic motivation (including status and responsibility) (Shah, 2006; von Hippel and von Krogh, 2003). This in turn potentially impacts the solution of other universal problems.

First, reward distribution is affected. Traditional systems of compensation weigh heavily, if not exclusively, on extrinsic motivators. As I noted in Chapter 2, organizations have goals, which may or may not correspond to the ultimate goals of their constituent individuals. In the traditional organization, a degree of sacrifice of discretion regarding task selection is a condition for membership (Simon, 1957). This is because the tasks assigned to individuals in traditional forms may not generate much intrinsic motivation. When they do not, extrinsic motivators—such as cash, status, power and promotion opportunities—will be particularly important. The greater the difference between organizational and individual goals, the greater the need to rely on extrinsic motivators. But conversely, if individuals can gain intrinsic motivation through self-selection into tasks, then the need for extrinsic motivators should decline. Under the right self-selection regime, one may see people do for free what they would only do for a fee under the shadow of authority in the traditional form of organizing.

Second, because task allocation is not centralized, exceptions in the form of both under- and over-provision of effort for critical tasks may arise. Key but mundane tasks for the organization may remain undone, and others may attract too much interest (e.g. Shah, 2008). Thus, some system for managing these exceptions—whether based on authority, slack, specific "residual claimant" roles who take on tasks left undone by others, or commonly shared norms—is still essential.

Third, to strike an optimistic note, self-selection may also make the emergence of stable norms of self-governance easier. When all the participants in an organization are aware that all other participants are there by choice too, and possibly attracted by similar ideologies and goals, reaching and enforcing agreements could in general be easier.

NOVELTY IN REWARD DISTRIBUTION

I have already noted above the alternatives to material compensation that can arise through self-selection into tasks. That is of course a major type of novelty relative to the traditional form. Here, I focus on another aspect of novelty in reward distribution—how the problem of excludability is solved (e.g. Ostrom, 2005). Traditional systems of compensation entail the distribution of a portion of organizational output (e.g. salary) as an inducement to individuals to ensure continued contribution. Such a system implicitly assumes that non-contributors can be excluded from sharing in these inducements. However, the reward distribution rule in some novel forms of organizing, such as open source software development (von Hippel and von Krogh, 2003) is very different—anyone can benefit from the achievement of the goals of the organization without even having to be a member of the organization. This particular reward distribution rule is well known to create the hazard of free-riding for rational self-interested agents.

The potential for free-riding exists in any situation where an individual can benefit by withholding contribution, given that others are contributing. (To use the terminology developed in Chapter 4, the valence of interdependence in such situations is negative.) The contribution can take the form either of abstention from consumption or investment in production. The tragedy of the commons is an instance of excessive consumption of a rivalrous, non-excludable good (Hardin, 1968); whereas under provision of a public good (i.e. a non-rivalrous non-excludable good)—is an instance of free-riding in terms of inadequate investment (Olson, 1971). How reward distribution can work in the absence of excludability therefore appears to be the key theoretical issue here.

The challenge of excludability is not limited to open source projects. Other public goods that exist despite the absence of mandated contribution include blood banks (Titmuss, 1970), enrolment in the army, and more generally charitable and voluntary service organizations. Elinor Ostrom (2005) has documented the sustainable existence of common pool natural resources (which like public goods feature low excludability, but unlike public goods, are rivalrous in use).

The mechanisms whereby the free-rider problem is effectively suppressed or mitigated in these situations are well known. These include social norms that encourage contributions and sanction non-contribution to a public good (e.g., Ostrom, 1990); the creation of what are termed Coasean islands—institutions in which the transaction costs of monitoring and selecting trustworthy contributors are reduced sufficiently for the potential beneficiaries of a public good to be able to pool their efforts effectively (Coase, 1960); and the existence of privileged groups that value the public good highly enough to contribute regardless of the (non-) contributions of others (Olson, 1971).

These mechanisms seem also in evidence in novel forms of organizing such as open source projects: social norms that govern fair contribution have been documented by O'Mahony (2003), Lee and Cole (2003), and Shah (2006), and noted by the founder of Wikipedia (TEDGlobal, 2005). Online platforms such as GitHub, SourceForge or Wikipedia represent Coasean islands; and founders and contributors to such projects represent privileged group members who gain sufficiently from their own user-needs and motivation to initiate and contribute to a project irrespective of whether others do so (Raymond, 1999; von Hippel and von Krogh, 2003).

NOVELTY IN INFORMATION PROVISION

Distributed work has now become so commonplace, that it no longer seems to merit inclusion in the category of novelty in forms of organizing. (In fact, "radical collocation" briefly became a slogan in the early 2000s as a novel form of organizing software development!) As we know from an extensive literature on distributed work, when *face-to-face* communication channels are unavailable, the burden shifts to one of two other mechanisms: creating and leveraging *common ground*—knowledge that is shared and known to be shared—to enable coordination of activities, and to creating a *modular task architecture* that enables different individuals to work in parallel without need for having to explicitly coordinate their actions (Hinds and Kiesler, 2002; Srikanth and Puranam, 2011, 2013).

In problem-solving contests, the specification of the task architecture is meant to stimulate as many independent efforts at providing solutions as possible, so that the need for information sharing across solution providers is rare. Modular task architectures are also important in open source communities though self-selection by contributors into tasks within the system may make it hard to fully maintain independence of action across them. The creation of common ground in such systems is known to rely on many of the same collaborative technologies as seen in other forms of organizing distributed work—including the use of email, bulletin boards and version control software (e.g., Lee and Cole, 2003; Raymond, 1999; Shah, 2006)—as are seen for instance in offshore software development (Srikanth and Puranam, 2011, 2013).

It is also true in communities producing software or other publicly visible information that the final product—the software or the online encyclopaedia—is its own representation. To the extent the code or content (and changes to it) are commonly visible and become a part of common ground, coordination across different agents contributing to it becomes easier.

NOVELTY IN TASK DIVISION

In general, there will be many ways to conduct task division, but a common heuristic approach is to think in terms of either activity-based or object-based task division (see Chapter 3). Tasks can be clustered based on how similar they are in how they transform inputs into outputs, leading to an *"activity"*-based division of labor. Activity-based task division enables specialization (Smith, 1776; Simon, 1962: 102). Alternately, tasks can be divided up and clustered in terms of distinctive intermediate objects they generate, leading to an *"object"*-based division of labor. Intermediate objects exist and have some value independent of each other. Primarily, object-based division of labor creates advantages through allowing more attention on the dependencies between the distinct tasks needed to produce an object (i.e. customization).

Novelty in task division may arise from the use of new criteria besides the gains from specialization or customization. One such is the ease of measurement. A division of labor that allows for easy measurement of task outputs may lower measurement costs (Barzel, 1982) and enhance *accountability*, enabling the use of sharp incentives that link rewards to outputs (Zenger and Hesterly, 1997). When individuals self-select into tasks (rather than be assigned to tasks by a hierarchical superior) then *transparency* of the task architecture may be another criterion for task division. As Carliss Baldwin and her colleagues have argued, in open source software development, a task division that is transparent—(i.e. makes visible as fine-grained a task structure as possible) allows potential contributors to select specific tasks so as to participate based on their personal skills and motivations, which increases the likelihood of them choosing to contribute instead of free-riding (e.g., Baldwin and Clark, 2006; Colfer and Baldwin, 2010; MacCormack et al., 2006, 2011). At least in theory, the criteria of measurability or transparency may run counter to that of enhancing gains from specialization or customization.

Task allocation and division may go hand in hand, when individuals simultaneously "carve out" a piece of work as well as allocate it to themselves (e.g. in an open source project where code architecture is fluid). In this case, the order of entry of contributing individuals into the system, and their skill and preference distribution will have significant implications for the nature of division of labor. These have yet to be investigated.

NOVELTY IN THE USE OF AUTHORITY

Corporate leaders around the world today are likely to be uncomfortable with words like "authority" or "hierarchical" when speaking of their organizations, even though their organizations very likely are formal authority hierarchies. In Chapters 5 and 6, I gave some reasons for this uneasy relationship with perhaps our most impressive organizational innovation, including some speculations on the evolutionary historical roots of our discomfort. Here I want to focus on the more prosaic question—what substitutes for formal authority?

Informal authority as an alternative to formal authority as a basis for organizing is of course quite well known. This could be based on expertise, reputation and status as well as bargaining power. It can result in stratified organizations even without any formal authority at work (Gulati, Puranam, and Tushman, 2012), though in the absence of delegation, it is less clear if multi-layered hierarchies of informal authority can develop.

Accounts of open-source projects demonstrate the exercise of authority by the project's founders in a number of ways (Raymond, 1999). In some open source collaborative platforms like Source Forge or GitHub, some exclusive founders' rights are even embedded into the project management software in use. Specifically, founders have the authority to assign certain project work to members of the project, accept or reject contributions, or to delegate this power to other members of the project. This authority differs from that seen in conventional business contexts in that it is not based on formal contracts, and lays a greater emphasis on the right to accept or reject contributions and claims of membership (Dahlander and O'Mahony, 2011)—rather than the right to direct an employee within a zone of indifference (Simon, 1951).

Norms of self-governance are a qualitatively distinct substitute for formal authority. Rules for resolving disputes or imposing sanctions based on voting or other forms of consensus—unless backed up by formal authority for enforcing such rules—are ultimately peer-to-peer in nature. Their spontaneous emergence cannot be taken for granted, nor are they always robust and self-reinforcing (Ostrom, 1990, 2005). Yet they do occasionally arise and seem stable from time to time, as Ostrom documented in her studies of common property resource management systems. Wikipedia's dispute resolution system based on voting is in this spirit. Page deletions (because of redundancy or poor quality) are voted on by contributors.[2] However, even this is tempered by the exercise of some degree of authority by the founder and the governing body. First, not all votes are weighted identically, as some contributors are seen as domain experts, and second, the founder can in principle step in to overrule a vote if he thinks the voting process has been "captured" by organized vested interests (TEDGlobal, 2005).

Holacracies (Robertson, 2015) are not truly non-hierarchical.[3] What is genuinely different about them is sometimes hard to see, in part because of the thicket of terminology that can be found in the publicly available documentation. But there are certain unique ways in which holacracies distribute

---

[2] Valve Corporation, a maker of video games, has become famous for having no bosses, and letting employees choose which project to join (and exit) whenever they like. It is believed that disagreements within project teams, if unable to be settled within the team, escalate laterally to members of other teams. The possibly adverse consequences to reputation (and therefore to the likelihood of participating in future projects) may thus act as a source of pressure against adopting unreasonable positions, and may thus serve as a dispute resolution mechanism (Puranam and Hakkanson, 2015).

[3] I point this out to students by showing them the usual representation of a holacracy—a series of concentric circles—and then asking what a traditional hierarchy would look like if we replaced the boxes with spheres, and looked down from above.

and delegate authority, which does make them different from traditional hierarchies. Holacracies appear to differ from traditional authority hierarchies on two key dimensions. First, there is a separation of authority into design and direction rights (vested in "Link leaders") and dispute resolution rights (vested in "Facilitators"). In Chapter 5, I discussed design, direction and dispute resolution as the fundamental functions of authority, and in many settings the three are bundled into a single role. In holacracies, these have been unbundled.

Second, design and direction rights flow from top to bottom as in a traditional hierarchy (flowing from the "anchor circle"—top layer—and the "lead link" of this circle appointed by the "ratifiers" of the constitution), but the right to resolve disputes within each circle is bestowed upwards on elected representatives. A third feature, which does not pertain to authority per se, is also worth mentioning: in traditional hierarchies, the boss is often a key information link between lower and higher layers. In holacracies, this is not necessarily the case, with elected representatives from lower circles participating in the higher circles. These changes serve to attenuate the directive authority which cascades from above (effectively increasing delegation), while enhancing the legitimacy of authority for dispute resolution (as it is bestowed from below). Or at least such is the claim made for holacracies, which remains to be robustly demonstrated at the time of writing.

Table 8.1 summarizes the aspects of novelty by each of the dimensions of the universal problems of organizing. A meta-theme that is visible in this table is that novel forms today implicitly or explicitly seem to avoid reliance on formal authority. As I noted in Chapter 6, authority hierarchies exist in tension with basic human preferences for egalitarianism, autonomy and task variety. One can summarize many of the experiments with new forms of organizing over the last few decades as the leveraging of information technologies to lower reliance on formal authority as an organizing principle.

The origins of novelty in organizing

Designing (or re-designing) anything, not just an organization, is a problem-solving activity driven by the gap between the current and the desired goal states (Simon, 1996: 111). Human problem-solving is a search process through a problem space (Newell and Simon, 1972). Each point in such a space is a possible solution, and better and worse solutions exist (also see reviews by Dunbar, 1998; Fischer et al., 2012). It is often assumed that organization design problems, like many managerial problems, are ill-defined (Rittel and Webber, 1973; Mintzberg, 1979; Cross, 2001).

However, as researchers now realize, the problem space for design problems in any domain is rarely completely free of structure (Goel and Pirolli, 1992). In the case of organization design, the deep structure of the problem space is defined by task division and allocation; reward distribution and information-provision, and finally the handling of exceptions arising from imperfect solutions to these. Designing an organization is the search for solutions in this problem space (Puranam et al., 2014).

Like many design spaces, the dimensions are very likely correlated in the case of organization design. Organizational research has many insightful and impactful papers on commonly occurring clusters of organizational attributes. Configuration theory (e.g., Doty, Glick, and Huber, 1993; Fiss, 2007; Meyer, Tsui, and Hinings, 1993) is an important instance, as are theories of adaptation on rugged landscapes (e.g., Levinthal, 1997) or complementarities between choices (e.g., Milgrom and Roberts, 1990, 1995). Such configurational approaches to organizations emphasize "commonly occurring clusters of attributes of organizational strategies, structures, and processes" (Ketchen, Thomas, and Snow, 1993: 1278). The occurrence of such clusters points to underlying complementarities in choices along different dimensions.

In the context of the universal problems of organizing, a pair of solutions to these problems are complements when adopting one increases the value of the other (Milgrom and Roberts, 1990, 1995). For instance, if the solution to task allocation relies on self-selection, then a solution to reward provision that relies on intrinsic motivation may be more valuable than one which does not; in this case, we would say that self-selection into tasks and intrinsic motivational rewards are complements in the resulting form of organizing. Thus, forms of organizing in which both solutions occur should be relatively more common than by chance.[4]

The implication of the existence of complementarities in the search space for the process of search can be derived from the large body of results that exist today from formal models about the process of search in such problem spaces (e.g., Levinthal, 1997 and the many papers on search on NK-landscapes that have since followed in the leading management journals). The key insights from the analysis of such models that are relevant for us are these: a) because of complementarities between choices on the solution dimensions, there are likely to be many local peaks; b) for the search process to avoid entrapment on a local peak, it must feature mechanisms for both expanding search efforts beyond the immediate neighborhood (exploration) as well as preserving a good solution (exploitation); c) complementarities in the search space (i.e., the degree of ruggedness of the landscape) influence the relative importance of

---

[4] For a Boolean qualitative comparative analysis of the co-occurrence of solutions in novel forms of organizing, see Alexy, Puranam, and Reitzig (2017).

these mechanisms (Rivkin and Siggelkow, 2003, 2007; Siggelkow and Levinthal, 2003; Siggelkow and Rivkin, 2005).

We would thus expect the process of search for new forms of organizing to stabilize around clusters of complementary solutions. The discovery of radically new forms of organizing (i.e. not just new to the comparison set, but new to the world—for instance the creation of the employment contract, the M-form, or online communities) should be a rare event triggered by organizations and individuals with strong incentives to explore, or due to changes in the landscape itself. Selection through competition among variations provided by unintentional experimentation may also throw up working solutions, with little or no foresight involved (Hodgson and Knudsen, 2010).

Of course, the bar for novelty need not be set this high, as we have argued. Novelty relative to peer organizations that share the same goals may also be achieved more frequently through imitation from outside the peer group. For instance, there seems little doubt that open source communities inspired the internal design of Valve Corporation. This borrowing by analogy from other domains (Gavetti, 2005) may well be the most common source of novelty in forms of organizing. At the same time, complementarities among solutions also should make it harder to imitate piecemeal the clusters of solutions that individual peaks—i.e. complementary solutions to the fundamental problems of organizing—represent (Rivkin, 2000). Either the entire form of organizing must be copied, or none at all.

This may explain why many of the novel forms of organizing tend to be greenfield attempts, rather than brownfield conversions of one form into another. A particularly well-documented attempt at novelty in a brownfield context is the case of the Danish hearing aids producer, Oticon (O'Keefe and Lovas, 2002). In response to poor performance, a dramatic attempt at organizational change was made in 1987. The company moved from a traditional form to one that relied heavily on self-selection into tasks (Lovas and Ghoshal, 2000). This restructuring has since received much attention and is often referred to as the "spaghetti" reorganization. Yet in a few years the system was apparently wound down and the traditional form re-instated (Foss, 2003).[5]

In sum, novelty in organizing may typically be the result of imitation, and less often, the discovery of fundamentally new clusters of solutions to the unchanging universal problems of organizing.

---

[5] The architect of these changes, then-CEO Lars Kolind, wrote an intriguing commentary on newer experiments of this sort at Valve (Puranam and Hakonnson, 2015).

Conclusion

Using the universal problems of organizing as a basic framework helps to expose novelty in forms of organizing in a precise manner. An important corollary is that even if a form of organizing is justifiably novel relative to the comparison group of organizations, it may well be that existing theory provides a sound basis for understanding much of this novelty, because the solutions are rarely novel to the world. For instance, I have described instances above of novelty in terms of a) task allocation through self-selection, b) reward distribution through intrinsic motivation and use needs as a solution to the excludability problem, c) information provision via modularity and common ground, d) task division based on transparency of task structures and self-selection, and e) exception management based on informal authority and norms of self-governance. Taking each by itself, it would be hard to argue that any of these mechanisms are theoretical novelties. However, there is undeniable novelty in a form of organizing even if it is but a new bundle of old solutions.

The implication is simple: the bar for novelty in organizing is significantly lower than the bar for theoretical novelty. Every new form of organizing that appears on our horizon need not lead us in fruitful quest for new theories of organizing. Rather, useful avenues for new theory development may lie in understanding the complementarities between the solutions to the problems of organizing that these new forms of organizing embody, rather than at the level of any particular solution (to one of the universal problems of organizing) itself.

9 Methodologies for microstructures

Any methodology aimed at understanding complex phenomena must necessarily rely on abstractions. The micro-structural approach to organization design employs a style of abstraction in which complex organizations are understood in terms of simpler, recurring organizational patterns. How we apply the typical research methodologies we use in the organizational sciences—statistical analysis, experiments, inductive studies and formal models—for studying organizations using the micro-structural approach, in part depends on this style of abstraction, and in part is due to the nature of the methodologies themselves. Reflections on these topics are the theme of this concluding chapter.[1]

I should begin with a disclaimer though: I do not profess to be a specialist in any particular methodology, and in fact have been embarrassingly promiscuous in my choice of methods for my research. The only excuse I can offer is the engineering sensibility of picking the tool for the problem, rather than the other way around. This lack of specialization has certainly not made me an authority on any one of these methods, but has taught me (as one colleague put it) "enough to be dangerous in many ways." It has also made the review process harder for some of my projects than it would have been for a specialist, showing that the danger may have been first and foremost to myself. These notes on methodology should therefore be seen as observations from a nonspecialist user, rather than a specialist of methodology.

Analyzing large samples of naturally occurring data

A single large organization may provide data on myriad micro-organizations. The microstructural approach is thus readily allied with traditional large-sample statistical techniques, albeit with smaller units of analysis (and possibly a greater need for considerations of representativeness). On the positive side, the ability to sample multiple organizational micro-units from the same macro-unit allows for a degree of control on contextual factors that may not

---

[1] This chapter draws on Puranam (2017).

otherwise be possible in organizational analysis. On the negative side, organizations seldom archive data conveniently on the micro-structures that they are composed of. Indeed, researchers succeed to a large extent in our field by finding ingenious ways to infer internal organizational constructs from archival sources not set up with that objective in mind (e.g. Karim, 2006, 2007; Karim and Williams, 2012; Gaba and Joseph, 2014; Joseph, Klingebiel, and Wilson, 2016; Aggarwal and Wu, 2012).

It is not inherently necessary that large samples be composed of archival data. Yet the costs and feasibility constraints of collecting primary data often direct us towards working with readily available archival data, particularly if it is available for many cases. This is still the modal type of measurement for researchers in organizations and strategy. It is the approach I was primarily taught as a doctoral student, and I was fortunate to have had the best in the field doing the teaching.

However, the review process swiftly brought home to me the limits of this kind of data for the kinds of questions I was interested in (that transcended my own possibly inept application of the methods). The difficulty of tying measures collected for an entirely different purpose to a theoretical construct of interest was the most obvious one. As somebody interested in understanding how organizations work, I had no illusions that finding plausible archival measures for the constructs I cared about—such as authority, coordination, cooperation, division of labor, the shape of hierarchies—would be easy. Less obvious (to me) was the realization that archival data was not necessarily more objective than primary data gathered by survey respondents. Once I learnt how commercially available databases often used by corporate strategists are put together, it was hard to retain my earlier degree of confidence in their objectivity. Similar deconstructive exercises have now taken their place in the domain of patenting data, to the discomfort of scholars relying extensively on such data to test ideas about knowledge flows.

Primary data collected through surveys offer, in theory, a means to measure more precisely the organizational constructs that matter to us, which are often perceptual. While some reviewers raised questions about the objectivity of such measurement, I did not see this as a major stumbling block, because a) the constructs we often care about are perceptual, b) we have a very sophisticated body of work on psychometric measurement to draw on to enhance reliability and validity of measurement, and c) the objectivity of many archival data sources I noted above is illusory. However, low response rates and the problem of common method bias are formidable obstacles (and these can interact—effective response rates are even lower when you need the independent and dependent variable to be provided by different sets of respondents). The latter problem is particularly relevant for organizational design scholars, because our theories tend to have dependent *and* independent variables that are hard to measure from archival sources.

Table 9.1 Empirical research strategies

	No Randomization	Randomization
Controlled manipulation	Quasi-experiment	Experimental design
Non-controlled (by researcher or subjects) manipulation	Quasi-(natural) experiment	Natural experiment
No manipulation	Observational study	*(Undefined)*

I believe the costs of collecting large samples of primary data (in the sense of collected for the purpose at hand, not necessarily through survey instruments) are now falling dramatically through access to so-called "big data." The label is a misnomer in some ways, because it is not the size per se, but the fine-grained nature of behavioral observation that makes big data so "big." Communication patterns as captured in email traffic, opinions as expressed on social media, and attitude as measured through the analysis of semantic units of text offer very promising avenues. Being proficient with the technologies that allow access to and manipulation of such data is likely to swiftly become central to doctoral training in the organizational sciences.

The other set of issues that confront those using large samples of naturally occurring data do with the challenge of causal inference (see Table 9.1). By definition, naturally occurring data are not obtained through experimental design. Studying organization designs is particularly challenging in this regard, as designs are extremely unlikely to be randomly assigned. Being aware of this limitation is valuable; being apologetic about it is not.[2]

THE ROLE OF CAUSAL INFERENCE IN ORGANIZATION SCIENCE

I take it as a premise that **the goal of the scientific process is to discover the causal mechanisms underlying phenomena of interest**. Therefore, little debate is needed about whether causal inference is desirable for this goal; by definition, it is. However, the statement above is sometimes incorrectly taken to imply two other statements. These are:

The fallacy of necessity: the belief that every step of the scientific process involves causal inferences. It does not. Other crucial steps, none of which involve causal inference include observation and documentation of pattern; induction, abductive theorizing, abstraction and generalization; and deduction of testable implications. The fallacy of necessity leads to the undervaluation of inductive and theoretical contributions, as well as of empirical contributions that do not involve causal inference.

---

[2] This section draws on my keynote speech to the Asian Management Research Consortium in 2016 titled "Causal inference: necessary, sufficient or irrelevant?"

The fallacy of sufficiency: the belief that establishing the causal effect of A on B is sufficient to establish scientific progress. It is not. Without enhancing knowledge on the underlying mechanism, or unless the effect itself is novel, there is no scientific progress, by definition. Instances of causal inference that do not constitute scientific progress would include establishing the causal effects of treatments that could be operating through multiple known mechanisms, without being able to tell which ones are operating. Of course, even when causal inference does not generate scientific progress, it may still be of use to decision-makers to know that a given treatment reliably produces an outcome (even though "how" remains a mystery).

The fallacy of sufficiency is not a problem arising from the mechanisms being too "obvious" or "not novel enough." Non-obviousness is a subjective property; what is not-obvious to me may be brutally obvious to you. Second, replication always has benefits in science (though naturally, there are diminishing marginal returns). Rather, the problem is typically about a lack of clarity about which among several possible mechanisms is operating, not replication beyond the point at which the benefits exceeds the costs (this is rare in our field).

The fallacy of sufficiency leads to an overvaluation of contribution for research involving causal inference which does not clarify which among several known underlying mechanisms could be operating. In the absence of auxiliary evidence and arguments for how the test enhanced our knowledge about underlying mechanisms (either by confirmation, refutation, or discovery— which is the rare case of documenting a pattern of causal effect with no known mechanism), there may in fact be no contribution at all.

There is a third problem, which is qualitatively different from the first two: it is not a logical fallacy about the role of causal inference in scientific progress (which I have argued above, is neither necessary nor sufficient; but of course, that does not mean it is irrelevant). Rather it springs from a belief that researchers can make causal inferences when they are not able to do so. It may simply be a form of overconfidence based on ignorance. I am tempted to call this "(far too) *casual* inference."

The fact is that if we are not operating with large samples of data involving randomized assignment into control and standardized treatment groups, our inference is unlikely to be causal. (Even if we are, the guarantee of causal inference is typically in a statistical sense i.e. consistency.) It does not matter whether what we are doing involves control variables, fixed effects, differences-in-differences, instrumental variables (unless based on shocks), matching (based on propensity or coarsened exact), regression discontinuity or quasi-experiments (i.e. non-randomly assigned shocks). If it is not data from an experiment with random assignment, then there is no guarantee of casual inference. In many cases, it is very hard to even tell conclusively which one of the above is more likely to get us closer to causal inference. The reason is that each one of these methods yields consistent estimates only under certain assumptions, at least some of which can never be verified (e.g. the exogeneity of instruments; that matching on observables produces sufficient comparability; that there are no undetectable non-linearities of functional form around the discontinuity, parallel trends as the counterfactual, etc.).

Note that I am not making a call for all of us to abandon these methods and only do experiments with randomized assignment; that is nothing but the fallacy of necessity all over again. I am simply pointing out that the methods above do not guarantee causal inference (which as I have said is neither necessary nor sufficient to advance science).

I believe the so-called "identification revolution" has done a lot of good to help mitigate this overconfidence bias. But it may also have done some harm, in generating the mistaken belief that causal inference is necessary and sufficient for an academic publication, coupled with overconfidence about what statistical methods can do with naturally occurring data by way of causal inference. More worryingly, it may also be crowding out the skills needed for the detective work that go into what I call, for lack of a better term, the method of raising the improbability of alternative explanations.

This method involves conducting a series of cleverly chosen correlational tests. It exploits the idea that the probability that alternative mechanisms exist that make the same set of widely different predictions derived from the hypothesized mechanism declines with the number of predictions and how different they are from each other (also see Lave and March, 1975; and Shadish, Cook, and Campbell, 2002: 105 on "coherent pattern matching"). Durkheim's classic analysis of suicide is a great illustration of this method. While alternate explanations may be found for each piece of evidence Durkheim produces, it is very hard to think of a single alternate explanation that explains all his diverse examples.

Where does this leave us? As authors, if we are not doing causal inference, I believe we should not feel diffident and undersell our contributions. Naturally occurring data has the unique virtue of being, to put it simply, natural. To the extent the scientific enterprise is about explaining what occurs in nature, this must have primacy. On the other hand, if we think we are doing causal inference, we should guard against the fallacy of sufficiency, and the tendency to be overconfident that we can make causal claims. As reviewers, we should not make the fallacy of necessity. Nor should we be taken in by authors who are themselves the victims of the fallacy of sufficiency or the mistaken belief that they have achieved causal inference with non-experimental data. I suggest we should aspire to be generous in accepting modest claims, and ruthless in destroying inflated ones.

Formal models

There are many appealing features (including aesthetic ones) of formal models—in which the mechanisms in a theory are described in formal languages rather than in natural languages. As Hernes (1979) puts it: "Models are to social sciences what metaphors are to poetry—the very heart of the matter" (quoted in Hedström and Swedburg, 1998). Yet, I find them useful primarily as a crutch to cognition. If I could achieve the level of precision and insight into interactions and dynamics that I need to theorize about a phenomenon with natural language models, I would use them exclusively. Unfortunately, very often I find that I cannot.

The key strength of formal models stems from the fact that they are written in a language that enables us to check their internal consistency much more easily than is the case for natural language models. They can be communicated in a more precise way, and assumptions can be made more transparent than is usually the case with natural languages (Kreps, 1990). These features are particularly valuable when models include interactions between mechanisms at a point in time, or over time. Examples of formal languages in which models about organizations have been written include causal maps, mathematical equations, Boolean algebras, computer programs (algorithms) and graphical analysis.

A useful way to classify models is to think in terms of those that A) describe a system by specifying the properties of its components and how they interact, or B) directly describe the aggregate behavior of the system, without explicit mention of its underlying components. In organization science, the Type A models are represented by agent-based models. Type B models are illustrated by systems dynamics/differential equation models. In economics, Type A are game theoretic models; Type B models can be found in classical macro-economics.

The reader should not be surprised that the author of a book on the microstructural approach to organization design prefers Type A models. They allow us to explicitly think about disaggregation and aggregation processes that are at the heart of this approach. But this does not imply that useful models at the system levels cannot be written that help us understand aggregate properties of the organization as a system in interaction with its environment (e.g. Sastry, 1997; Romme, 2001; Rahmandad, 2012; also see Sterman and Rahmandad, 2008 for an insightful discussion comparing the approaches).[3]

Independent of this distinction, there is also the question of how one analyzes a model and what results one gets from them. One can distinguish between models that yield "proofs," vs. those that yield "graphs." Models whose solution can be written in closed form are necessary for the first but not the

---

[3] In fact, these are hierarchically linked; the assumptions about agent behavior in an agent-based model are aggregate descriptions of sub-systems within the agent.

second, which can instead be obtained by (essentially) Monte Carlo simulation within a parameter space. The easy access to high power computing increasingly makes it possible to explore very large parameter spaces, but it will nonetheless be true that the graphs describe the results only for the sampled points in the parameter space. Even the lines joining points in the graphs are interpolations or extrapolations; whereas a proof tells us the result is true for every point in a specified parameter space (which may not even be specified in a particular functional form).

It follows that proofs are always better in terms of a rigorous understanding of mechanisms, if they are possible for the problem we are analyzing. At the same time, I think it would be absurd to change the problem to use models from which we can get proofs! Between a choice of a model formulation that yields proofs but does not capture the phenomena being studied, and one which does but can at best yield graphs, it seems sensible to prefer the latter. This raises immediately the question of proofs being "possible" for whom—for me, or a better mathematician?

Sometimes the problems I studied have been such that setting up models with closed-form solutions was possible, even with my meager mathematical skills. Sometimes it has not, or I could only derive such results for special simplified versions of the more general model. In the latter cases, my instinct has been to trust to the division of labor between researchers, and blunder on. I focus on what I think I can do well in these situations—understand phenomena in terms of mechanisms, formalize these and study their behavior at least inductively with the tools at my disposal. I am content to wait for somebody to come along and do better mathematics, to show that my simulation results were a special case of a more general theorem (or even an interesting anomaly).

There are interesting differences though in how one approaches these two kinds of models (i.e. those that yield proofs vs. graphs). In the closed form models, we often knew what result we wanted to prove, and often had simple numerical examples before we started. We then set up the simplest possible equation system that seemed to capture key features of interest in the phenomena, which enabled us to prove our point mathematically. The key mode of reasoning was deductive.[4]

In contrast in the models where simulation was the key means of generating results, it seemed better to ask open-ended questions to begin with. The philosophy broadly was to build a toy replica of a phenomenon and "play with it" to see what happens, and perform (logical) experiments on the model to see how changing something affects outcomes. We could raise questions as we went along, and we could also begin with more open-ended questions.

---

[4] Examples in this category would be Kretschmer and Puranam, 2008; Gulati and Puranam, 2009; Puranam and Vanneste, 2009; and Puranam, Gulati, and Bhattacharya, 2013.

The key mode of reasoning here was inductive to begin with, but became deductive as we understood the dynamics of the model better, and ran "confirmatory tests" to check our understanding.[5] Both approaches have their charms and thrilling moments.

The key challenge in the review process for modeling papers in the field of organization science, in my view, remains the widespread skepticism about the abstractions that models require, coupled with unfamiliarity with the methods. I have sometimes tried to console myself with Bertrand Russell's words: "The power of using abstractions is the essence of intellect...Many people have a passionate hatred of abstraction, chiefly I think because of its intellectual difficulty; but as they do not wish to give this reason they invent all sorts of others that sound grand." (Chapter 3, 2001). But ultimately, I did come to realize that if the reviewers didn't get it, it was my fault (and certainly my problem).

As doctoral programs increase training in modeling skills, some of these challenges should decline. But setting aside my vested interests as a producer of models, I also recognize that it may be better for the field if the bar continues to be high for justifying formalized abstraction—for reviewers to continue to demand a high "insight to Greek (letters)" ratio. What we choose to abstract into a model is ultimately a matter of taste and tractability, however much we pretend otherwise. Accepting the constraint that we should be forced to show what is gained, to get readers to accept our possibly idiosyncratic simplifications, seems healthy.

I also think the challenge of convincing reviewers about the value of our formalization exercises will likely remain (and probably should remain) severe as long as our models remain primarily metaphorical (i.e. they propose a mechanism to explain a general stylized pattern of data, rather than make specific falsifiable predictions). Once calibration is possible with empirical evidence, models will automatically be easier to sell (though harder to produce). This is as it should be in my view, as I do not think our field would be well served if more than a minority of researchers started producing models; empirical research should still comprise the bulk of efforts, and this is what will help us keep the "science" in organization science.

Behavioral lab experiments

Experiments enable causal inference through randomization, whether they are conducted in the field or in the lab. This fact is used across a wide variety of

---

[5] Examples in this category would be Puranam and Swamy (2015), Lee and Puranam (2016), and Clement and Puranam (2017).

sciences. But here I want to emphasize a unique strength of lab experiments for organization design researchers. While I would not undermine the importance of continuing to study organization designs *in situ* (i.e. in organizations not designed for the purpose of studying them), it is important to recognize how hard it is to find the data that enables even close to causal inference to do so (e.g. Sorensen, 2003; Agarwal and Wu, 2014; Valentine and Edmondson, 2015; Stan and Puranam, 2016). As a complement to traditional methods, we should think about the promise of behavioral lab experiments on groups (Argote, 2013) to help advance our understanding of organization design.

The micro-structural approach of this book takes as a premise that groups of any size can be treated as organizations if they are goal-directed multi-agent systems. As I noted in Chapter 1, there is no basis (besides convention) on which one can say that a three-person firm is an organization but a four-person team is not (Puranam, Stieglitz, Osman, and Pillutla, 2015). To the extent these are goal-directed multi-agent systems, they are both organizations, albeit solving their problems of division of labor and integration of effort in different ways.

This implies that we can think of task-oriented groups in the behavioral lab as synthetic organizations. They offer a direct test-bed for our micro-structural theories. There is a natural complementarity between modeling and lab experimental work in that they both deal with interaction structures among a small number of agents, in carefully controlled task environments (Billinger et al., 2014; Reitzig and Maciejovsky, 2014).

Most importantly, both are analytical technologies for focusing on one or a few mechanisms underlying phenomena—rather than to recreate complex phenomena in full verisimilitude. Indeed, the critiques of both methods are often the same, and hinge on the (to some) uncomfortable levels of abstraction involved. But the defense is also the same for these methodologies, and rests on the reductionism inherent in expressing phenomena in terms of constituent mechanisms (also see Dennett, 1985 for a useful distinction between "good" and "greedy" reductionism). Precisely for these reasons, lab experiments on groups can provide a very direct test of the predictions emerging from models about organization. Elinor Ostrom and her colleagues have demonstrated, in a most inspirational manner, how effective such an approach can be (Ostrom, 2005).

Half a century ago, Zelditch famously asked: "Can we really study the army in a laboratory?" (Zelditch, 1969). He gave an affirmative answer, as long as the goal was testing theoretical mechanisms rather than completely explaining phenomena (which are inherently multi-mechanism driven). In other words, to the extent we believe that reducing phenomena down to their core mechanisms and studying them one by one is a sound analytic strategy, there is no reason why experiments or models cannot be used to study organizations (any more than in general, theorize about them in terms of mechanisms).

Interestingly, Zelditch also acknowledged the caveat that no synthetic organization could ever hope to recreate a "primary group"—one in which norms have been created. Yet researchers have now created norms and even shared languages within synthetic groups in the laboratory (Brennan and Clark, 1996; Weber and Camerer, 2003). Today, we would answer Zelditch's question in the affirmative as he did, but with even more confidence (also see Falk and Heckman, 2009).

Recent studies have taken such a perspective in examining search (Billinger et al., 2014), evaluation (Reitzig and Maciejovsky, 2014), exploration (Hakonsson et al., 2016), trust in contracting (Malhotra and Murnighan, 2002; Agarwal et al., 2012), and division of labor in organizations (Raveendran et al., 2015; Reagans, Miron-Spektor, and Argote, 2016). The promise of experiments as a methodology to study organization design seems to be increasing with the possibility of creating virtual organizations that involve online interactions (e.g. Centola and Baronchelli, 2015).

It should also be clear that results from a lab experiment (or from a model) cannot directly aspire to explain real world phenomena; at most, we can claim to have shown the empirical plausibility (experiment) or internal consistency (model) of a theoretical mechanism that can provide a sufficient explanation for a phenomenon. At the least, though, we will have shown that the mechanism in question is sufficient to causally produce the observed phenomenon.

Inductive methods

Observational studies (that feature neither randomization nor manipulation—see row 3 in Table 9.1) are a primary source for inductive theory generation. The important role played by qualitative research methods—of either the interpretive or comparative type—to understand organizations is obvious and does not require repetition here (Eisenhardt, 1989; Gioia, Corley, and Hamilton, 2013; Ragin and Amoroso, 2010; Gerring, 2004). Many important contributions to the field of organization design have drawn on these inductive methods (e.g. Siggelkow, 2002; Shah, 2006; Davis and Eisenhardt, 2011), and some level of skill at these methods seems universally necessary to me for at least initiating a meaningful investigation of an empirical phenomenon.

Perhaps less obvious is the promise of quantitative induction based on data-mining and machine-learning. These statistical techniques are primarily meant to build predictive models from large samples of data (rather than test hypotheses about particular mechanisms). This functionality has many applications, but for the purposes of the current discussion, the point I wish to highlight is that the estimated models are inductively derived patterns in the data. For microstructural researchers, I believe that mastering these techniques of quantitative induction can be very useful because of the expansion in data made possible by studying sub-units within larger organizations as organizations in their own right, as well as the expansion in the types of behavioral data itself.

While machine-learning at its current state of development cannot guarantee assumption-free causal inference in the way that randomization can, it can guarantee that the associations found in the data are robust (i.e. they are not idiosyncratic to a sample). The techniques through which machine-learning algorithms avoid the well-known problem of overfitting, or "finding correlations just by looking hard enough," include regularization and cross-validation. Regularization acts as a constraint on model complexity (e.g. preventing too many parameters being estimated). Cross-validation involves partitioning data into sub-samples and fitting models to one sub-sample and testing fit on others. Through these methods, algorithms can produce correlations that are robust (though still not causal). The theorists can then start with these stylized facts and produce theories that account for them, to be tested in additional data (possibly through randomized experiments).

To what extent such quantitative induction techniques will come to belong to the portfolio of techniques used by inductive theorists is unknown at this point. The irony is that machine-learning principles are not that new to us: they help us do data mining in a more sophisticated and honest way than what many in the field, we suspect, are already doing in a less sophisticated way (i.e. p-hacking; see Gelman and Loken, 2014). Machine-learning helps to separate clearly data-mining from hypothesis-testing, and helps us do data-mining in a way that mitigates the risk of overfitting.

An important psychological barrier to the adoption of machine-learning to inductive research is that the role of human intuition and understanding in producing the robust associations is small. The process of poring over individual case details, and the thrill of seeing a gestalt emerge from the diverse strands of data is fundamentally different from that involved in algorithmic induction. These can however be complementary. I believe a case can be made that finding the pattern through induction, and abductively generating the explanation for it could be usefully separated (in most current qualitative work, the two go hand-in-hand). The separation may help to mitigate the motivated reasoning biases that may lead to overfitting explanations that do not generalize beyond the cases being studied.

In closing, I should acknowledge that advances in computer science and data analytics now make it at least theoretically possible to conduct quantitative induction (e.g. what product features seem to correlate with purchase behavior), followed by the establishment of validated causal effects through randomized control trials (e.g. random assignment of customers to exposure to products with varying features), all without human understanding at *any* point. It's hard to say where such trends will lead.

The ability to predict and to understand were strongly coupled when the key information processing constraint was our own mind. With expanded computational power, the ability of algorithms to predict may far outpace our human ability to understand. This raises the provocative question as to why the latter is necessary, or at least when it is necessary (see also the debate between Duncan Watts and critics, 2014).

Conclusion: from studying to creating organization designs

As I noted in Chapter 8, novelty in forms of organizing is a topic of great interest to organizational scholars. Yet we have restricted ourselves to studying these innovations, rather than creating them. I take as a premise that progress in a design-centric science, like organization design, is enabled rather than hindered when its students are willing to embody their hypotheses in prototypes and pilots (Simon, 1996). The developments in theory and methodology discussed in this book may allow us to begin creating innovative forms of organizing, rather than rest content with studying them after they have emerged.

One of these developments is the conceptualization of organizing as a problem-solving process, with a reasonably well-defined set of problem dimensions (i.e. the universal problems of organizing). While these problems are universal, the solutions are not. If we can recognize the underlying structural similarity of problems between organizations in very different domains, then we can copy solutions from one context to the other. Our copying need not be limited to other human organizations. For instance, collaboration among insects has some surprising isomorphisms to human collaboration without leadership and under communication constraints (Gelblum, Pinkoviezky, Fonio, Ghosh, and Feinerman, 2015).

Of course, we may also be able to create, and not only copy. This is where the theoretical advance represented by the micro-structural approach, as well as the resurgence of methodologies like experiments and models come in. While these are useful to the researcher to specify and test individual theoretical mechanisms, they can also be used to "prototype" organizational designs at the micro-structural level. To implement an organizational re-design requires us to be confident that the proposed change will causally produce the effects we desire.

The highest confidence in such a premise comes with data from a randomization-based experiment. When conducted in the context of the organization we are trying to redesign, we call this a field experiment, or a randomized control trial. It is an expensive but convincing test of the efficacy of a small set of potential re-design solutions.

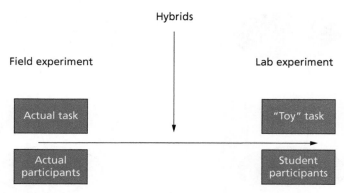

Figure 9.1 Hybrids between lab and field experiments

An alternative is to conduct the experiment in a behavioral laboratory, or through putting individuals in a scenario or thought experiment, which is a hybrid between a field and a lab experiment (see Figure 9.1). This establishes the existence (or not) of a causal effect, but because the context is so different from that of a real organization, it can be thought of at most as a "proof of concept" (Ostrom, 2005). Yet another alternative is to build an agent-based model with calibration to data, to use as an environment within which we can experiment with alternative designs at relatively low cost when we run them *in silico* (Benabeau, 2003).

The process of organization re-design can thus be seen in terms of multiple stages. It begins with careful observation of phenomena (Step 1, Figure 9.2). Qualitative or indeed quantitative induction (i.e. data mining through machine learning) can play a critical role here. Once we have some understanding or at least conjectures about underlying mechanisms, we can use the behavioral lab or an agent based model (Step 2) to run cheap experiments to adjust the design (Step 3). Once we have formulated a new design, we may want to run a field experiment with randomization in Step 4. If the results look satisfactory, we scale up and implement (Step 5).

We now have the conceptual and technical apparatus to prototype organization designs at small scale, cheaply and fast. With proper care and attention to detail, we can transform how we do organizational science, which is after all a science of the artificial (Simon, 1996).

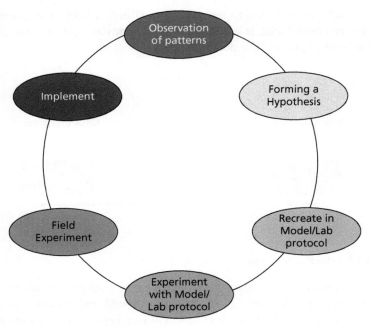

Figure 9.2 The full cycle of organizational (re)-design

■ BIBLIOGRAPHY

Aarts, H., Gollwitzer, P. M., and Hassin, R. R. (2004). Goal contagion: perceiving is for pursuing. *Journal of Personality and Social Psychology*, 87(1): 23.

Adams, J. S. (1965). Inequity in social exchange. *Advances in Experimental Social Psychology*, 2, 267–99.

Agarwal, R., Anand, J., Bercovitz, J., and Croson, R. (2012). Spillovers across organizational architectures: The role of prior resource allocation and communication in post-acquisition coordination outcomes. *Strategic Management Journal*, 33(6): 710–33.

Aggarwal, V. A., Posen, H. E., and Workiewicz, M. (2017). Adaptive capacity to technological change: A microfoundational approach. *Strategic Management Journal*, 38(6): 1212–31.

Aggarwal, V. A., and Wu, B. (2014). Organizational constraints to adaptation: intrafirm asymmetry in the locus of coordination. *Organization Science*, 26(1): 218–38.

Aghion, P. and Tirole J. (1997). Formal and Real Authority in Organizations. *Journal of Political Economy*, 105(1): 1–29.

Ahl, V. and Allen, T. F. H (1996). *Hierarchy Theory: A vision, vocabulary and epistemology.* New York: Columbia University Press.

Alchian, A. A. (1965). The basis of some recent advances in the theory of management of the firm. *The Journal of Industrial Economics*, XIV(I): 30–41.

Alchian, A. A. and Demsetz, H. (1972). Production, Information Costs, and Economic Orgnaization. *American Economic Review*, 62(5): 777–95.

Aldrich, H. (1979). *Organizations and Environments.* Englewood Cliffs, NJ: Prentice-Hall.

Alexander, C. (1964). *Notes on the Synthesis of Form* (Vol. 5). Cambridge, MA: Harvard University Press.

Alexy, O., Reitzig, M., Puranam, P. (2017). *Innovation in organizing: A descriptive analysis.* Working Paper.

Altman, E. J., Nagle, F., and Tushman, M. (2013). *Technology and Innovation Management.* Oxford Bibliographies in Management. New York: Oxford University Press.

Andersen, S. M., Moskowitz, G. B., Blair, I. V., and Nosek, B. A. (2007). Automatic thought. *Social Psychology: Handbook of basic principles*, 2: 138–75.

Anderson, C., and Franks, N. R. (2001). Teams in animal societies. *Behavioral Ecology*, 12(5): 534–40.

Argote, L. (2013). Organization Learning: A Theoretical Framework. In *Organizational Learning* (pp. 31–56). New York: Springer.

Arrow, H., McGrath, J. E., Berdahl, J. L. (2000). *Small Groups as Complex Systems: Formation, coordination, development, and adaptation.* Thousand Oaks, CA: SAGE.

Arrow, K. J. (1974). *The Limits of Organization.* New York: W.W. Norton.

Augsdorfer, P. (2005). Bootlegging and path dependency. *Research Policy*, 34(1): 1–11.

Aumann, R., and Brandenburger, A. (1995). Epistemic conditions for Nash equilibrium. *Econometrica*, 63: 1161–80.

Baker, G. (2002). Distortion and risk in optimal incentive contracts. *Journal of Human Resources*, 37(4): 728–51.

Baker, G., Gibbons, R., and Murphy, K. J. (1999). Informal authority in organizations. *Journal of Law, Economics, and Organization*, 15(1): 56–73.

Baker, G., Gibbons, R., Murphy, K. J. (2002). Relational Contracts and the Theory of the Firm. *Quarterly Journal of Economics*, 117(1): 39–84.

Baldwin, C., and Clark, K. (2000). *Design Rules: The power of modularity*. Cambridge, MA: MIT Press.

Baldwin, C. Y., and Clark, K. B. (2006). The architecture of participation: Does code architecture mitigate free riding in the open source development model? *Management Science*, 52: 1116–27. doi: 10.1287/mnsc.1060.0546.

Barley, S. R. (1990). The alignment of technology and structure through roles and networks. *Administrative Science Quarterly*, 35(1), Special Issue: Technology, Organizations, and Innovation: 61–103.

Barnard, C. (1938). *The Functions of the Executive*. Harvard University Press.

Barnard, C. I. (1939). *Dilemmas of leadership in the democratic process*. Pub. under the University Extension Fund, Herbert L. Baker Foundation, Princeton Univerity.

Barney, J., and Felin, T. (2013). What are microfoundations? *The Academy of Management Perspectives*, 27(2): 138–55.

Barzel, Y. (1982). Measurement cost and the organization of markets. *Journal of Law and Economics*, 25(1): 27–48. doi: 10.1086/467005.

Baumann, O., and Stieglitz, N. (2014). Rewarding value-creating ideas in organizations: The power of low-powered incentives. *Strategic Management Journal*, 35(3): 358–75.

Bazerman, M. H., Giuliano, T., and Appelman, A. (1984). Escalation of commitment in individual and group decision making. *Organizational Behavior and Human Performance*, 33(2): 141–52.

Becker, H. S., and Geer, B. (1960). Latent culture: A note on the theory of latent social roles. *Administrative Science Quarterly*, 5(2): 304–13.

Bendix, R. (1956). *Work and Authority in Industry: Ideologies of Management in the Course of Industrialization,* Classics of the Social Sciences. New Orleans, LA: Quid Pro Books.

Benner, M. J., and Tushman, M. (2002). Process management and technological innovation: A longitudinal study of the photography and paint industries. *Administrative Science Quarterly*, 47(4): 676–707.

Benner, M. J., and Tushman, M. L. (2003). Exploitation, exploration, and process management: The productivity dilemma revisited. *Academy of Management Review*, 28(2): 238–56.

Billinger, S., Stieglitz, N., and Schumacher, T. R. (2013). Search on rugged landscapes: An experimental study. *Organization Science*, 25(1): 93–108.

Blau, P. M., and Scott, W. R. (1962). *Formal Organizations: A comparative approach*. Stanford, CA: Stanford University Press.

Bloom, N., Sadun, R., and Van Reenen, J. (2009). *The organization of firms across countries*, NBER Working Paper 15129.

Boehm, C. (1997). Impact of the human egalitarian syndrome on Darwinian selection mechanics. *The American Naturalist*, 150(S1): S100–S121.

Boehm, C. (1999). *Hierarchy in the Forest: The evolution of egalitarian behavior*. Cambridge, MA: Harvard University Press.

Bonabeau, E. (2002). Predicting the unpredictable. *Harvard Business Review*, 80(3): 109–16.

Bouas, K. S., and Komorita, S. S. (1996). Group Discussion and Cooperation in Social Dilemmas. *Personality and Social Psychology Bulletin*, 22: 1144–50.

Bower, J. L. (1970). *Managing the Resource Allocation Process: A Study of Corporate Planning and Investment*. Boston, MA: Harvard Business School, Division of Research.

Brass, D. J., Galaskiewicz, J., Greve, H. R., and Tsai, W. (2004). Taking stock of networks and organizations: A multilevel perspective. *Academy of Management Journal*, 47(6): 795–817.

Brennan, S. E., and Clark, H. H. (1996). Conceptual pacts and lexical choice in conversation. *Journal of Experimental Psychology: Learning, Memory, and Cognition*, 22(6): 1482–93.

Brewer, M. B. (2007). The importance of being we: Human nature and intergroup relations. *American Psychologist*, 62(8): 728.

Brewer, M. B., and Kramer, R. M. (1986). Choice behavior in social dilemmas: Effects of social identity, group size, and decision framing. *Journal of Personality and Social Psychology*, 50(3): 543.

Brosnan, S. F., and de Waal, F. (2004). Socially learned preferences for differentially rewarded tokens in the brown capuchin monkey (Cebus apella). *Journal of Comparative Psychology*, 118(2): 133.

Brown, D. E. (1991). *Human universals*. New York: McGraw-Hill.

Burgelman, R. A. (1983). A process model of internal corporate venturing in the diversified major firm. *Administrative Science Quarterly*, 28(2): 223–44.

Burt, R. S. (1992). *Structure Holes. The Social Structure of Competition*. Cambridge MA: Harvard University Press.

Burton, R. M., and Obel, B. (1980). A computer simulation test of the M-form hypothesis. *Administrative Science Quarterly*, 25: 457–66.

Burton, R. M., and Obel, B. (1984). *Designing Efficient Organizations: Modelling and Experimentation*, Amsterdam: North Holland.

Burton, R. M., and Obel, B. (1998). Introduction. In *Strategic Organizational Diagnosis and Design* (pp. 1–40). Boston, MA: Springer.

Cabigiosu, A., and Camuffo, A. (2012). Beyond the "mirroring" hypothesis: Product modularity and interorganizational relations in the air conditioning industry. *Organization Science*, 23(3): 686–703.

Camerer, C. (2003). *Behavioral Game Theory: Experiments in strategic interaction*. Princeton, NJ: Princeton University Press.

Camerer, C. F. (1997). Progress in behavioral game theory. *The Journal of Economic Perspectives*, 11(4): 167–88.

Camerer, C. F., and Ho, T. (1999). Experience-weighted attraction learning in normal form games. *Econometrica*, 67(4): 827–74.

Camerer, C. F., and Knez, M. (1996). Coordination, organizational boundaries and fads in business practices. *Industrial and Corporate Change*, 5: 89–112. doi: 10.1093/icc/5.1.89.

Camerer, C. F., and Knez, M. (1997). Coordination in organizations: A game-theoretic perspective. In Z. Shapira (Ed.): *Organizational Decision Making*: 158–88. Cambridge: Cambridge University Press.

Caporael, L. R. (2007). Evolutionary theory for social and cultural psychology. *Social psychology: Handbook of basic principles*, 2: 3–18.

Centola, D., and Baronchelli, A. (2015). The spontaneous emergence of conventions: An experimental study of cultural evolution. *Proceedings of the National Academy of Sciences*, 112(7): 1989–94.

Chandler, A. (1977). *The Visible Hand*. Cambridge, MA: Harvard University Press.

Chandler, A. D. (1962). *Strategy and Structure: Chapters in the history of industrial enterprise.* Cambridge, MA: MIT Press.

Child, J., and McGrath, R. G. (2001). Organizations unfettered: Organizational form in an information-intensive economy. *Academy of Management Journal,* 44(6): 1135–48.

Christensen, M., and Knudsen, T. (2010). Design of decision-making organizations. *Management Science,* 56(1): 71–89.

Clark, H. H. (1996). *Using Language.* Cambridge: Cambridge University Press.

Clark, K. B., and Fujimoto, T. (1991). *Product Development Performance: Strategy, Organisation and Management in the World Auto Industry.* Boston, MA: Harvard University Press.

Clauset, A., Newman, M. E. J., and Moore, C. (2004). Finding community structure in very large networks, *Physical Review E,* 70(6): 1–6.

Clement, J., and Puranam, P. (2017). Searching for structure: Formal organization design as a guide to network evolution. *Management Science:* Forthcoming.

Coase, R. H. (1937). The nature of the firm. *Economica,* 4(16): 386–405.

Coase, R. H. (1960). The problem of social cost. *Journal of Law and Economics,* 3: 1–44. doi: 10.1086/466560.

Cohen, M. D., and Bacdayan, P. (1994). Organizational routines are stored as procedural memory: Evidence from a laboratory study. *Organization Science,* 5(4): 554–68.

Cohen, M. D., Levinthal, D. A., and Warglien, M. (2014). Collective performance: modeling the interaction of habit-based actions. *Industrial and Corporate Change,* 23(2): 329–60.

Coleman, J. S. (1990). *Foundations of Social Theory.* Cambridge, MA: Harvard University.

Colfer, L., and Baldwin, C. Y. (2010). *The mirroring hypothesis: Theory, evidence and exceptions.* Working Paper No. 10–058, Harvard Business School, Cambridge, MA.

Colombo, M. G., and Delmastro, M. (2007). *The Economics of Organizational Design: Theoretical Insights and Empirical Evidence.* New York: Palgrave Macmillan.

Cooper, D. J., and Kagel, J. (2013). Other regarding preferences: A selective survey of experimental results. Forthcoming in *The Handbook of Experimental Economics,* Vol. 2, eds. Kagel, J. and Roth, A.

Cosmides, L., and Tooby, J. (1997). *Evolutionary Psychology: A primer.*

Cross, N. (2001). Design cognition: Results from protocol and other empirical studies of design activity. In: Eastman, C., Newstatter, W., and McCracken, M. (eds.): *Design Knowing and Learning: cognition in design education.* Oxford: Elsevier, pp. 79–103.

Csaszar, F. A., and Eggers, J. P. (2013). Organizational decision making: An information aggregation view. *Management Science,* 59(10): 2257–77.

Cyert, R. M., and March, J. G. (1963). *A Behavioral Theory of the Firm.* Englewood Cliffs. NJ: Prentice-Hall.

Daft, R. L. (2001). *Essentials of Organization Theory and Design.* South Western Educational Publishing.

Daft, R. L. (2007). *Understanding the Theory and Design of Organizations.* Mason: Thomson South-Western.

Daft, R. L., and Lengel, R. H. (1986). Organizational information requirements, media richness and structural design. *Management Science,* 32(5): 554–71.

Dahlander, L., and O'Mahony, S. (2011). Progressing to the center: Coordinating project work. *Organization Science,* 22: 961–79.

Davis, J. P., and Eisenhardt, K. M. (2011). Rotating leadership and collaborative innovation: Recombination processes in symbiotic relationships. *Administrative Science Quarterly*, 56(2): 159–201.

Daw, N. D., O'Doherty, J. P., Dayan, P., Seymour, B., and Dolan, R. J. (2006). Cortical substrates for exploratory decisions in humans. *Nature*, 441(7095): 876–79.

Dawes, R. M. (1980). Social dilemmas. *Annual Review of Psychology* 31: 169–93.

Dawkins, R. (1986). *The Blind Watchmaker: Why the evidence of evolution reveals a universe without design*. New York: W.W Norton and Company.

Deci, E. L., Koestner, R., and Ryan, R. M. (1999). A meta-analytic review of experiments examining the effects of extrinsic rewards on intrinsic motivation. *Psychological Bulletin*, 125(6): 627.

Deci, E. L., and Ryan, R. M. (2000). The "what" and "why" of goal pursuits: Human needs and the self-determination of behavior. *Psychological Inquiry*, 11(4): 227–68.

De Dreu, C. K., and Nauta, A. (2009). Self-interest and other-orientation in organizational behavior: Implications for job performance, prosocial behavior, and personal initiative. *Journal of Applied Psychology*, 94(4): 913–26.

Demsetz, H. (1988). The theory of the firm revisited. *Journal of Law, Economics, and Organization*, 4(1): 141–61.

Dewar, R. D., and Simet, D. P. (1981). A level specific prediction of spans of control examining the effects of size, technology, and specialization. *Academy of Management Journal*, 24: 5–24.

Dewey, J. (1930). The quest for certainty: A study of the relation of knowledge and action. *The Journal of Philosophy*, 27(1): 14–25.

DiMaggio, P., and Powell, W. W. (1983). The iron cage revisited: Collective rationality and institutional isomorphism in organizational fields. *American Sociological Review*, 48(2): 147–60.

Dobrajska, M., Billinger, S., and Karim, S. (2015). Delegation within hierarchies: How information processing and knowledge characteristics influence the allocation of formal and real decision authority. *Organization Science*, 26(3): 687–704.

Døjbak Håkonsson, D., Eskildsen, J. K., Argote, L., Mønster, D., Burton, R. M., and Obel, B. (2016). Exploration versus exploitation: emotions and performance as antecedents and consequences of team decisions. *Strategic Management Journal*, 37(6): 985–1001.

Domjan, M. (2010). *Principles of Learning and Behavior*, 6th ed. Stamford, CT: Cengage/Wadsworth.

Donaldson, L. (1995). *American Anti-management Theories of Organization: A critique of paradigm proliferation* (Vol. 25). Cambridge: Cambridge University Press.

Donaldson, L. (2001). *The Contingency Theory of Organizations*. Thousand Oaks, CA: Sage Publications.

Dosi, G., Levinthal, D. A., and Marengo, L. (2003). Bridging contested terrain: Linking incentive-based and learning perspectives on organizational evolution. *Industrial and Corporate Change*, 12(2): 413–36.

Doty, D. H., Glick, W. H., and Huber, G. P. (1993). Fit, equifinality, and organizational effectiveness: A test of two configurational theories. *Academy of Management Journal*, 36: 1196–1250.

Dougherty, D. (1992). Interpretive barriers to successful product innovation in large firms. *Organization Science*, 3(2): 179–202.

Doz, Y., Evans, P., and Laurent, A. (Eds.). (1989). *Human Resource Management in International Firms: Change, Globalization, Innovation*. New York: Palgrave Macmillan.

Doz, Y. L., Santos, J., and Williamson, P. J. (2001). *From Global to Metanational: How companies win in the knowledge economy*. Cambridge, MA: Harvard Business Press.

Drazin, R., and Van de Ven, A. H. (1985). Alternative forms of fit in contingency theory. *Administrative Science Quarterly*, 30(4): 514–39.

Dunbar, R. I. (1998). The social brain hypothesis. *Brain*, 9(10): 178–90.

Durkheim, E. (1893). *The Division of Labor in Society*. New York: Free Press.

Eisenberger, R., and Cameron, J. (1996). Detrimental effects of reward: Reality or myth? *American Psychologist*, 51(11): 1153–66.

Eisenhardt, K. M. (1988). Agency- and institutional-theory explanations: The case of retail sales compensation. *Academy of Management Journal*, 31(3): 488–511.

Eisenhardt, K. M. (1989). Building theories from case study research. *Academy of Management Review*, 14(4): 532–50.

Eisenhardt, K. M., and Bourgeois, L. J. (1988). Politics of strategic decision making in high-velocity environments: Toward a midrange theory. *Academy of Management Journal*, 31(4): 737–70.

Emerson, R. M. (1962). Power-dependence relations. *American Sociological Review*, 27(1): 31–41.

Epley, N., and Dunning, D. (2000). Feeling "holier than thou": are self-serving assessments produced by errors in self- or social prediction? *Journal of Personality and Social Psychology*, 79(6): 861–75.

Eppinger, S. D. (1991). Model-based approaches to managing concurrent engineering. *Journal of Engineering Design*, 2: 283–90.

Eppinger, S. D. (2001). Innovation at the speed of innovation. *Harvard Business Review*, 79(1): 149–58.

Ericsson, K., and Charness, N. (2006). *The Cambridge Handbook of Expertise and Expert Performance*. Cambridge: Cambridge University Press.

Ethiraj, S. K. and Levinthal, D. A. (2004a). Bounded rationality and the search for organizational architecture: An evolutionary perspective on the design of organizations and their evolvability. *Administrative Science Quarterly*, 49(3): 404–37.

Ethiraj, S. K., and Levinthal, D. A. (2004b). Modularity and innovation in complex systems. *Management Science*, 50(2): 159–73.

Ethiraj, S. K., Levinthal, D., and Roy, R. R. (2008). The dual role of modularity: Innovation and imitation. *Management Science*, 54(5): 939–55.

Etzioni, A. (1964). *Modern Organizations*. Englewood Cliffs, NJ: Prentice-Hall.

Evans, J. S. B., and Stanovich, K. E. (2013). Dual-process theories of higher cognition: Advancing the debate. *Perspectives on Psychological Science*, 8(3): 223–41.

Falk, A., and Heckman, J. J. (2009). Lab experiments are a major source of knowledge in the social sciences. *Science*, 326: 535–38.

Fayol, H. (1949). *General and Industrial Management*. Accession Number: 00838929. UC Berkeley.

Fehr, E., and Gintis, H. (2007). Human motivation and social cooperation: Experimental and analytical foundations. *Annu. Rev. Sociol.*, 33: 43–64.

Fehr, E., Herz, H., and Wilkening, T. (2013). The lure of authority: Motivation and incentive effects of power. *American Economic Review*, 103(4): 1325–59.

Fehr, E., and Schmidt, K. M. (1999). A theory of fairness, competition, and cooperation. *Quarterly Journal of Economics*, 114(3): 817–68.

Festinger, L. (1957). *A theory of Cognitive Dissonance*. Stanford, CA: Stanford University Press.

Fischbacher, U., and Gächter, S. (2006). *Heterogeneous social preferences and the dynamics of free riding in public goods*. CeDEx Discussion Paper No. 2006/01.

Fischer, A., Greiff, S., and Funke, J. (2012). The process of solving complex problems. *Journal of Problem Solving*: 4: 19–42.

Fishbach, A., and Ferguson, M. J. (2007). The goal construct in social psychology. In Kruglanski, A. W., and Higgins, E. T. (Eds.): *Social Psychology: Handbook of basic principles*. New York: Guilford Press, pp. 490–515.

Fiss, P. C. (2007). A set-theoretic approach to organizational configurations. *Academy of Management Review*, 32: 1180–98.

Fligstein, N., and Dauber, K. (1989). Structural change in corporate organization. *Annual Review of Sociology*, 15: 73–96.

Folger, R. (1977). Distributive and procedural justice: Combined impact of voice and improvement on experienced inequity. *Journal of Personality and Social Psychology*, 35(2): 108–19.

Forsyth, D. R. (2009). *Group Dynamics*. Cengage Learning.

Foss, N. (2007). The emerging knowledge governance approach: Challenges and characteristics. *Organization*, 14(1): 29–52.

Foss, N. J. (2003). Selective intervention and internal hybrids: Interpreting and learning from the rise and decline of the Oticon spaghetti organization. *Organization Science*, 14(3): 331–49.

Foss, N. J., and Lindenberg, S. (2013). Microfoundations for strategy: A goal-framing perspective on the drivers of value creation. *The Academy of Management Perspectives*, 27(2): 85–102.

Freeland, R. F. (1996). The myth of the M-form? Governance, consent, and organizational change. *American Journal of Sociology*, 102(2): 483–526.

Gaba, V., and Joseph, J. (2013). Corporate structure and performance feedback: Aspirations and adaptation in M-form firms. *Organization Science*, 24(4): 1102–19.

Galbraith, J. R. (1973). *Designing Complex Organizations*. Reading, MA: Addison-Wesley.

Galbraith, J. R. (1977). *Organizational Design*. Reading, MA: Addison-Wesley.

Galbraith, J. R. (2012). *Designing Matrix Organizations that Actually Work: How IBM, P&G and others design for success*. San Francisco, CA: Jossey-Bass.

Gargiulo, M., and Benassi, M. (2000). Trapped in your own net? Network cohesion, structural holes, and the adaptation of social capital. *Organization Science*, 11(2) 183–96.

Garicano, L. (2000). Hierarchies and the organization of knowledge in production. *Journal of Political Economy*, 108(5): 874–904.

Gavetti, G. (2005). Cognition and hierarchy: Rethinking the microfoundations of capabilities' development. *Organization Science*, 16(6): 599–617.

Gavetti, G., Greve, H. R., Levinthal D. A., and Ocasio, W. (2012). The behavioral theory of the firm: Assessment and prospects. *The Academy of Management Annals*, 6(1): 1–40.

Gavetti, G., and Levinthal, D. (2000). Looking forward and looking backward: Cognitive and experiential search. *Administrative Science Quarterly*, 45(1): 113–37.

Gavetti, G., Levinthal, D., and Ocasio, W. (2007). Perspective—Neo-Carnegie: The Carnegie school's past, present, and reconstructing for the future. *Organization Science*, 18(3): 523–36.

Gelblum, A., Pinkoviezky, I., Fonio, E., Ghosh, A., Gov, N., and Feinerman, O. (2015). Ant groups optimally amplify the effect of transiently informed individuals. *Nature Communications*, 6(7729): 6.

Gelman, A., and Loken, E. (2014). The statistical crisis in science data-dependent analysis—a "garden of forking paths"—explains why many statistically significant comparisons don't hold up. *American Scientist*, 102(6): 460.

Gentner, D. (1981). Some interesting differences between nouns and verbs. *Cognition and Brain Theory*, 4: 161–78.

Gentner, D. (1982). Why nouns are learned before verbs: Linguistic relativity versus natural partitioning. In S. Kuczaj (Ed.): *Language Development*: Vol. 2. Language, thought and culture (pp. 199–241). London: Cambridge University Press.

Gentner, D., and Boroditsky, L. (2001). Individuation, relativity and early word learning. In M. Bowerman and S. Levinson (Eds.): *Language Acquisition and Conceptual Development* (pp. 215–56). Cambridge: Cambridge University Press.

Gerring, J. (2004). What is a case study and what is it good for? *American Political Science Review*, 98(2): 341–54.

Gibbons, R. (1998). Incentives in organizations. *Journal of Economic Perspectives*, 12(4): 115–32.

Gibbons, R., (2018). *Foundations of Organizational Economics*. Princeton, NJ: Princeton University Press, forthcoming.

Gigerenzer, G., and Goldstein, D. G. (1996). Reasoning the fast and frugal way: models of bounded rationality. *Psychological Review*, 103(4): 650–69.

Gilbert, P., Price, J., and Allan, S. (1995). Social comparison, social attractiveness and evolution: How might they be related? *New Ideas in Psychology*, 13(2): 149–65.

Gioia, D. A., Corley, K. G., and Hamilton, A. L. (2013). Seeking qualitative rigor in inductive research: Notes on the Gioia methodology. *Organizational Research Methods*, 16(1): 15–31.

Gittell, J. H. (2001). Supervisory span, relational coordination, and flight departure performance: A reassessment of postbureaucracy theory. *Organization Science*, 12: 468–83.

Goel, V., and Pirolli, P. (1992). The structure of design problem spaces. *Cognitive Science*, 16(3): 395–429.

Gokpinar, B., Hopp, W. J. and Iravani, S. M. R. (2010). The impact of misalignment of organizational structure and product architecture on quality in complex product development. *Management Science*, 56(3): 468–84.

Gottschalg, O., and Zollo, M. (2007). Interest alignment and competitive advantage. *Academy of Management Review*, 32(2): 418–37.

Granovetter, M. (1985). Economic action and social structure: The problem of embeddedness. *American Journal of Sociology*, 91(3): 481–510.

Greenberg, J. (1987). Reactions to procedural injustice in payment distributions: Do the means justify the ends? *Journal of Applied Psychology*, 72(1): 55.

Greenwald, A. G. (2012). There is nothing so theoretical as a good method. *Perspectives on Psychological Science*, 7(2): 99–108.

Gresov, C., and Drazin, R. (1997). Equifinality: Functional equivalence in organization design. *Academy of Management Review*, 22: 403–28.

Greve, H. R. (2003). *Organizational learning from performance feedback: A behavioral perspective on innovation and change*. Cambridge: Cambridge University Press.

Greve, H. R. (2008). A behavioral theory of firm growth: Sequential attention to size and performance goals. *Academy of Management Journal*, 51(3): 476–94.

Griesinger, D. W., and Livingston, J. W. (1973). Toward a model of interpersonal motivation in experimental games. *Behavioral Science*, 18(3): 173–88.

Gulati, R., Lawrence, P. R., and Puranam, P. (2005). Adaptation in vertical relationships: Beyond incentive conflict. *Strategic Management Journal*, 26(5): 415–40.

Gulati, R., and Puranam, P. (2009). Renewal through reorganization: The value of inconsistencies between formal and informal organization. *Organization Science*, 20(2): 422–40.

Gulati, R., Puranam, P., and Tushman, M. (2012). Meta-organization design: Rethinking design in interorganizational and community contexts. *Strategic Management Journal*, 33(6): 571–86.

Gulick, L., and Urwick, L. (1937). *The Theory of Administration*. New York: Institute of Public Administration.

Hackman, J. R. (1990). *Groups that work and those that don't*. San Francisco, CA: Jossey-Bass.

Hackman, J. R., and Oldham, G. R. (1976). Motivation through the design of work: Test of a theory. *Organizational Behavior and Human Performance*, 16: 250–79.

Hamel, G. (1991). Competition for competence and interpartner learning within international strategic alliances. *Strategic Management Journal*, 12(S1): 83–103.

Hannan, M. T., and Freeman, J. (1977). The population ecology of organizations. *American Journal of Sociology*, 82: 929–64.

Hansen, M. T. (1999). The search-transfer problem: The role of weak ties in sharing knowledge across organization subunits. *Administrative science quarterly*, 44(1): 82–111.

Hardin, G. (1968). The tragedy of the commons. *Science*, 162: 1243–48.

Harhoff, D., and Lakhani, K. R. (2016) *Revolutionizing Innovation: Users, Communities, and Open Innovation*. Cambridge, MA: MIT Press.

Heath, C., and Staudenmayer, N. (2000). Coordination neglect: How lay theories of organizing complicate coordination in organizations. *Research in Organizational Behavior*, 22: 153–91.

Hedström, P., and Swedberg, R. (Eds.) (1998). *Social mechanisms: An analytical approach to social theory*. Cambridge: Cambridge University Press.

Helfat, C. E., and Peteraf, M. A. (2015). Managerial cognitive capabilities and the microfoundations of dynamic capabilities. *Strategic Management Journal*, 36(6): 831–50.

Henderson, R. M., and Clark, K. B. (1990). Architectural innovation: The reconfiguration of existing product technologies and the failure of established firms, *Administrative Science Quarterly*, 35: 9–30.

Herzberg, F. I. (1966). *Work and the Nature of Man*. New York: World Publishing.

Hinds, P. J., and Kiesler, S. (2002). *Distributed Work*. Cambridge, MA: MIT Press.

Ho, T. H., and Su, X. (2009). Peer-induced fairness in games. *American Economic Review*, 99(5): 2022–49.

Hodgson, G. M. (2004). Opportunism is not the only reason why firms exist: Why an explanatory emphasis on opportunism may mislead management strategy. *Industrial and Corporate Change*, 13(2): 401–18.

Hodgson, G. M., and Knudsen, T. (2010). *Darwin's conjecture: The search for general principles of social and economic evolution*. Chicago: University of Chicago Press.

Holland, J. H. (1998). *Emergence: From chaos to order*. Redwood, CA: Addison-Wesley.

Holland, P. W., and Leinhardt, S. (1976). Local structure in social networks. *Sociological Methodology*, 7: 1–45.

Hölmstrom, B. (1979). Moral hazard and observability. *Bell Journal of Economics*, 10(1): 74–91.

Hölmstrom, B. (1982). Moral hazard in teams. *Bell Journal of Economics*, 13: 324–40.

Hölmstrom, B., and Milgrom, P. (1991). Multitask principal-agent analyses: Incentive contracts, asset ownership, and job design. *Journal of Law, Economics, and Organization*, 7: 24–52.

Hölmstrom, B., and Milgrom, P. (1994). The firm as an incentive system. *American Economic Review*, 84(4): 972–91.

Hölmstrom, B., and Roberts, J. (1998). The boundaries of the firm revisited. *Journal of Economic Perspectives*, 12(4): 73–94.

Hoopes, D. G., and Postrel, S. (1999). Shared knowledge, "glitches," and product development performance. *Strategic Management Journal*, 20(9): 837–65.

Hsu, G., and Hannan, M. T. (2005). Identities, genres, and organizational forms. *Organization Science*, 16: 474–90.

Inkpen, A. C., and Tsang, E. W. (2007). 10 learning and strategic alliances. *The Academy of Management Annals*, 1(1): 479–511.

Jaques, E. (1990). In praise of hierarchy. *Harvard Business Review*, 1: 127–33.

Jensen, M. C., and Meckling, W. H. (1976). Theory of the firm: Managerial behavior, agency costs and ownership structure. *Journal of Financial Economics*, 3(4): 305–60.

Jensen, M. C., and Meckling, W. H. (1979). Rights and production functions: An application to labor-managed firms and codetermination. *Journal of Business*, 52(4): 469–506.

Jensen, M. C., and Meckling, W. H. (1992). Specific and general knowledge and organizational structure. In L. Werin and H. Wijkander (eds.) *Contract Economics*. Oxford: Blackwell Publishers.

Jeppesen, L. B., and Lakhani, K. R. (2010). Marginality and problem-solving effectiveness in broadcast search. *Organization Science*, 21(5): 1016–33.

Jimmy Wales on the birth of Wikipedia (2005). http://www.ted.com/talks/lang/eng/jimmy_wales_on_the_birth_of_wikipedia.html.

Joseph, J., Klingebiel, R., and Wilson, A. J. (2016). Organizational structure and performance feedback: Centralization, aspirations, and termination decisions. *Organization Science*, 27(5): 1065–83.

Joseph, J., and Ocasio, W. (2012). Architecture, attention, and adaptation in the multibusiness firm: General Electric from 1951 to 2001. *Strategic Management Journal*, 33(6): 633–60.

Kahneman, D. (2011). *Thinking, Fast and Slow*. Macmillan.

Kahneman, D., Slovic, P., and Tversky, A. (1982). *Judgment Under Uncertainty: Heuristics and Biases*. New York: Cambridge University Press.

Karim, S. (2006). Modularity in organizational structure: The reconfiguration of internally developed and acquired business units. *Strategic Management Journal*, 27(9): 799–823.

Karim, S. (2009). Business unit reorganization and innovation in new product markets. *Management Science*, 55(7): 1237–54.

Karim, S., and Williams, C. (2012). Structural knowledge: How executive experience with structural composition affects intrafirm mobility and unit reconfiguration. *Strategic Management Journal*, 33(6): 681–709.

Kates, A., and Galbraith, J. R. (2007). *Designing your Organization. Using the Star Model to Solve 5 Critical Design Challenges.* San Francisco, CA: Jossey-Bass.

Katz, D., and Kahn, R. L. (1978). *The social psychology of organizations* (Vol. 2). New York: Wiley.

Kelley, H. H., and Thibaut, J. W. (1978). *Interpersonal relations: A theory of interdependence.* New York: John Wiley.

Ketchen, D. J., Jr., Thomas, J. B., and Snow, C. C. (1993). Organizational configurations and performance: A comparison of theoretical approaches. *Academy of Management Journal,* 36: 1278–313.

Kleinbaum, A., and Stuart, T. (2014). Network Responsiveness: The Social Structural Micro-foundations of Dynamic Capabilities. *Academy of Management Perspectives,* 28(4): 353–67.

Knudsen, T., and Srikanth, K. (2014). Coordinated exploration organizing joint search by multiple specialists to overcome mutual confusion and joint myopia. *Administrative Science Quarterly,* 59(3): 409–41.

Kogut, B., and Zander, U. (1996). What firms do? Coordination, identity, and learning. *Organization Science,* 7(5): 502–18.

Kollock, P. (1998). Social dilemmas: The anatomy of cooperation. *Annual Review of Sociology,* 24: 183–214.

Kozlowski, S. W., and Bell, B. S. (2013). *Work groups and teams in organizations: Review update.* Cornell University ILR School Working Paper.

Krackhardt, D. (1994). Graph theoretical dimensions of informal organizations. *Computational Organization Theory,* 89(112): 123–40.

Kreps, D. M. (1990). *Game theory and economic modelling.* Oxford: Oxford University Press.

Kretschmer, T., and Puranam, P. (2008). Integration through incentives within differentiated organizations. *Organization Science,* 19(6): 860–75.

Kugler, T., Kausel, E. E., and Kocher, M. G. (2012). Are groups more rational than individuals? A review of interactive decision making in groups. *Wiley Interdisciplinary Reviews: Cognitive Science,* 3(4): 471–82.

Lakhani, K., Lifshitz-Assaf, H., and Tushman, M. (2012). *Open innovation and organizational boundaries: the impact of task decomposition and knowledge distribution on the locus of innovation.* Harvard Business School Technology and Operations Mgt. Unit Working Paper No. 12–57.

Lamont, B. T., Williams, R. J., and Hoffman, J. J. (1994). Performance during "M-Form" reorganization and recovery time: the effects of prior strategy and implementation speed. *Academy of Management Journal,* 37(1): 153–66.

Langlois, R. N. (2002). Modularity in technology and organization. *Journal of Economic Behavior and Organization,* 49: 19–37.

Larkin, I., Pierce, L., and Gino, F. (2012). The psychological costs of pay-for-performance: Implications for the strategic compensation of employees. *Strategic Management Journal,* 33(10): 1194–1214.

Laureiro-Martinez, D., Brusoni, S., Canessa, N., and Zollo, M. (2015). Understanding the exploration–exploitation dilemma: An MRI study of attention control and decision-making performance. *Strategic Management Journal,* 36(3): 319–38.

Lave, C. A., and March, J. G. (1993). *An Introduction to Models in the Social Sciences.* University Press of America.

Lawrence, P. R., and Lorsch, J. W. (1967). *Organization and environment: Managing differentiation and integration.* Boston, MA: Harvard University Press.

Lazear, Edward P. (2000). The power of incentives. *The American Economic Review,* 90(2): 410–14.

Lecuona, J. R. and Reitzig, M. (2014). Knowledge worth having in "excess": The value of tacit and firm-specific human resource slack. *Strategic Management Journal,* 35: 954–73.

Lee, C. H., Hoehn-Weiss, M. N., and Karim, S. (2016). Grouping interdependent tasks: Using spectral graph partitioning to study complex systems. *Strategic Management Journal,* 37(1): 177–91.

Lee, E., and Puranam, P. (2015). The nature of expertise in organization design: Evidence from an expert–novice comparison. In *Cognition and Strategy* (pp. 181–209). Emerald Group Publishing Limited.

Lee, E., and Puranam, P. (2016). The implementation imperative: Why one should implement even imperfect strategies perfectly. *Strategic Management Journal,* 37(8): 1529–46.

Lee, G. K., and Cole, R. E. (2003). From a firm-based to a community-based model of knowledge creation: The case of the Linux kernel development. *Organization Science,* 14: 633–49.

Lee, S., and Meyer-Doyle, P. (2017). How performance incentives shape individual exploration and exploitation: Evidence from microdata. *Organization Science,* 28(1): 19–38.

Lee, S., and Puranam, P. (2017). incentive redesign and collaboration in organizations: Evidence from a natural experiment. *Strategic Management Journal,* 38(12): 2333–52.

Leijonhufvud, A. (1986). Capitalism and the Factory System. In Langlois, R. N. (ed.) *Economics as a Process: Essays in the New Institutional Economics.* New York: Cambridge University Press, pp. 203–23.

Levi Martin, J. (2009). *Social Structures.* Princeton University Press.

Levi Martin, J. (2011). *The Explanation of Social Action.* OUP.

Levinthal, D. (1988). A survey of agency models of organizations. *Journal of Economic Behavior and Organization,* 9(2): 153–85.

Levinthal, D., and Workiewicz, M. (2017). Near decomposability and organizational structure: The adaptive rationality of multi-authority. *Academy of Management Annual Meeting Proceedings,* 2017(1): 15299.

Levinthal, D. A. (1997). Adaptation on rugged landscapes. *Management Science,* 43: 934–50.

Levinthal, D. A. (2011). A behavioral approach to strategy—what's the alternative? *Strategic Management Journal,* 32(13): 1517–23.

Levinthal, D. A., and March, J. G. (1993). The myopia of learning. *Strategic Management Journal,* 14(S2): 95–112.

Lewis, D. (1969). *Convention: A Philosophical Study.* Cambridge, MA: Harvard University Press.

Liang, D. W., Moreland, R. L., and Argote, L. (1995). Group versus individual training and group performance: The mediating role of transactive memory. *Personality and Social Psychology Bulletin* 21(4): 384–93.

Lind, E. A., and Tyler, T. R. (1988). *The social psychology of procedural justice.* Springer Science and Business Media.

Lindenberg, S. (2008). Social rationality, semi-modularity and goal-framing: What is it all about? *Analyse and Kritik,* 30(2): 669–87.

Lindenberg, S. (2013). Cognition and governance: why incentives have to take a back seat. In Grandori, A. (Ed.): *Handbook of Economic Organization. Integrating Economic and Organization Theory.* Cheltenham: Elgar, pp. 41–61.

Lindenberg, S., and Foss, N. J. (2011). Managing joint production motivation: The role of goal framing and governance mechanisms. *Academy of Management Review,* 36(3): 500–25.

Lindenberg, S., and Frey, B. S. (1993). Alternatives, frames, and relative prices: A broader view of rational choice theory. *Acta Sociologica,* 36(3): 191–205.

Lounama, P. H., and J. G. March. (1987). Adaptive coordination of a learning team. *Management Science,* 33: 107–23.

Lounsbury, M. (2002). Institutional transformation and status mobility: The professionalization of the field of finance. *Academy of Management Journal,* 45: 255–66.

Lovas, B., and Ghoshal, S. (2000). Strategy as guided evolution. *Strategic Management Journal,* 21: 875–96.

Luce, R. D. (1959). *Individual Choice Behavior a Theoretical Analysis.* John Wiley and Sons.

MacCormack, A., Baldwin, C., and Rusnak, J. (2012). Exploring the duality between product and organizational architectures: A test of the "mirroring" hypothesis. *Research Policy,* 41: 1309–24.

MacCormack, A. D., Rusnak, J., and Baldwin, C. Y. (2006). Exploring the structure of complex software designs: An empirical study of open source and proprietary code. *Management Science,* 52: 1015–30.

Mael, F., and Ashforth, B. E. (1992). Alumni and their alma mater: A partial test of the reformulated model of organizational identification. *Journal of Organizational Behavior,* 13(2): 103–23.

Malhotra, D., and Murnighan, J. K. (2002). The effects of contracts on interpersonal trust. *Administrative Science Quarterly,* 47(3): 534–59.

Malone, T. W., and Crowston, K. (1994). The interdisciplinary study of coordination. *ACM Computing Surveys,* 26(1), 87–119.

Mandelbrot, B. B. (1983). *The Fractal Geometry of Nature.* New York: W. H. Freeman Publishers.

March, J. G. (1991). Exploration and exploitation in organizational learning. *Organization Science,* 2: 71–87.

March, J. G. (1994). *Primer on decision making: How decisions happen.* New York: Simon and Schuster.

March, J. G., and Olsen, J. P. (2010). *Rediscovering institutions.* New York: Simon and Schuster.

March, J. G., and Simon, H. A. (1958). *Organizations.* New York: Wiley.

March, J. G., and Simon, H. A. (1993). Introduction to the second edition. *Organizations* (2nd ed., pp. 1–19). Cambridge, MA: Blackwell Publishers.

Martin, J. (1982). The fairness of earnings differentials. An experimental study of the perceptions of blue-collar workers. *Journal of Human Resources,* 17: 110–22.

Marx, K. (1906). *Capital.* New York: Modern Library.

Mawhood P. (1983) Decentralization: The Concept and the Practice. In Mawhood, P. (ed.) *Local Government in the Third World: The Experience of Tropical Africa.* London: John Wiley and Son.

McEvily, B., Soda, G., and Tortoriello, M. (2014). More Formally: Rediscovering the Missing Link between Formal Organization and Informal Social Structure. *The Academy of Management Annals,* 8(1): 299–345.

McGraw, K. O., and McCullers, J. C. (1979). Evidence of a detrimental effect of extrinsic incentives on breaking a mental set. *Journal of Experimental Social Psychology*, 15(3): 285–94.

McPherson, M., Smith-Lovin, L., and Cook, J. M. (2001). Birds of a feather: Homophily in social networks. *Annual Review of Sociology*, 27: 415–44.

Megarry, T. (1995). *Society in Prehistory: The Origins of Human Culture*. New York: NYU Press.

Meyer, A. D., Tsui, A. S., and Hinings, C. R. (1993). Configurational approaches to organizational analysis. *Academy of Management Journal*, 36: 1175–95.

Meyer, J. W., and Rowan, B. (1977). Institutionalized organizations: Formal structure as myth and ceremony. *American Journal of Sociology*, 83(2): 340–63.

Meyer, M. W. (1978). *Environments and Organizations*. San Francisco, CA: Jossey-Bass Inc Pub.

Michels, R. (1966). Democracy and the iron law of oligarchy. In *Political Parties: A sociological study of the oligarchical tendencies of modern democracies*, trans. Eden and Cedar Paul. New York: Free Press.

Milgrom, P. R., and Roberts, B. M. (1990). The economics of modern manufacturing technology, strategy and organization. *American Economic Review*, 80: 511–28.

Milgrom, P. R., and Roberts, B. M. (1995). Complementarities and fit: Strategy, structure and organizational change in manufacturing. *Journal of Accounting and Economics*, 19: 179–208.

Milgrom, P. R., and Roberts, J. D. (1992). Economics, organization and management. *American Economic Review*, 80: 511–28.

Miller, D., and Friesen, P. H. (1984). *Organizations: A quantum view*. Englewood Cliffs, NJ: Prentice-Hall.

Miller, J. H., and Page, S. E. (2007). *Complex Adaptive Systems. An Introduction to Computational Models of Social Life*. Princeton, NJ: Princeton University Press.

Milo, R., Shen-Orr, S., Itzkovitz, S., Kashtan, N., Chklovskii, D., and Alon, U. (2002). Network motifs: simple building blocks of complex networks. *Science*, 298(5594): 824–27.

Mintzberg, H. (1979). *The structuring of organizations: A synthesis of the research*. Englewood Cliffs, NJ: Prentice-Hall.

Mintzberg, H. (1980). Structure in 5's: A Synthesis of the Research on Organization Design. *Management Science*, 26(3): 322–41.

Mollgaard, A., Zettler, I., Dammeyer, J., Jensen, M. H., Lehmann, S., and Mathiesen, J. (2016). Measure of node similarity in multilayer networks. *PloS one*, 11(6): e0157436.

Moore, D. A., and Healy, P. J. (2008). The trouble with overconfidence. *Psychological Review*, 115(2): 502.

Moreland, R. L. (1999). Transactive memory: Learning who knows what in work groups and organizations. In Thompson, L., Messick D., and Levine, J. (Eds.): *Shared Cognition in Organizations: The management of knowledge* (pp. 3–31). Mahwah, NJ: Erlbaum.

Moreland, R. L., Argote, L., and Krishnan, R. (1996). Socially Shared Cognition at Work: Transactive memory and group performance, In Nye, J. L. and Brower, A. M. (Eds.): *What's Social about Social Cognition? Research on socially shared cognition in small groups* (pp. 57–84). Thousand Oaks, CA: Sage.

Moreland, R. L., and Myaskovsky L. (2000). Exploring the performance benefits of group training: Transactive memory or improved communication? *Organizational Behavior and Human Decision Processes* 82(1): 117–33.

Moskowitz, G. B., and Grant, H. (Eds.). (2009). *The Psychology Of Goals*. New York: Guilford Press.

Nadler, D., and Tushman, M. (1997). *Competing by design: The power of organizational architecture*. Oxford: Oxford University Press.

Nadler, D. A., and Tushman, M. L. (1990). Beyond the charismatic leader: Leadership and organizational change. *California Management Review*, 32(2): 77–97.

Nelson, R. R. (2008). Bounded rationality, cognitive maps, and trial and error learning. *Journal of Economic Behavior and Organization*, 67(1): 78–89.

Nelson, R. R., and Winter, S. G. (1982). *An Evolutionary Theory of Economic Change*. Cambridge, MA: Belknap/Harvard University Press.

Newell, A., and Simon, H. A. (1972). *Human problem solving*. Englewood Cliffs, NJ: Prentice-Hall.

Newman, M. E. J. (2006). Modularity and Community Structure in Networks. *Proceedings of the National Academy of Sciences*, 103(23): 8577–82.

Nicholson, N. (1997). Evolutionary psychology: Toward a new view of human nature and organizational society. *Human Relations*, 50(9): 1053–78.

Nickerson, J. A., and Zenger, T. R. (2008). Envy, comparison costs, and the economic theory of the firm. *Strategic Management Journal*, 29(13): 1429–49.

Nickerson, N. A., and Zenger, T. R. (2002). Being efficiently fickle: A dynamic theory of organizational choice. *Organization Science*, 13(5): 547–66.

Nisbett, R. E. (2005). *The Geography of Thought: How Asians and Westerners Think Differently… and Why*. London, Boston: Nicholas Brealey Publishing.

North, D. C. (1981). *Structure and Change in History*. New York and London: Norton.

Nowak, M., and Sigmund, K. (1993). A strategy of win-stay, lose-shift that outperforms tit-for-tat in the Prisoner's Dilemma game. *Nature*, 364(6432): 56–8.

Ocasio, W. (1997). Towards an attention-based view of the firm. *Strategic Management Journal*, 18: 187–206.

Ocasio, W. (2005). The opacity of risk: Language and the culture of safety in NASA's space shuttle program. Organization at the limit: Lessons from the Columbia disaster. In Starbuck, W. H. and Farjoun, M. (Eds.): *Organization At the Limit: Lessons from the Columbia Disaster* (pp. 101–21). Malden, MA: Blackwell.

O'Keefe, B., and Lovas, B. (2002). *Oticon A/S*. London Business School Case.

Oldham, G. R. and Hackman, J. R. (2010). Not what it was and not what it will be: the future of job design research. *Journal of Organizational Behavior*, 31(2–3): 463–79.

Olson, M. (1971). *The logic of collective action: Public goods and the theory of groups* (2nd ed.). Cambridge, MA: Harvard University Press.

O'Mahony, S. (2003). Guarding the commons: How community managed software projects protect their work. *Research Policy*, 32: 1179–98.

Onnela, J. P., Saramäki, J., Hyvönen, J., Szabó, G., Lazer, D., Kaski, K., and Barabási, A. L. (2007). Structure and tie strengths in mobile communication networks. *Proceedings of the National Academy of Sciences*, 104(18): 7332–36.

Ostrom, E. (1990). *Governing the commons: The evolution of institutions for collective action*. Cambridge: Cambridge University Press.

Ostrom, E. (2005). *Understanding institutional diversity*, Vol. 241. Princeton, NJ: Princeton University Press.

Ostrom, E., Walker, J., and Gardner, R. (1992). Covenants with and without a sword: Self-governance is possible. *American Political Science Review*, 86(2): 404–17.

Parnas, D. L. (1972). On the criteria to be used in decomposing systems into modules. *Comm. ACM*, 15(12): 1053–8.

Perrow, C. (1972). *Complex organizations*. New York: Scott, Foresman.

Petersen, T. (1992). Individual, collective, and systems rationality in work groups: Dilemmas and market-type solutions. *American Journal of Sociology*, 98(3): 469–510.

Pfeffer, J. (1981). *Power in Organizations*, Vol. 33. Marshfield, MA: Pitman.

Pfeffer, J. and Salancik, G. R. (1978). *The External Control of Organizations: A Resource Dependence Perspective*. New York: Harper and Row.

Pillutla, M. M., and Chen, X. P. (1999). Social norms and cooperation in social dilemmas: The effects of context and feedback. *Organizational Behavior And Human Decision Processes*, 78(2): 81–103.

Pinker, S. (2002). *The Blank Slate: The Modern Denial of Human Nature*. New York: Viking.

Pittman, T. S., and Zeigler, K. R. (2007). Basic human needs. *Social psychology: Handbook of basic principles*, 2: 473–89.

Prendergast, C. (1999). The provision of incentives in firms. *Journal of Economic Literature*, 37(1): 7–63.

Prendergast, C. (2000). What trade-off of risk and incentives? *American Economic Review*, 90(2): 421–25.

Puranam, P. (2012). A Future for the Science of Organization Design. *Journal of Organization Design*, 1(1): 18–19.

Puranam, P. (2017). When will we stop studying innovations in organizing, and start creating them? *Innovation*, 19(1): 5–10.

Puranam, P., Alexy, O., and Reitzig, M. (2014). What's "new" about new forms of organizing? *Academy of Management Review*, 39(2): 162–80.

Puranam, P., Gulati, R., and Bhattacharya, S. (2013). How much to make and how much to buy? An analysis of optimal plural sourcing strategies. *Strategic Management Journal*, 34(10): 1145–61.

Puranam, P., and Håkonsson, D. D. (2015). Valve's Way. *Journal of Organization Design*, 4(2): 2–4.

Puranam, P., and Maciejovsky, B. (2017). Organizational Structure and Organizational Learning. In: L. Argote and J. M. Levine (Eds.): *The Oxford Handbook of Group and Organizational Learning*. Oxford University Press, Forthcoming.

Puranam, P., and Raveendran, M. (2013). Interdependence and organization design. In *Handbook of Economic Organization: Integrating Economic and Organization Theory*. Cheltenham: Edward Elgar Publishing.

Puranam, P., Raveendran, M., and Knudsen, T. (2012). Organization design: The epistemic interdependence perspective. *Academy of Management Review*, 37(3): 419–40.

Puranam, P., Singh, H., and Chaudhuri, S. (2009). Integrating acquired capabilities: When structural integration is (un)necessary. *Organization Science*, 20: 313–28.

Puranam, P., Singh, H., and Zollo, M. (2006). Organizing for innovation: Managing the coordination-autonomy dilemma in technology acquisitions. *Academy of Management Journal*, 49(2): 263–80.

Puranam, P., and Srikanth, K. (2007). What they know vs. what they do: How acquirers leverage technology acquisitions. *Strategic Management Journal*, 28(8): 805–25.

Puranam, P., Stieglitz, N., Osman, M., and Pillutla, M. M. (2015). Modelling bounded rationality in organizations: Progress and prospects. *Academy of Management Annals*, 9(1):
337–92.

Puranam, P., and Swamy, M. (2010). Expeditions without Maps: Why Faulty Initial Representations May Be Useful in Join Discovery Problems. Keynote paper, DRUID London Confer-
ence, May 2010.

Puranam, P., and Swamy, M. (2016). How initial representations shape coupled learning
processes. *Organization Science*, 27(2): 323–35.

Puranam, P., and Vanneste, B. (2016). *Corporate strategy: Tools for analysis and decision-making.*
Cambridge: Cambridge University Press.

Puranam, P., and Vanneste, B. S. (2009). Trust and governance: Untangling a tangled web.
Academy of Management Review, 34(1): 11–31.

Radner, R. (1993). The organization of decentralized information processing. *Econometrica:
Journal of the Econometric Society*, 61(5): 1109–46.

Ragin, C. C, and Amoroso, L. M. (2010). *Constructing social research: The unity and diversity of
method.* Pine Forge Press.

Rahmandad, H. (2012). Impact of growth opportunities and competition on firm-level capability
development trade-offs. *Organization Science*, 23(1): 138–54.

Rahmandad, H., and Sterman, J. (2008). Heterogeneity and network structure in the dynamics of
diffusion: Comparing agent-based and differential equation models. *Management Science*,
54(5): 998–1014.

Ratner, R. K., and Miller, D. T. (2001). The norm of self-interest and its effects on social action.
Journal of Personality and Social Psychology, 81(1): 5.

Raveendran, M., Puranam, P., and Warglien, M. (2015). Object salience in the division of labor:
Experimental evidence. *Management Science*, 62(7): 2110–28.

Raymond, E. S. (1999). *The cathedral and the bazaar: Musings on Linux and open source by an
accidental revolutionary.* Sebastopol, CA: O'Reilly.

Reagans, R., Miron-Spektor, E., and Argote, L. (2016). Knowledge utilization, coordination, and
team performance. *Organization Science*, 27(5): 1108–24.

Reitzig, M., and Maciejovsky, B. (2015). Corporate hierarchy and vertical information flow inside
the firm—a behavioral view. *Strategic Management Journal*, 36(13): 1979–99.

Ribot, J. (2001). Local actors, powers and accountability in African decentralizations: A review of
issues. *International Development Research Centre of Canada Assessment of Social Policy
Reforms Initiative*, 25: 104.

Rittel, H. W., and Webber, M. M. (1973). Dilemmas in a general theory of planning. *Policy
Sciences*, 4(2): 155–69.

Rivkin, J. W. (2000). Imitation of complex strategies. *Management Science*, 46(6): 824–44.

Rivkin, J. W., and Siggelkow, N. (2003). Balancing search and stability: Interdependencies among
elements of organizational design. *Management Science*, 49: 290–311.

Rivkin, J. W., and Siggelkow, N. (2007). Patterned interactions in complex systems: Implications
for exploration. *Management Science*, 53: 1068–85.

Robertson, B. J. (2015). *Holacracy: The new management system for a rapidly changing world.*
Macmillan.

Roethlisberger, F. J., and Dickson, W. J. (1939). *Management and the worker.* Cambridge:
Harvard University Press.

Romme, A. G. L. (2004). Unanimity rule and organizational decision making: A simulation model. *Organization Science*, 15(6): 704–18.

Rouse, W. B., and Morris, N. M. (1986). On looking into the black box: Prospects and limits in the search for mental models. *Psychological bulletin*, 100(3): 349.

Rueffler, C., Hermisson, J., and Wagner, G. P. (2012). Evolution of Functional Specialization and Division of Labor. *Proceedings of the National Academy of Science of the USA*, 109: E326-E335.

Russell, B. (2001). *The scientific outlook*. Psychology Press.

Ryan, R. M., and Deci, E. L. (2000). Intrinsic and extrinsic motivations: Classic definitions and new directions. *Contemporary Educational Psychology*, 25(1): 54–67.

Sah, R. K., and Stiglitz, J. E. (1985). Human Fallibility and Economic Organization. *The American Economic Review*, 75(2): 292–97.

Sah, R. K., and Stiglitz, J. E. (1988). Committees, hierarchies and polyarchies. *The Economic Journal*, 98(391): 451–70.

Salancik, G. R. (1995). WANTED: A Good Network Theory of Organization. *Administrative Science Quarterly*, 40(2): 345–49.

Sanchez, R., and Mahoney, J. (1996). Modularity, flexibility, and knowledge management in product and organization design. *Strategic Management Journal*, 17: 63–76.

Sastry, M. A. (1997). Problems and paradoxes in a model of punctuated organizational change. *Administrative Science Quarterly*, 42(2): 237–75.

Schein, E. H. (1985). *Organisational culture and leadership: A dynamic view*. San Francisco, CA: Jossey-Bass.

Schein, E. H. (1993). SMR forum: How can organizations learn faster? The challenge of entering the green room. *Sloan management review*, 34(2): 85.

Schelling, T. C. (1960). *The strategy of conflict*. Cambridge, MA: Harvard University Press.

Scott, W. R. (1998). *Organizations: Rational, natural, and open systems* (4th ed.). Upper Saddle River, NJ: Prentice-Hall.

Selznick, P. (1957). *Leadership in administration*. New York: Harper and Row.

Sendova-Franks, A. B. and Franks, N. R. (1999). Self-assembly, self-orgnaization and division of labor. *Phil Trans R Soc Lond B*, 354: 1395–1405.

Shadish, W. R., Cook, D. T., and Campbell, D. T. (2002). *Experimental and Quasi- Experimental Designs for Generalized Causal Inference*. New York: Houghton Mifflin.

Shah, S. K. (2006). Motivation, governance, and the viability of hybrid forms in open source software development. *Management Science*, 52(7): 1000–14.

Shaw, J. D., Gupta, N., and Delery, J. E. (2002). Pay dispersion and workforce performance: Moderating effects of incentives and interdependence. *Strategic Management Journal*, 23(6): 491–512.

Shearer, B. (2004). Piece rates, fixed wages and incentives: Evidence from a field experiment. *The Review of Economic Studies*, 71(2): 513–34.

Siggelkow, N. (2002). Misperceiving interactions among complements and substitutes: Organizational consequences. *Management Science*, 48(7): 900–16.

Siggelkow, N., and Levinthal, D. A. (2003). Temporarily divide to conquer: Centralized, decentralized, and reintegrated organizational approaches to exploration and adaptation. *Organization Science*, 14: 650–69.

Siggelkow, N., and Rivkin, J. W. (2005). Speed and search: Designing organizations for turbulence and complexity. *Organization Science*, 16: 101–22.

Simon, H. A. (1946). The proverbs of administration. *Public Administration Review*, 6(1): 53–67.

Simon, H. A. (1947). *Administrative Behavior*: A study of decision-making processes in administrative organization. New York: Macmillan.

Simon, H. A. (1951). A formal theory of the employment relationship. *Econometrica*, 19: 293–305.

Simon, H. A. (1955). A behavioral model of rational choice. *Quarterly Journal of Economics*, 69(1): 99–118.

Simon, H. A. (1957). *Administrative Behavior: A study of decision-making processes in administrative organization*. New York: Free Press.

Simon, H. A. (1962). New Developments in the Theory of the Firm. *The American Economic Review*, 52(2): 1–15.

Simon, H. A. (1977). Scientific discovery and the psychology of problem solving. In *Models of discovery* (pp. 286–303). Netherlands: Springer.

Simon, H. A. 1996 (1992). *The Sciences of the Artificial* (2nd ed.). Cambridge, MA: MIT Press.

Simsek, Z., Fox, B. C., and Heavey, C. (2015). "What's past is prologue": A framework, review, and future directions for organizational research on imprinting. *Journal of Management*, 41(1): 288–317.

Slater, S. F., Hult, G. T. M., and Olson, E. M. (2010). Factors influencing the relative importance of marketing strategy creativity and marketing strategy implementation effectiveness. *Industrial Marketing Management*, 39(4): 551–59.

Sloane, S., Baillargeon, R., and Premack, D. (2012). Do infants have a sense of fairness? *Psychological Science*, 23(2): 196–204.

Smith, A. (1776). *An Inquiry into the Nature and Causes of the Wealth of Nations*. London: W. Strahan and T. Cadell.

Smith, A. (1909). *An Inquiry into the Nature and Causes of the Wealth of Nations*. New York: P. F. Collier and Son, pp. 364–661.

Smith, J. E., Gavrilets, S., Mulder, M. B., Hooper, P. L., Mouden, C. E., Nettle, D. and Smith, E. A. (2016). Leadership in mammalian societies: Emergence, distribution, power, and payoff. *Trends in Ecology and Evolution*, 31(1): 54–66.

Smith, V. L. (1998). The two faces of Adam Smith. *Southern Economic Journal*, 65: 2–19.

Smith-Doerr, L. and Powell, W.W. (2005). Networks and economic life. *The Handbook of Economic Sociology*, 2: 379–402.

Soda, G., and Zaheer, A. (2012). A network perspective on organizational architecture: Performance effects of the interplay of formal and informal organization. *Strategic Management Journal*, 33(6): 751–71.

Sorenson, O. (2003). Interdependence and adaptability: organizational learning and the long-term effect of integration. *Management Science*, 49(4): 446–63.

Sosa, M. E. (2008). A structured approach to predicting and managing technical interactions in software development. *Research in Engineering Design*, 19(1): 47–70.

Sosa, M. E., Eppinger, S. D., and Rowles, C. M. (2004). The misalignment of product architecture and organizational structure in complex product development. *Management Science*, 50(12): 1674–89.

Srikanth, K., and Puranam, P. (2011). Integrating distributed work: Comparing task design, communication, and tacit coordination mechanisms. *Strategic Management Journal*, 32: 849–75.

Srikanth, K., and Puranam, P. (2014). The firm as a coordination system: Evidence from software services offshoring. *Organization Science*, 25(4): 1253–71.

Stan, M., and Puranam, P. (2017). Organizational adaptation to interdependence shifts: The role of integrator structures. *Strategic Management Journal*, 38(5): 1041–61.

Stanovich, K. E., and West, R. F. (2000). Advancing the rationality debate. *Behavioral and Brain Sciences*, 23(05): 701–17.

Staw, B. M., and Boettger, R. D. (1990). Task revision: A neglected form of work performance. *Academy of Management Journal*, 33(3): 534–59.

Stea, D., Foss, K., and Foss, N. J. (2015). A neglected role for organizational design: Supporting the credibility of delegation in organizations. *Journal of Organization Design*, 4(3): 3–17.

Steward, D. V. (1981). *Systems analysis and management: Structure, strategy and design.* New York: Petrocelli Books.

Stigler, G. (1951). The division of labor is limited by the extent of the market. *Journal of Political Economy*, 59(3): 185–93.

Stinchcombe, A. L. (1965). Social structure and organizations. In J. G. March (Ed.): *Handbook of Organizations*. Chicago: Rand McNally, pp. 142–93.

Sutton, R. S., and Barto, A. G. (1998). *Reinforcement learning: An Introduction* (Vol. 1, No. 1). Cambridge: MIT Press.

Tajfel, H., Billig, M. G., Bundy, R. P., and Flament, C. (1971). Social categorization and intergroup behaviour. *European Journal of Social Psychology*, 1(2): 149–78.

Taylor, F. W. (1911). *Principles of Scientific Management*. New York: Harper.

Tetlock, P. E., and Mellers, B. A. (2002). The great rationality debate. *Psychological Science*, 13(1): 94–99.

Thagard, P. (2005). Mind. Introduction to *Cognitive Science* (2nd ed.). Bradford Books.

Thomke, S. H. (1997). The role of flexibility in the development of new products: An empirical study. *Research Policy*, 26(1): 105–19.

Thompson, J. D. (1967). *Organizations in action*. New York: McGraw-Hill.

Thorndike, E. L. (1911). *Individuality*. Houghton, Mifflin.

Titmuss, R. M. (1970). *The gift relationship: From human blood to social policy*. London: Allen and Unwin.

Tomasello, M., Carpenter, M., Call, J., Behne, T., and Moll, H. (2005). In search of the uniquely human. *Behavioral and Brain Sciences*, 28(5): 721–27.

Turner, A. N., and Lawrence, P. R. (1965). *Industrial jobs and the worker: An investigation of response to task attributes.* Harvard University, Division of Research, Graduate School of Business Administration.

Tushman, M. L., and Nadler, D. A. (1978). Information processing as an integrating concept in organizational design. *Academy of Management Review*, 3: 613–24.

Tushman, M. L., and O'Reilly, C. A. (1996). The ambidextrous organizations: Managing evolutionary and revolutionary change. *California Management Review*, 38(4): 8–30.

Valentine, M. A., and Edmondson, A. C. (2014). Team scaffolds: How mesolevel structures enable role-based coordination in temporary groups. *Organization Science*, 26(2): 405–22.

Van Maanen, J. (1978). People processing: Strategies of organizational socialization. *Organizational Dynamics*, 7(1): 19–36.

Van Maanen, J., and Schein, E. H. (1979). Toward a theory of organizational socialization. In B. M. Staw (Ed.): *Research in Organizational Behavior*: Vol. 1. Greenwich, CT: JAI Press, pp. 209–64.

Van Vugt, M. (2006). Evolutionary origins of leadership and followership. *Personality and Social Psychology Review*, 10(4): 354–71.

Vanneste, B. S., and Puranam, P. (2010). Repeated interactions and contractual detail: Identifying the learning effect. *Organization Science*, 21(1): 186–201.

Von Hippel, E. (1990). Task partitioning: an innovation process variable. *Research Policy*, 19(5): 407–18.

Von Hippel, E., and Von Krogh, G. (2003). Open source software and the "private-collective" innovation model: Issues for organization science. *Organization Science*, 14: 209–33.

Von Neumann, J., and Morgenstern, O. (1944). *Theory of Games and Economic Behavior*. Princeton, NJ: Princeton University Press.

Wageman, R. (1995). Interdependence and group effectiveness. *Administrative Science Quarterly*, 40(1): 145–80.

Wageman, R., and Baker, G. (1997). Incentives and cooperation: The joint effects of task and reward interdependence on group performance. *Journal of Organizational Behavior*, 18: 139–58.

Watts, D. J. (2014). Common sense and sociological explanations. *American Journal of Sociology*, 120(2): 313–51.

Weber, R. A., and Camerer, C. F. (2003). Cultural conflict and merger failure: An experimental approach. *Management Science,* 49(4): 400–15.

Wegner, D. M., and Bargh, J. A. (1998). *Control and automaticity in social life*. New York: McGraw-Hill.

Wildschut, T., Pinter, B., Vevea, J. L., Insko, C. A., and Schopler, J. (2003). Beyond the group mind: A quantitative review of the interindividual-intergroup discontinuity effect. *Psychological Bulletin*, 129(5): 698–722.

Williamson, O. E. (1967). Hierarchical control and optimum firm size. *Journal of Political Economy*, 75(2): 123–38.

Williamson, O. E. (1975). *Markets and hierarchies: Analysis and antitrust implications*. New York: Free Press.

Williamson, O. E. (1985). *The economic institutions of capitalism*. New York, NY: Free Press.

Williamson, O. E. (1991). Comparative economic organization: The analysis of discrete structural alternatives. *Administrative Science Quarterly*, 36(2): 269–96.

Wilson, E. O. (1998). *Consilience*. New York: Alfred A. Knopf.

Woodward, J. (1958). *Management and technology: Problems and progress in technology*. London: Her Majesty's Stationery Office.

Wyer, R. S. (2007). Principles of mental representation. *Social Psychology: Handbook of Basic Principles*, 2: 285–307.

Yamagishi, T., and Mifune, N. (2008). Does shared group membership promote altruism? Fear, greed, and reputation. *Rationality and Society*, 20(1): 5–30.

Zelditch Jr, M. (1962). Some methodological problems of field studies. *American Journal of Sociology*, 67(5): 566–76.

Zelditch Jr, M. (1969). Can you really study an army in the laboratory? In Etzioni, A. (Ed.): *Complex Organizations*, 2nd ed. New York: Holt, Rinehart, Winston, pp. 528–39.

Zenger, T. R. (1994). Explaining organizational diseconomies of scale in R&D: Agency problems and the allocation of engineering talent, ideas, and effort by firm size. *Management Science*, 40(6): 708–29.

Zenger, T. R., and Hesterly, W. S. (1997). The disaggregation of corporations: Selective intervention, high-powered incentives, and molecular units. *Organization Science*, 8: 209–22.

▣ INDEX

Figures and tables are denoted by an italic *f* or *t* following a page number.